Recollecting Lotte Eisner

FEMINIST MEDIA HISTORIES

Shelley Stamp, Series Editor

Their Own Best Creations: Women Writers in Postwar Television, by Annie Berke

Violated Frames: Armando Bó and Isabel Sarli's Sexploits, by Victoria Ruetalo

Recollecting Lotte Eisner: Cinema, Exile, and the Archive, by Naomi DeCelles

Recollecting Lotte Eisner

CINEMA, EXILE, AND THE ARCHIVE

Naomi DeCelles

UNIVERSITY OF CALIFORNIA PRESS

The publisher and the University of California Press Foundation gratefully acknowledge the generous support of the Robert and Meryl Selig Endowment Fund in Film Studies, established in memory of Robert W. Selig.

University of California Press
Oakland, California

© 2022 by Naomi DeCelles

Library of Congress Cataloging-in-Publication Data

Names: DeCelles, Naomi, author.
Title: Recollecting Lotte Eisner : cinema, exile, and the archive / Naomi DeCelles.
Other titles: Feminist media histories (Series) ; 3.
Description: Oakland, California : University of California Press, [2022] | Series: Feminist media histories ; 3 | Includes bibliographical references and index.
Identifiers: LCCN 2022025051 (print) | LCCN 2022025052 (ebook) | ISBN 9780520388123 (cloth) | ISBN 9780520388130 (paperback) | ISBN 9780520388147 (epub)
Subjects: LCSH: Eisner, Lotte H. | Women film critics—Biography. | Mass media—20th century.
Classification: LCC PN1998.3.E358 D43 2022 (print) | LCC PN1998.3.E358 (ebook) | DDC 791.43092—dc23/eng/20220720
LC record available at https://lccn.loc.gov/2022025051
LC ebook record available at https://lccn.loc.gov/2022025052

31 30 29 28 27 26 25 24 23 22
10 9 8 7 6 5 4 3 2 1

CONTENTS

Acknowledgments vii

Introduction 1

1 . Fräulein Doktor Eisner 22

2 . A Reluctant Bellwether: Dr. L. H. Eisner and Flapper at the *Film-Kurier*, 1927–1933 40

3 . "*La seule historienne*": Exile, Salvage, and Community at the Cinémathèque Française 75

4 . "Lacunae Everywhere": Iterative Historiography and the Midcentury Palimpsests 106

Conclusion: The Woolly Mammoth of the Cinémathèque 142

Appendix: *Film-Kurier* Bibliography, by the Numbers 163

Notes 167

References 207

Index 221

ACKNOWLEDGMENTS

This book began its life as a doctoral dissertation; throughout the metamorphosis of that project into this one, I was sustained by Charles Wolfe, Patrice Petro, and Ross Melnick, who were unstintingly generous with their time and counsel. Chuck and Patrice have been selfless, tireless advocates, consistently embodying the highest standards of scholarship and collegiality. They opened doors to public fora in which I was able to road-test my ideas, and stood by the project (and me) through thick and thin; it is scarcely possible to convey the extent of my admiration for them in these few lines. Naoki Yamamoto joined Chuck, Patrice, and Ross in advising my doctoral research and writing; his wealth of knowledge and expertise helped to shape the initial framing of my research inquiry, and his perceptive reading and observations strengthened it further at later stages of its development. The years-long exchange with Janet Bergstrom that began during my time at the University of California, Los Angeles was valuable, and I thank her for her interest in and engagement with this project, as well as for sharing her own digital copies of several important books with me while I lived and worked overseas, relying on a skeleton research library that had come over with me in a single, heavy backpack and on my three-pound tether to the cloud. The inimitable Bishnupriya Ghosh, Bhaskar Sarkar, and Cristina Venegas fed me an embarrassment of riches, intellectual and alimentary alike; my gratitude to them for their care knows no end. With skill and profound kindness, Ryan Kendle and Wendy Luc steered me through treacherous waters. Private citizens, including Alex, Alexa, Andrews D. and M., Bailey, Barbara, Ben, Bhargavi, Bianka, Caitlin, Clare, Elif, Eric, Eric', Gabi, G. T., Hannah, Ivan, Jason, Jenni, Jodi, John, Katie, Kerry, Kevin, Meredith, Papa, Pat, Pete, Ruth, Sarah, Scott, Sis, Tasch, Tay, and Tyler lightened my load, restored my spirit, and steadied me in moments of uncertainty and adversity. The pandemic brought unexpectedly extended stays with Ruth and Ivan, Pete and Barbara, Jodi and John, Tyler and Alexa, and the Schlakpeople; they were abundantly gracious, tolerant, and generous, and it is thanks to them that I was able to work and live well in spite of the circumstances.

Raina Polivka and Shelley Stamp have been tremendously supportive and thoughtful guides in the publication process. Not least among their numerous contributions to the project are the superb readers they recruited. Attentive engagement by Mila Ganeva, Catherine Russell, Tami Williams, Gary Hamel, and an anonymous reader refined the arguments and style of the manuscript. Helpful translation notes from Robert E. Goodwin improved my understanding of Eisner's early writing on the film archive; his friendly, interested address of the draft I sent him was enormously encouraging. Nathaniel Greenberg led the Society for Cinema and Media Studies Translation Committee—whose members included Fabrizio Cilento, Hongwei Thorn Chen, and Lisa Rabin—that provided discerning, thorough feedback on a selection of the translations I address in the second chapter. Their efforts, along with those of Sara Bakerman and Caetlin Benson-Allott, were greatly appreciated.

Responding with humane generosity to my unsolicited email, Mark Horowitz shared his experience of making *Lotte Eisner in Germany*, and later magnanimously granted permission to use the stills included in this book; I am grateful to him for his images, his time, and his interest in the project. I am indebted to Mark along with Michelle Langford, Giaime Alonge, Nicholas Baer, Werner Herzog, Sam Pressman, Mila Ganeva, Noah Isenberg, Stefan Kloo at the Goethe-Institut Los Angeles, Gilles Veyrat at the Cinémathèque française, Mark Quigley at UCLA Film and Television Archive, and the unflappable Meghan Johnson at UCSB's Interlibrary Loan Department for the research leads they gave me. Each of these interlocutors fortified and enriched the project at different stages, helping clue me into a tool or document here, an insight there; I thank all of them for their collaborative contributions.

With expertise and aplomb, Emily Zinn, Paula Firth, Catherine Cox, Evelyn Godinez, and Kathy Murray helped make overseas travel for this work feasible. Joe Palladino, Matt Ryan, and Dana Welch helped me track down and operate the projection equipment I needed to study some of the films I consulted in researching this book; Matt and Dana were also fun, congenial colleagues at the Carsey-Wolf Center. The programming we mounted with Chuck, Cristina, Patrice, Emily, Paula, and Kathy was vital to my research, and their support and encouragement were always buoying. The Council for European Studies, the Carsey-Wolf Center, and the Albert and Elaine Borchard Fellowship funded my research, conference travel, and writing time. Azadeh Fatehrad organized the Sohrab Shahid Saless conference of 2017 that was hosted by the Goethe-Institut London, and Julia Eisner and Erica Carter put together the Lotte Eisner Symposium of 2018 that was hosted by King's College; each of these gatherings helped to distill ideas I had developed for the second chapter and conclusion of this book. Julia Eisner and Luke Ingram have taken special interest in promoting scholarship on Lotte Eisner, and I wish to acknowledge and thank them for their engagement and their assiduous attention to detail. I'm grateful to David Sterritt for the opportunity to hone my thinking about Eisner's mythic years on the strop of public scrutiny with the publication of "Mediating Displacement: Lotte Eisner's Exile on Film," in *Quarterly Review of Film and Video*. In Autumn 2021, *Screen* published "Out and About: Lotte Eisner at the *Film-Kurier*, 1927–1933," along with my translation of Eisner's 1928 article, "From One Who Went Forth to Learn What 'Cinema' Was [...]," in the dossier that emerged from the Lotte Eisner Symposium, titled "Lotte Eisner: A Reappraisal"; the ideas I presented in that dossier are each engaged in greater depth in the second and third chapters of this book. Some of the arguments I make in this book's introduction and third chapter saw the light of day sooner (under the title, "The Case for (Re)collecting Lotte Eisner's Work"), thanks to the early-rising Patrice and Emily, who sped *Uncanny Histories in Film and Media Studies* along its path with alacrity and verve. Similarly, in the second chapter of this book, I deal with a suite of translations that were published (along with a brief introduction that drew on the insights of this book at large) in *Journal of Cinema and Media Studies* under the title, "A Critic at Large: Lotte Eisner at the *Film-Kurier* (1927–1933)."

The greatest debt and the humblest thanks I owe to Eric. He solved a number of the daunting and varied problems that presented themselves along the way to this book, such as how to process several thousand pages of material in high resolution on a tight timeline without permanently crooking my neck, and how we were going to eat when the fish weren't biting. He has made the last several years of my work possible at all, and he has been a true and steady partner in it from the start; I couldn't have wished for a more brilliant, supportive, or thoroughly enjoyable teammate.

Introduction

IT IS BROADLY UNDERSTOOD that Lotte Eisner's interventions in the field of academic film and media studies are twofold: she established a major archive of interwar German cinema at the Cinémathèque française, and she wrote some of the first postwar scholarly studies about the aesthetic and historical contexts of Weimar-era films and filmmakers. It is also known that she had a PhD in art history, that she worked as a film critic in the 1920s, and that she lived in exile for many years. Often, she is remembered as a satellite of the larger-than-life company she kept: Louise Brooks, Werner Herzog, Fritz Lang, Henri Langlois. Over the course of decades, she has become a dusty fixture of the dutiful literature review. Eisner's best-known publication, *The Haunted Screen*, has been reissued at regular intervals in English since its 1969 translation and, gradually, consensus has calcified around an assessment of the book as rather dated, to the point that assertions to this effect have taken on the routine quality of a refrain in introductory remarks to English-language Weimar cinema surveys.

Yet, for having become so familiar, Eisner has receded in the discipline's intellectual history; we think we know her work, and we assume that the edges and extent of its generative potential have been reached. Embedded in this assumption, however, is a central paradox: her archival and scholarly work is widely used and often cited, but no substantial study of Eisner's corpus at large has been made, and her work is often acknowledged in ways that diminish the significance of its contributions. Her doctoral dissertation and journalism have remained obscure, glancingly engaged when they are mentioned at all. The fact that her archival and scholarly work in the postwar period were shaped by her status as an exile is usually assumed, but, aside from the occasional reference to her memoirs, she rarely figures in studies of the German expatriates who fled the Nazi regime and the war.

One reason a survey of her interwar work hasn't been done may be that Eisner herself disparaged it in her later years. In the interviews she gave to journalists, cineastes, and scholars, she often described this period of her life with reference to a set of anecdotes featuring the celebrities of 1920s Berlin, preferring to regale her interlocutors with irreverent, sometimes outlandish stories about Leni Riefenstahl or Bertolt Brecht, rather than describe in detail the scope or importance of her own work. Another explanation of this oversight is that her later work has been understood by some influential commentators to bear the strong influence of her training in art history and film criticism and to have, as a consequence, less traction in the realm of film studies proper, less portability beyond the ken of Weimar cinema. However, the work of other prominent film theorists of the period who approached film aesthetics and politics from an art historical vantage point—such as Erwin Panofsky and Rudolf Arnheim—has been engaged in depth and at length. There are also notable examples of film critics and archivists, some of whom published in the same journals as Eisner did—including Béla Balázs, Iris Barry, André Bazin, and Siegfried Kracauer—the translation and exegesis of whose work has occupied generations of film scholars.

It is also possible that in addition to Eisner's cues and the meanderings of scholastic fashion, a decisive factor in the relegation of her work has been the series of interruptions visited upon her career by political, economic, and social turmoil, which resulted in the fragmentation of her work in academic, journalistic, archival, and film historiographical domains, all of it scattered across four languages and six decades. Added to these practical difficulties of access is the problem of the work's metaphorical legibility; for some of the same reasons that it was possible and interesting, her work is also peculiar, sometimes difficult, and, like its author, resistant. Eisner was born into and raised with a great deal of privilege, yet she also experienced grave hardship and inequity throughout her adult life. The qualities that give her early work its verve—her powers of observation, intellectual independence, and deep reservoir of cultural reference—find their verso in the characteristics that make her a slippery or troubling subject for recuperation today: her single-mindedness, a measure of prejudice, and, in certain contexts, a propensity toward disputatious individualism. A voracious and discerning consumer of culture, she often wrote with striking clarity, yet her judgment could be harsh, sometimes hasty. In her memoirs, which she dictated to her caretaker,

Martje Grohmann, Eisner summed up her life's work as the refinement of this power:

> MARTJE GROHMANN: Why did you want to write your memoirs? Bluntly put: who cares about your life, which you have dedicated to other creative people? One reads the memoirs of Buñuel because he is a great director, but the memoirs of a film historian?
>
> LOTTE EISNER: You may as well ask: why does the principal witness keep her mouth shut during a murder trial, although she might exonerate the accused? I am something of a witness of our cultural history. My private life, which I have never taken very seriously, has repeatedly crossed with the lives of our most important intellectual innovators.... I believe in destiny. My destiny was to discover people like Bert Brecht, Peter Lorre, Satyajit Ray, Shadi Abdel Salam, and Henri Langlois. I had a nose for originality and a gift for putting my discoveries into words. I saw that as my life's task, rather than marrying and raising children. Others can do that better than I. Fate has helped me, though I was often in mortal danger. It has saved me so that I might finish my work.[1]

About a quarter century before this weighty destiny befell her, Lotte Eisner was an eccentric and creative child. Bridling at convention and its enforcers, she was possessed of an appetite for literary and theatrical fiction matched in its intensity only by her boisterous imaginative faculty. How she came to see herself as a key witness, rather than a defendant—and to understand murder, justice, and cultural history as intertwined with one another in her own narrative of identity—is as much a story of her professional life as it is of her personal life, in spite of her protestations of not having taken the latter very "seriously." Why the only and undesirable alternative to such testimony would have been marriage and children, in Eisner's view, was likewise a function of the period, places, and circumstances under which she lived.

In the five chapters to follow, I trace Eisner's upbringing, her doctoral work, and her careers as a journalist, as an archivist, and as a film historian, indicating both continuities and interruptions, and highlighting aspects of Eisner's work that can be clarified with reference to certain contemporary film studies discourses. While this study is framed chronologically, makes extensive use of Eisner's memoirs and personal reflections, and indicates salient life events as influences on her work and legacy, it is primarily concerned with charting Eisner's development as a key figure in the intellectual history of film studies and with embedding her professional trajectory within the larger histories that shaped the reception of her work; that is to say, I do not attempt to provide an exhaustive study of Eisner's biography. This is both a methodological choice—the disciplinary context in which I have researched and written is that of film studies, and my interest is in contributing to that field in particular—and a practical one. Eisner's personal papers have a somewhat fraught history in terms of ownership, and while there exist several troves of her correspondence in publicly accessible archival collections, a current project by one of her great-nieces, Julia Eisner, draws on exclusive access to the primary archive of Lotte Eisner's personal papers, and it promises to offer a biographical study of its subject. In certain respects, this coincidence has functioned as a limitation on the present project: the absence of any previous dedicated secondary studies or biographical literature on Eisner, compounded with the opacity of the personal archive has meant that it has not been possible to verify certain claims made in Eisner's memoirs and interviews, and there are indications that a great deal of the correspondence she conducted in the postwar period—some of it personal, some of it professional, much of it hybrid—was diverted to her home addresses; if it survives, it may be in the family's archive.

Given the dearth of attention to Eisner's early work, however, there is no shortage of fresh material outside that archive. I have focused on Eisner's contributions to the aesthetic, economic, and historiographical analysis of film and film industries, attending to the intellectual and cultural histories from which Eisner emerged and in which she participated. I have worked with Eisner's numerous publications and the portion of her correspondence that is held in public archives, including the voluminous administrative archives of the Cinémathèque française, the personal papers of Herman G. Weinberg held at the New York Public Library, some personal correspondence of Fritz Lang's held at the University of Southern California, Edouard Roditi's at the University of California, Los Angeles, and Sohrab Shahid Saless's at Werkstatt Film, Oldenburg, Germany. Eisner's memoirs and the interviews she gave serve throughout this study as important sources of biographical information and historical context, yet as I discovered in my research, Eisner reflected on the people and experiences that had marked her life most strongly—particularly in her later years—in strategic, self-consciously rhetorical narratives. As feminist media historiographers have shown, autobiography and personal testimony can take on a critical and generative significance beyond the individual or the anecdotal in cases where the standard historiography fails or refuses to take account of minority groups. I have looked to the self-reflexive praxis of scholars working in the domains of feminist and queer historiography for guidance in my own efforts to understand and historicize Eisner's work and its legacy in the field of scholarly film study.

In addition to offering a few framing remarks, this brief introduction surveys the reception of Eisner's work in English-language film and media studies, emphasizing the gaps and inconsistencies in that discourse. I describe the ways I dealt with certain of these gaps, how I contextualized some of the inconsistencies, as well as how I gauged the frictions between Eisner's early ambitions and the tumultuous circumstances under which most of her professional life was lived. This approach draws strength from comparative readings of Eisner's autobiographical remarks and a critical address of the strategic qualities and rhetorical investments of these narratives, as much as it does from a wide-ranging survey of her scholarly and journalistic work. With attention throughout to the issues of historiography in what reception there has been of Eisner's work in the secondary literature, I show that reading her doctoral dissertation, interwar journalism, and archival correspondence together with her memoirs can reframe the conventional wisdom on Eisner and her work.

At stake is not only the recognition of a marginalized female scholar and a revision of the intellectual history of academic film studies, but an opportunity to observe the ways that gendered, linguistic, and institutional privilege shapes historiography. The development and institutionalization of film studies in the popular and trade press, as well as in archival and scholarly contexts, involved the legitimation of certain ethics and poetics of the archive and cultural history over others; one of the fundamental and broadly relevant findings of this study is that the latter are ripe with potentialities in our contemporary moment.

THE POLITICS OF CITATION, CRITIQUE, AND RE/MEMBERING

Citations, acknowledgments, and commentary—typically engaging either Eisner's academic or archival work, largely ignoring her film criticism—tend to fall into three general categories: critiques of her Weimar cinema survey *The Haunted Screen* (*L'écran démoniaque*, 1952, 1965; English editions 1969, 1973), citations of *F. W. Murnau* (French, 1964; German, 1967, 1979; English, 1973) and *Fritz Lang* (English, 1976; French, 1984) recounting biographical or historical information reported therein, and accounts, often framed as personal remembrances, of her archival work at the Cinémathèque française. While *The Haunted Screen* remains Eisner's best-known publication, it is frequently misunderstood and misrepresented. Many familiar with *The Haunted Screen* think of it as a catalog of Weimar cinema that demonstrates how certain films prefigure the aesthetics and politics of Nazism: an inaccurate assumption based on a common elision. Eisner does discuss a reified Germany and German mentality, but these are addressed in the context of Romanticism, rather than Nazism, and her analysis is rigorously constrained to film and art historical contexts. For Eisner's readers familiar with the sociology and history of Weimar-era right-wing political theory, Romanticism bridges, albeit crookedly, to Nazism via reactionary modernisms and the Conservative Revolution, by dint of what Jeffrey Herf calls a "selective tradition."[2] Although pointed references—including the book's epigraph by Leopold Ziegler—indicate a familiarity on Eisner's part with the literature of that selective tradition, it is not the case that *The Haunted Screen* speculates on the connections between Romanticism and Nazism via Weimar cinema; indeed, quite the opposite. This widespread misreading is probably due, in part, to the long shadow of Siegfried Kracauer's *From Caligari to Hitler* (1947) and to the fact that the two volumes are often read in conjunction. Both books were written by former film critics and German Jews in exile, both were published in the postwar period, and both deal with (and to an extent, codify) a Weimar film canon; because of these passing similarities, *The Haunted Screen* is often discussed as a foil or counterpart to *From Caligari to Hitler*. For her own part, Eisner resented these comparisons, expressing her frustration candidly in private correspondence and publicly in oblique references to the tendentiousness of certain methods of film historiography that cut their evidence to measure.

Arriving about a generation after the first English-language Weimar cinema scholarship boom in the 1980s—a wave which itself followed the earliest postwar studies of the period by several decades—the impulse to compare *The Haunted Screen* and *From Caligari to Hitler* in the same breath is common to many of the revisionist histories of Weimar cinema published around the turn of the millennium.[3] These third-wave histories offered fresh archival and historiographical insights, in part as a function of their own historical moment; *die Wende*, the centenary of cinema, and a reinvigoration of early cinema studies in the United States beginning in the mid-1990s all contributed to this increase in scholarly attention. As Sabine

FIGURE 1. Eisner the *raconteuse*, in her Neuilly-sur-Seine apartment. Still from *Lotte Eisner in Germany* (S. M. Horowitz, 1980).

Hake points out, "German unification has allowed cultural critics to think about central aspects of German culture, history, and national identity," in no small part due to the increased accessibility of the DEFA (Deutsche Film-Aktiengesellschaft) archives and catalogs.[4] In a review of the edited collection, *Expressionist Film: New Perspectives* (2003), Noah Isenberg observes that "film scholars have been knocking heads with Kracauer and Eisner since their respective works first appeared," and goes on to describe "Kracauer's teleological understanding of Weimar cinema" as "an easy target."[5] This passage is paradigmatic in that Isenberg groups Kracauer and Eisner together, but outlines a critique of Kracauer's methodology alone; even the most self-reflexive comparisons of Kracauer and Eisner tend to conform to this pattern. Claudia Lenssen's thoughtful essay on the history of reception of Eisner and Kracauer, for example, identifies some of the key problems in the existing literature and clearly articulates the need for a complete study of Eisner's work, including the interwar journalism. However, the bulk of Lenssen's short essay is focused on Kracauer's work and its reception; Lenssen's engagement of Eisner is restricted to a rehashing of select biographical details from the memoirs and a gloss on Eisner's postwar books.[6] In *Weimar*

Cinema and After, Thomas Elsaesser remarks that "There have been many objections to *From Caligari to Hitler* and *The Haunted Screen,* ever since they were published, with Kracauer's methodology and Eisner's assumptions continuing to arouse criticism," but all seven works Elsaesser references in this claim's corresponding footnotes critique *From Caligari to Hitler.* Not a single one deals in detail with Eisner's work.[7]

When Eisner's work, especially *The Haunted Screen,* is directly engaged, it is almost always in parallel to Kracauer's; evocatively, Elsaesser has referred to Kracauer and Eisner as "the Scylla and Charybdis" of Weimar film studies. Although he grants that Eisner is "persuasive on the intertextualities between film, theater and painting," he maintains that "the term 'influence' fails as an explanatory concept."[8] Instead, Elsaesser suggests that attention to the "institutional, semi-industrial, profit-driven context in which these individuals were constrained or encouraged to work" is a more productive avenue of inquiry.[9] Granted, Eisner's commentary in *The Haunted Screen* on industrial workflows is typically—although not always—couched as supporting detail for her stylistic analysis. As a prime counterexample to Elsaesser's claim, I would highlight Eisner's interest in the industry-standard *Regiensitzungen,* or production meetings, in *The Haunted Screen.*[10] Moreover, such interest in the industrial labor practices and their import for film style is indisputably central to the monographs she wrote on both Murnau and Lang, and in the introductions to each, she anticipates Elsaesser's criticism, remarking that interested parties might read *F. W. Murnau, The Haunted Screen,* and *Fritz Lang* as part of one larger, overarching project.[11] Indeed, in the private and administrative correspondence spanning decades that is held at the Cinémathèque française, Eisner discussed a planned volume devoted exclusively to the work of interwar German set designers, in which she hoped to more clearly make the case that the production culture of filmmaking teams and the collective spirit in which they worked contributed to a hallmark style of the German industry in that period.

Elsaesser further argues that *The Haunted Screen* suffers from a preoccupation with the individual filmmaker, to whom is attributed what he calls a "will-to-style."[12] From this argument also flows the critique that the book is apolitical in its single-minded focus on aesthetics; or that it is retrograde in its interest in the auteur and his psyche. Along these lines, Hake has made the claim that both *The Haunted Screen* and *From Caligari to Hitler* evince a "profoundly anti-modernist" bent and can only be construed as "self-consciously German in [their] preoccupation with problems of identity and the metaphysics of space."[13] The first of these claims is belied by the methodological and rhetorical significance of interviews and testimony by the presumed auteur's collaborators: for *The Haunted Screen*, Max Reinhardt is less a lone mastermind than a node in a network, Murnau's vaunted stylistics are the product of an innovative team comprised of set designers, cameramen, screenwriters, and actors, and the genius of Pabst consists entirely in his collaboration with brilliant actors.[14] Thus, "Reinhardt," "Murnau," and "Pabst" serve as shorthand references to artistic, industrial, and social clusters. Furthermore, a careful survey of her interwar writing reveals that Eisner's interest in filmmaking teams as collaborative creative units began in her first months at the *Film-Kurier*. Over her five-and-a-half year tenure there (August 1927–March 1933), she published scores of articles, opinion pieces, reports, interviews, and reviews treating the topic, and she initiated a column that would grow to include the contributions of other *Film-Kurier* editors, titled "Das Feuilleton des Autors," which emphasized the importance of collaboration in the German industry by way of short profiles of the conceptualization and production processes of prominent German filmmakers, including screenwriters, art directors, and cinematographers. In her work at the Cinémathèque française, and in the numerous scholarly publications that emerged from this archival work, Eisner continued to develop her thesis that the characteristic feature of the interwar German film industry was the production collective, an argument that preceded and contrasted in important ways with the branch of auteur theory propounded by the influential French critics and cineastes associated with the *Cahiers du cinéma*. Without reference to a comprehensive survey of Eisner's interwar work, much less a thorough study of her archival praxis or her extensive correspondence on the topic in the postwar period, the claims Elsaesser and Hake make seem plausible, but reading across Eisner's oeuvre it is clear that her conception of authorship and style is more nuanced and more firmly grounded in a firsthand, fine-grained understanding of the production culture of the period than either Elsaesser or Hake are inclined to grant.

Superficially, the archetypal reactionary preoccupation with authenticity—a cardinal concern for conservative aesthetic and nationalist discourses of purity and entitlement, including many of the long twentieth century's European fascisms—appears to be fundamental to the discussion of many films in both *The Haunted Screen* and *From Caligari to Hitler*, as Hake suggests. Yet attentive tracking of the contexts in which the notion of authenticity figures for each reveals that in *The Haunted Screen* it is typically deployed either as a synonym for verisimilitude, adherence to genre convention, or on-location shooting, all stylistic and aesthetic questions that Eisner engaged from her very first *Film-Kurier* contributions onward. In *From Caligari to Hitler*, authenticity is at stake in discussions of artifice or fakery (as contrasted to nature or the natural, under the aegis of stylistic realism), and it is the criterion of Kracauer's assessments of ideology—that is, the relative explanatory powers of various ideological constructions.

The contrast between Eisner's medium-specific application and Kracauer's much broader, ponderously value-laden usage rhymes with another important divergence: throughout *The Haunted Screen*, Eisner's operative unit of film analysis is the sequence and, as a result, emphasis is placed on movement and composition in time, whereas in *From Caligari to Hitler*, the fundamental units of Kracauer's analysis are text, plot, and, on occasion, the still image. Eisner's discussion of *Pandora's Box* (*Die Büchse der Pandora*, G. W. Pabst, 1929) is exemplary:

> [Lulu] is the centre of attraction, and Pabst succeeds in devising an infinite variety of seduction scenes to show her to advantage, as when Dr. Schön comes into the flat wondering how to tell his mistress that he is getting married. The camera catches his nervousness as he paces up and down the room; the ash from his cigarette burns a table-runner, and he fiddles with a bibelot, as Jannings had fidgeted with a liqueur glass in *Variety*. Then a skilful [*sic*] shot-and-reverse shot shows us Lulu observing him. She sinks back into the cushions, moves, lies on her front half-reared like a sphinx, while Schön goes up to her and sits down.[15]

Eisner makes the case that Pabst's films are distinguished by the subtlety of characterization and mood achieved in collaboration with his actors, building her critique around an analysis of movement, space, and body language. Picking out Fritz Kortner's agitated characterization of Dr. Schön—his back to Lulu, we cut to a close-up of him turning the toylike lamb figurine on the mantelpiece slightly in its place, so it, too, can avoid Lulu's inquiring gaze—Eisner compares this detail to the trifling petulance of Emil Jannings's Boss Huller in *Variety* (*Varieté*, E. A. Dupont, 1925). As his wife, played by Maly Delschaft, washes their dinner dishes, Huller childishly tips a small liqueur glass to and fro with one hand, bickering with her about going back to the thrills of his acrobatic work in favor of his domestic post-injury routine, a notion suggested by the arrival of their scantily clad houseguest, Bertha-Marie (Lya de Putti). Schön and Huller are each in conflict with a woman whose will they resist, and the idle, toying characterization given by Kortner and Jannings, respectively, emits in each case a powerful affective charge; this man is dissembling and manipulative, that one, fickle and selfish. By contrast, Kracauer's address of the film focuses on what might be called paratextual critique:

> Contemporaries considered *Pandora's Box* a failure. A failure it was, but not for the reason most critics advanced. They held that Pabst was fundamentally wrong in making a silent film from a literary play whose meaning depended mainly upon the fine points of its dialogue. However, the film's weakness resulted not so much from the impossibility of translating this dialogue into cinematic terms as from the abstract nature of the whole [Frank] Wedekind play. It was a texture of arguments; its characters, instead of living on their own, served to illustrate principles. Pabst blundered in choosing a play that because of its expressive mood belonged to the fantastic postwar era rather than to the realistic stabilized period. The outcome of his misplaced endeavors was a film which, as [Harry Alan] Potamkin puts it, "is 'atmosphere' without content."16

For Kracauer, questions of critical reception, adaptation, and textuality notwithstanding, the fundamental problem with the film is that it was stylistically out of step with the progression identified in *From Caligari to Hitler*; it is the exception that proves the rule. When he does attend to visual stylistic analysis in this volume, Kracauer tends to cite still images, rather than sequences. A pose, carefully tracked by Kracauer from *New Year's Eve* (*Sylvester*, Lupu Pick, 1923) through *Warning Shadows* (*Schatten*, Arthur Robison, 1923), *The Street* (*Die Straße*, Karl Grune, 1923), *The Holy Mountain* (*Der heilige Berg*, Arnold Fanck, 1926), *Secrets of a Soul* (*Geheimnisse einer Seele*, G. W. Pabst, 1926), and *Tragedy of the Street* (*Dirnentragödie*, Bruno Rahm, 1927) is illustrative: in *New Year's Eve* (*Sylvester*), "while his mother caresses him as if he were a child, [the protagonist] rests his head helplessly on her bosom." In Kracauer's view, "It is noteworthy that, far from being repudiated, his singular gesture of capitulation reappeared, almost unchanged, in various German films, indicating that his instinctive reluctance to attempt emancipation might be considered a typical German attitude. It is an attitude which results from the prolonged dependence of the Germans upon a feudal or half-feudal military regime—not to mention the current social and economic motives enforcing the perpetuation of this attitude within the middle class."17

For Kracauer, the image figures less as a filmic composition, or an aspect of characterization in acting style than as a static relational trope to be dissected with the aid of historical economic, social, and political contexts. In this particular case, the vulnerabilities of his argumentative strategy are laid bare: Kracauer proposes a scathing, patriarchal interpretation—presumably, it is a perverse "capitulation" because grown men shouldn't be comforted by their mothers—yet the embrace itself might just as plausibly be construed through less toxic optics as a gesture of affection, solidarity, or care. Furthermore, the other six instances of male characters being comforted by female characters that Kracauer inveighs against and describes as a pervasive, reprehensible tendency among German men appear in a mere 1.3 percent of the total body of films cited in his book at large: they are hardly "typical," then, in any usual sense.[18]

Leaving aside questions of language and translation, Eisner's work seems to suffer in almost all instances for being associated with Kracauer's; the political impetus and implications of *The Haunted Screen* have been deemed objectionable on the grounds both that they are too strident (and too similar to Kracauer's in *From Caligari to Hitler*) and that they aren't quite strident enough.[19] Tellingly, the most recent edition of *From Caligari to Hitler* contains a six-page appendix listing inaccuracies in the text—mostly consisting of mistakes in the reported release dates of films, although some are more troubling, such as citations that have not been substantiated or gross errors in the characterization of a film's plot or production—but it also contains a thirty-six page, painstaking introduction by Leonardo Quaresima that frames and qualifies the errata and opens up the work in valuable ways. None of the English-language editions of *The Haunted Screen* contains supplements as scrupulous or as generous as these. In fact, they have no supplements at all.[20]

The second general category of acknowledgments—citations and references to Eisner's work, rather than commentary on it—is the most prolific. By and large, *F. W. Murnau* and *Fritz Lang* are cited by contemporary scholars in neutral tones; the depth and breadth of research represented therein have made these monographs indispensable to studies of individual films, filmmakers, and technologies alike. These volumes have come to be so widely relied upon that it would be a challenge to find a study dealing with Weimar cinema culture that does not use or cite Eisner's work in some capacity. Yet in narratives about the intellectual history of Weimar cinema studies, even straightforward citations of her work tend to fall back on diminutive language in describing Eisner and her work. Barry Salt's pugnacious article-length survey of Weimar cinema studies scholarship on Expressionism circa 1979, "From Caligari to Who?," takes aim, as its title suggests, first and foremost at Kracauer, and it differs from most second-wave studies in that Salt declines to lump Eisner's work in with his critique of Kracauer's.[21] However, in the service of his larger argument—that Expressionism in the interwar German cinema has been too vaguely defined to date—Salt makes a handful of misleading, even false claims about the existing literature, mostly concerning what has or has not been addressed. Citing only John Willett's previous work on Expressionism as a positive influence on his own understanding, Salt overlooks Rudolf Kurtz's 1926 *Expressionismus und Film* along with a raft of short articles and encyclopedia entries Eisner published in the postwar period, and he misrepresents what little work of Eisner's he does engage.

Among the mistakes Salt makes in his survey are the following: first, he claims that nobody has yet addressed the stylistic variations within a single film's mise en scène, costume, and acting styles, or allowed that single elements might be properly considered Expressionist while the rest of the film might not. In point of fact, Eisner made this argument as early as 1949— thirty years prior to Salt—in an article for *La Revue du cinéma*, titled, "Aperçus sur le costume dans les films allemands," as well as in all editions of *L'écran démoniaque* and *The Haunted Screen*. Salt also boldly claims that the Danish influence on German film, especially in terms of lighting, "seems to be unknown to everyone who has written on German cinema of the 20s," yet Eisner treats this theme in an exhaustive 1957 entry on Expressionism and cinema for the *Enciclopedia dello spettacolo*, elements of which she reprised in the third chapter of *The Haunted Screen*, titled, "The Spell of Light: The Influence of Max Reinhardt." In the latter, she argues, "Max Reinhardt was far from being the sole source of the German cinema's celebrated treatment of light and shade. There was also the contribution of the Nordic filmmakers (the Danes in particular) who invaded the German studios: Stellan Rye, Holger Madsen, Dinesen, for example. They brought with them, at a time when Expressionism had still not crystallized into a recognizable style, their love for nature and their feeling for chiaroscuro."[22] Salt wrongly claims to have inaugurated the study of numerous stylistic features and producers of Weimar cinema, including: the importance of Asta Nielsen's acting style; the supernatural themes in the work of Henrik Galeen and Paul Wegener; German attitudes toward the French seen through the lens of the Frederick the Great films of the twenties; the influence of Murnau's collaborative approach on his film style; and the importance of formalized directorial control for the interwar German cinema style. In reality, Eisner had discussed each one of these topics with subtlety and specificity decades prior to Salt's intervention.[23] But his address of Eisner is most obtrusively problematic when it is direct. Arguing that previous work has overlooked Expressionist theater as an influence on German cinema, Salt claims: "Even Lotte Eisner's *The Haunted Screen*, which has a deal of pertinent information on the influence of Max Reinhardt on the German cinema, says nothing on this point."[24] Begrudging Eisner the standard phrasal modifier (e.g., "a good deal") and implying that her original analysis is less useful than the "information" she reports, Salt also misrepresents her work; aside from the shorter passages and numerous footnotes discussing Expressionist theater that a hurried glance might not catch, the book's thirteenth chapter, "The Handling of Crowds" begins with a section on *Metropolis* subtitled, "The Influence of the Expressionist Choruses and Piscator": a beacon all but the most lackadaisical reader ought to notice. He continues by offering the ostensibly novel insight that Karl Heinz Martin, César Klein, and Robert Neppach all directly influenced German cinematic Expressionism, a fact Eisner had established thirty years earlier in the pages of *La Revue du cinéma*, and that even Salt's target, Kracauer, well knew.

Salt's difficulties might be chalked up to a lack of familiarity with Eisner's work and the German-, Italian- and French-language secondary literature in which she participated, but no such explanation can be offered in the case of other commentators who were aware of the extent of Eisner's scholarship and belittled it nevertheless. Perhaps due to his investment in staking a distinct space in the secondary literature for his own work, Elsaesser characterizes Eisner's analysis of the Mayer-Murnau collaborations of the early twenties as too focused on "a specific art historical style or . . . a unique or unified *Weltanschauung*," in contrast with his own interest in the team as a subgenre unto themselves (which he calls "Murnau's 'corporate identity'") within the larger genre of Expressionist filmmaking, itself "a *genus* with a strong family resemblance between its individual specimen[s], and a collectively worked (proto-)type."[25] Elsaesser goes on in the next paragraph to explain the consistency of style and thematics as a result of the imbrication of all levels of above- and below-the-line labor on these films, using Eisner's original research as the source and substantiation of these claims, acknowledged in a brusque footnote.

Paradoxically, Eisner functions as the problem and the source of its solution: the task *Weimar Cinema and After* mandates for itself is to correct misunderstandings Elsaesser claims Eisner set in motion, but the new information and fresh perspectives brought to bear on these alleged misunderstandings are in fact the cornerstones of Eisner's own monograph and are implicit in *The Haunted Screen*. Yet Elsaesser's balky relationship to Eisner's work is perhaps nowhere more obvious than in his chapter on Murnau. Bafflingly, Elsaesser states midway through the first page of the chapter that "As with so many other directors of the silent era, chief honour [for contemporary access to and appreciation of Murnau's work] must go to Henri Langlois, his assistant Lotte Eisner and the members of the *nouvelle vague*, whom Langlois's Paris Cinémathèque provided with their filmic education," in spite of the fact that the second sentence of this very chapter had been annotated with the admission that Eisner's monograph "is still the most important study of Murnau's life and work, and the source I am drawing on for much of the biographical information."[26] The chapter's first in-text acknowledgment of Eisner—the one that will register most prominently for the majority of Elsaesser's readers—is as Langlois's "assistant" and second fiddle, yet as the footnotes and an attentive reading of the chapter at large attest, it is as sole author of a seminal text in the field of film studies that Eisner matters for this chapter.[27]

It's worth dwelling for a moment longer on this assertion, since it offers a useful example of another problematic tendency in the secondary literature: the description of Eisner as a helper and subordinate to Langlois. Without an understanding of the distinctive, independent archival and historiographical praxis Eisner forged in her time there, particularly in terms of the philosophical differences between Eisner and Langlois and the degree to which Eisner directed the Cinémathèque française's interwar German acquisitions efforts, Elsaesser's description of her merely as Langlois's "assistant," and his claim that *The Haunted Screen* was addressed to Langlois as her "benefactor," might pass muster.[28] In view of the evidence to the contrary—in the Cinémathèque's administrative archives, and in Eisner's scholarly work—it is clear that not only do such descriptions misallocate credit, but they fundamentally misunderstand the dynamics of labor, publicity, and mythmaking that have been well documented in the literature about the Cinémathèque's turbulent midcentury organizational politics.

A third family of texts about Eisner is comprised of tributes and celebrations published during her lifetime and after her death in 1983 that work to articulate—in the connective and enunciative senses—and to reanimate a particular narrative of her life and legacy.[29] While they usually gesture at the connections among her critical, scholarly, and archival work, these essays tend to do so in a biographical mode and along a linear chronology, their authors slipping into anecdotal, sometimes worshipful registers. Richard Roud's exemplary "The Moral Taste of Lotte Eisner" is peppered with pithy details and aperçus gathered from conversations with Eisner, and it closes with the remark: "To have met Lotte Eisner was a privilege; to have known her was to have known a representative of the best of German intelligence, wit and warmth."[30] A moving tribute to their relationship, Roud's reflections on Eisner's work and contributions are displaced by memorialization of a bygone, of the trope of the noble German: the emphasis is placed on what has been lost, rather than what might persist or remain vital past the point of her death. In addition to their resonances in the postwar period, particularly in terms of denazification, the tributes in this vein to Eisner qua German can be read, to a certain extent, as exchanges in the marketplace of social capital. Werner Herzog, for example, has been particularly effusive about Eisner's involvement in his early career, but, as I explore in the conclusion, the benefits of that imprimatur flowed both ways, and they can be difficult to parse. It is clear that Herzog's take on Eisner's significance, in the absence of any substantial, positive arguments to the contrary, has come to be widely accepted. However, I argue that there are important aspects of her work that go entirely unaddressed in that frame of reference. Furthermore, coded narratives about Eisner proffered by Herzog and other young filmmakers who knew her in her last decades—focused on her physical frailty, her fragility, her nurturing impulses—have contributed, in concert with the underlying assumptions made by many film scholars, to an informal consensus that revisiting her better-known work, let alone looking into her little-known work, is unlikely to yield much.

Yet there have been important exceptions to the larger trends in the secondary literature identified above. Laurent Mannoni was one of the young men at the Cinémathèque française whom Eisner mentored, but, unlike others, he has consistently advocated in his own scholarly work for a revision of the mythology around Eisner's role there, recuperating her archival work and, to a limited extent, her postwar scholarship in his 2006 volume dedicated to the history of the Cinémathèque française, as well as several articles.[31] Mannoni's work, while illuminating, is oriented exclusively toward the context of the Cinémathèque française, works primarily with source materials held there, and engages the broader contexts of academic film study or Eisner's other careers only peripherally.

More recently, there has been further work in key areas. Julia Eisner's research in the family archive promises to shed further light on Lotte Eisner's postwar years and her work at the Cinémathèque française. A symposium convened by Erica Carter and Julia Eisner in the fall of 2018 also showcased the work of Janet Bergstrom, who affirmed the importance of Lotte Eisner's archival and scholarly work. Bergstrom indicated in her presentation the relevance of Eisner's work on Murnau in particular, but Bergstrom's work is by no means alone today in reverberating with the impact of Eisner's scholarship and archival praxis. Michael Wedel's contribution to the symposium took some steps toward placing Eisner's dissertation in context, although the bulk of his talk was devoted to a comparative reading of Eisner's and Éric Rohmer's uses of the terms *Stimmung* and *Umwelt* and to the reasons that Rohmer may have drawn on Eisner's work without citing her, rather than on the original context of her dissertation, or the somewhat complicated problem of Eisner's own modes of citation and reference with regard to these terms.[32] Classicist Patrick Schollmeyer recently echoed the call for a comprehensive intellectual historicization and disciplinary contextualization of Eisner's dissertation and career in film journalism and scholarship, suggesting that reservoirs of interest beyond Anglophone film study continue to precipitate.[33]

The reception of Eisner's postwar work and the neglect of her interwar journalism have as much to do with the dynamics and politics of institutionalized film study in the academy as they do with the ways Eisner described and contextualized the work and herself as its producer. Therefore, these recent stirrings suggest that the present moment is opportune for reexamination of both those descriptions on Eisner's part and the work itself.

STRUCTURE AND SCOPE

In the first chapter, "Fräulein Doktor Eisner," I open by discussing Eisner's commentary on her family life and her disclosures in the memoirs and interviews on her childhood experience of gender dysphoria. In reading Eisner's later recollections of her first days, we gain an understanding both of how she understood herself to have moved in the world as a child and young person and what she would later conceive of as the larger forces shaping that movement—that is, her experience of choice and the later reflections on what had conditioned, or, in some cases, voided her choices. Important historical factors include the changing, contested status of women in the academy in Germany during this period and the ways that gender and class figure in Eisner's narrative—set forth in her memoirs, as well as in numerous interviews given from the 1950s through the 1980s—about her education, writing style, and intellectual interests. From there, I move to place Eisner's doctoral training as an art historian and her 1924 dissertation in context, providing a stylistic analysis of the text and a summary of her contributions therein. Indicating the ways it participated in contemporaneous academic art historical and archaeological discourse, I highlight the elements of her dissertation that anticipate her later journalistic and scholarly work.

In the second chapter, "A Reluctant Bellwether: Dr. L. H. Eisner and Flapper at the *Film-Kurier*," I present a detailed assessment of Eisner's journalism published in the *Film-Kurier* from 1927 to 1933 and offer an analysis of some of the political, aesthetic, and philosophical commitments evinced by this voluminous body of work. Glossing the characteristics of the publication at large, and the larger trends during the period of Eisner's tenure, I show the ways her writing style and areas of coverage changed over time, and the themes and approaches that persisted throughout, bringing to light selections from this corpus that have not been reproduced or discussed elsewhere in English-, German-, or French-language scholarship to date. I situate this body of work within the larger debates of the period about film aesthetics and politics. I pay special attention to the publications in which she broached novel perspectives on key contemporaneous discourse, and the areas in which Eisner thought and wrote outside the mainstream. In the latter cases, I argue, we discover the vital interwar cinema culture anew and find new opportunities and points of engagement for film studies in the present.

The third chapter, "*La seule historienne*: Exile, Salvage, and Community at the Cinémathèque Française," traces the early years of Eisner's exile and her time in hiding during the Occupation, showing how these experiences shaped her archival work at the Cinémathèque française, where she honed a theory and practice of transnational, multilingual collection, preservation, and access as chief curator. I argue that the historiographical underpinnings of her archival work in the postwar period were shaped by the wholesale destruction wrought on the social, economic, political, and institutional networks that she and many of her colleagues and peers from the interwar period had relied upon for sustenance and community. Grounded in original research I conducted in the administrative archives of the Cinémathèque française, this chapter engages contemporary secondary literature on archive theory and queer historiography to flesh out a description and analysis of

Eisner's methods in the context of the period. I argue that the received wisdom regarding Eisner's role at the Cinémathèque and the value of her often highly personalized archival praxis is overdue for a revision, and I suggest several angles from which I believe particularly productive rereadings are possible.

In the fourth chapter, "'Lacunae Everywhere': Iterative Historiography and the Midcentury Palimpsests," I focus on Eisner's scholarly publications—comprising over seventy articles and several books, including *L'écran démoniaque* and *The Haunted Screen*, *F. W. Murnau*, and *Fritz Lang*—which she continued to revise, expand, and reshape in each successive edition. Taking its title quotation from Eisner's own assessment of the state of film historiography circa 1953, this chapter performs a close comparative analysis of Eisner's postwar publications, tracing her research methodology, the historiographical stakes of her work, and the ways she nuanced signal concepts and lines of argumentation. The problematic ways that Eisner has been cited and elided find some explanation in the organizational, institutional, and social dynamics of the postwar milieux in which she worked and published; yet they also spring from the ways Eisner explained her work and addressed her intended audiences, and from the associations she avoided and alliances she spurned. One of the key interventions this chapter makes is to place these postwar scholarly publications in context, both in terms of Eisner's doctoral work and interwar journalism, and in the emergent field of academic film studies in France and the United States.

The conclusion, "The Woolly Mammoth of the Cinémathèque," covers Eisner's later years as a symbolic figure for young filmmakers associated with New Wave movements in France and Germany. During this period, Eisner enjoyed greater recognition within a larger community of filmmakers and scholars than at any other point in her life, yet the narrative that began to solidify then about the scope and significance of her work was incomplete and ultimately foreclosed many of its most interesting potentialities. Returning to the mythmaking process alluded to in this introduction that Eisner, Roud, Herzog, and others set in motion, I assess what was lost in the fashioning of these myths and demonstrate what is gained by a more robust understanding of her work. I ground this discussion in the comparative narrative and stylistic analysis of a pair of documentaries about Eisner—*Die langen Ferien der Lotte H. Eisner* (*The Long Vacation of Lotte H. Eisner*, Sohrab Shahid Saless, 1979) and *Lotte Eisner in Germany* (S. M. Horowitz, 1980)—that take divergent approaches to mediating displacement and exile; one conforming to received notions about the nature of her accomplishments and legacy, the other suggesting a more complex, open-ended approach to her life and work. I close this final chapter with a reflection on the stakes and risks of recuperative reading and on what my own historiographical commitments have been.

In excavating Eisner's early work and evaluating the impact of exile and displacement on her career, I bring her work and the arc of her career into sharper focus and highlight a novel opportunity to consider the relation of labor and gender to the emergence and circulation of theories of film history, aesthetics, and culture. I am wary of the additive model of historical recuperation and have made an effort to relate my critique in this particular case to larger structures and norms. Eisner's rich and generative body of work over multiple domains has been hiding in plain sight, and the ways of seeing characterized by this occlusion have resulted in many other oversights. In conversation with feminist historiography, this project brings new evidence to bear on long-standing debates about popular culture, historiography, and the archive in the context of seismic political and economic shifts in twentieth-century European and US history. Reading Eisner's memoirs, dissertation, interwar journalism, and the extensive administrative and personal correspondence from the postwar period alongside her more familiar scholarly publications, I argue, may not only help us to reorient the lodestars of early film theory, but to sketch new constellations in the intellectual history of the field, thereby freeing up lines of inquiry that have been hitherto blurred or dimmed by habits of seeing and the vantage points from which a disciplinary imaginary has been plotted.

All translations from German, French, and Italian into English, unless otherwise noted, are my own; in the cases of authors whose work has already circulated for many years in English translation, such as André Bazin, I have opted to quote from previously published translations rather than to retranslate excerpts myself. Eisner's writing voice in German, particularly during her time at the *Film-Kurier*, is expressive and highly original. In her later years, she often remarked that writing style was among the most important aspects of her journalistic craft, in addition to being a special point of pride. In my translations of German-language source texts, I have worked to give a sense in English of my own impressions of the style, tone, and diction in German, resulting in looser, more idiomatic renderings where possible: a "domesticating" translation per Lawrence Venuti's dichotomy. In contemporaneous reviews of her postwar French-language publications—particularly

L'écran démoniaque and *F. W. Murnau* (not, as far as I'm aware, *Fritz Lang*, which was translated into French from English with the help of Bernard Eisenschitz)—some commentators remarked that her writing style lacked a certain native-language elegance or expansiveness; the passages excerpted here from her French-language writing are, in the main, less self-consciously stylish, far less numerous, and in all cases I attempted to give close translations.

ONE

Fräulein Doktor Eisner

LOTTE HENRIETTE REGINA EISNER was born on March 5, 1896, to Margarethe Feodora Aron and Hugo Eisner, a textile exporter and magistrate. Preceded in 1893 by an elder brother, Fritz, she would be followed in 1906 by a sister, Stefanie. Eisner's descriptions in her memoirs of her family and upbringing emphasize, for the most part, the continuities between her early and mature interests and self-image. In common with interviews and anecdotes recorded elsewhere, she seems to delight in irreverent characterization, verging on caricature. At the outset, Eisner traces her lineage and middle name from a glamorous maternal grandmother, Henriette Cahn—a woman who, Eisner proudly notes, shared with her granddaughter a preference for the novels of Stendhal and once fielded a marriage proposal from a French count—noting that among Henriette's daughters, only one, an aunt of Eisner's, was graced with their mother's beauty or wit: "Why my father married my mother, of all people, remains unclear to me to this day. As a child I resented it and pictured what might have been had he married the pretty English pastor's daughter, memorably named 'Minny Pretty,' instead of my mother. [Minny] had rejected his marriage proposal on the (in my opinion, irrelevant) grounds that she was three years older than he. From this affair my father retained an Anglomania my brother and I inherited."[1] This passage is exemplary of Eisner's recollections in the memoirs in three important ways: first, in terms of its conversational style, salted with asides and put-downs. The memoirs lean toward historical accounting, in some ways; reproducing extended passages from select publications of Eisner's with careful citations, the text is also generously seasoned with archival photos and extracts of personal correspondence. But they are billed "as told to" co-author Martje Grohmann and strongly marked by the tropes of the celebrity

FIGURE 2. Eisner in her youth. Still from *Lotte Eisner in Germany* (S. M. Horowitz, 1980).

biography, including near-incessant name-dropping and the inclusion of dubiously sourced, gossipy, sometimes ludicrous anecdotes.[2] A second representative feature of this passage is that Eisner allies herself in it with her father and brother in opposition to her mother; this is a consistent feature of the reflections in her memoirs on her childhood and early adult years, and it is an important commonality among the memoirs of many other women of Eisner's generation who grew up in similar environments and went on to pursue higher education and careers outside the domestic sphere.

Finally, and perhaps most importantly, this sample gives a good flavor of the experience of reading the memoirs at large in terms of how difficult it is to identify and place Eisner's tone. The jocular, sardonic spirit in which she doles out such criticism does little to mute its harshness; cruel teasing curdles virtually all of Eisner's commentary in the memoirs on her early family life.[3] One imagines, not without some amusement, what a trying child she might have been when she says that in spite of his past as a ladies' man, her father remained true to her mother until his death, and that she "resented this, too," continuing, "Of course, I held my mother solely responsible for the fact that I had been born neither a boy nor an Indian, qualities deemed by me essential preconditions to leading a happy life."[4] An unflattering portrait of Eisner in childhood and old age alike as an unrepentant, even gleeful maligner of her mother emerges from the memoirs. Arch and cutting, yet with moments of awkward vulnerability, she appears before the reader in her own telling as a young person struggling with certain boundaries and expectations, especially those related to her gender, yet it remains unclear whether Eisner's animus in the memoirs toward her mother is primarily personal or symbolic. Many of her mother's appearances in the text take place in the context of a binary dynamic, either contrasted with Eisner's father, or allied with Eisner's sister against Eisner herself. In these anecdotes, her mother is the embodiment of qualities Eisner deems undesirable and unnatural in her own person: feminine dress and mannerisms, interest in socializing with other women, a lack of interest or aptitude in intellectual pursuits, and a preoccupation with her physical appearance.[5]

In the passage above, and in others dotted throughout the memoir, Eisner alludes to her sense of dysphoria in a complicated, multivalent expression of difference. She comments most directly in the memoirs on her gender identity and sexuality during her twenties and thirties, stating that she felt unfulfilled both by romantic relationships and by the norms structuring gender. Claiming that her love life wasn't eventful enough to warrant chronicling in the memoirs, Eisner explains: "Either the man who fell in love with me lost his dignity because he wanted to pamper and cherish me—gentleness and worshipful behavior only encourage maliciousness in me—or else when I was the one in love, it was usually with an empty-headed handsome man, whose stupidity would bore me stiff, and I'd break things off." She goes on to offer the following intriguing explanation for her difficulties: "I was perhaps not entirely normal, or rather masculine. . . . When I was dancing I always wanted to take the lead; in love, the passive role of the woman disturbed me. I wanted to be the dominant one myself."[6] Eisner seems to have chafed under gendered norms of sexuality and power, dissatisfied with the opportunities she had been presented to negotiate sexual, romantic, and professional relationships on her own terms. This frustration is articulated both in terms of a rejection of femininity, as she understands it, and an affirmation of masculinity, largely in terms of what she perceived as its entitlements.[7]

In Eisner's somewhat sheltered upper-middle-class milieu, girls and women had less opportunity and freedom than boys and men to pursue intellectual and physical achievements, and she was, by her own account, an ambitious, creative child who saw in her father's hobbies, interests, and his encouragement of these in her greater fulfillment than those modeled or enforced by her mother. In this, Eisner was not alone; as Harriet Pass Freidenreich noted in her study of Jewish Central European university women from 1900 to 1933, "It was not uncommon for academically oriented adolescent girls to feel uncomfortable or ambivalent about their own sexuality or femininity. In their memoirs, university women tended to attribute their conflicting attitudes, on the one hand, to their relationships with their parents or siblings, and, on the other hand, to uncertainty about their physical attractiveness and hence their marriage possibilities."[8] The expression of gender dysphoria and ambivalence is a theme among the memoirs of many of these women. Freidenreich points out that in some cases this was expressed as resentment about having not been born a boy, while in others it was articulated as an affinity with fathers and brothers in preference to mothers and sisters, or as a lament that they might never partake of affordances like higher education, professional careers, personal freedoms, even military service, which were mostly, if not exclusively, available to men. In the memoirs of Margaret Schoenberger Mahler, a physician born just one year after Eisner, Freidenreich isolates a passage exemplifying this tendency, one which bears a strong resemblance to Eisner's description of her own experience: "Existing well outside the narcissistic orbit of my mother and sister . . . I tended to deny my own femininity entirely. I refused to believe that any man worth having could love me; if one per chance expressed any feeling for me, he was instantly devalued."[9] The similarities between Mahler's self-portrait and Eisner's—particularly in terms of their scornfulness—are striking; interestingly, Mahler ultimately did marry, whereas Eisner did not. In her memoirs, Eisner links this decision directly to exile and to her professional ambitions, arguing that being single made her career possible, and during her years in hiding, it allowed her to move freely and to evade capture.[10]

ADOLESCENCE AND EARLY EDUCATION

In spite of these difficulties, Eisner describes her teenage years as relatively untroubled by the usual emotional and physical tribulations. She was by her own account a voracious reader who found creative outlets in writing and putting on plays, and who nurtured an abiding passion for the outdoors, particularly hiking and bathing.[11] While she denies having been troubled by angst or self-doubt during her teens, she admits that she was observed to be rather anxious and withdrawn. She attributes any outward displays of awkwardness to a growing aversion to her mother and sister and an increasing difference between her sense of how she identified and what she began to feel was expected of her with regard to gender, religion, and class performance.[12] Her memoirs describe a young person who felt encouraged within certain limits to think of herself as an intellectual; Eisner's assumption, seemingly from an early age, was that her education might be pursued as far as and in whatever direction she desired. In this way, she was among a privileged and rare subset of girls who would go on to university, according to Freidenreich; the majority of Jewish university women pursued professional degrees and were supported in this by their families with the expectation that a profession would help bolster the family's economic security, or would allow a daughter disinclined to marry to become financially independent.[13] Eisner felt included by her father and brother in conversation, debate, and common interests, and she was proud to have had a close relationship with her father, sharing his appreciation for music, literature, and classical studies.[14]

Tutored from an early age by governesses, Eisner attended a Protestant primary school for several years, but was later withdrawn from it by her parents and placed under private tutelage arranged in common among the wealthy families of their neighborhood, where she and a dozen or so other young women of her age and class were instructed at a more advanced level in classics, religion, dancing, music, and languages.[15] Eisner recalls this private education circle as more academically rigorous than her previous schooling, in spite of its clear fixation on inculcating gender and class norms; one of the chief benefits of this private education, as far as she was concerned, was the freedom it gave parents to withdraw their children at any point for extended travel. She claims to have been awkwardly uncoordinated in the realm of feminine tasks such as sewing, cooking, and dancing, in spite of her dexterity and discernment when the same fine motor skills were applied in the service of artistic or creative tasks: "All feminine skills escaped me. The sewing and knitting teacher, who also taught drawing and handicrafts, once said to me: 'Lotte, it's funny: you've got two different pairs of hands. When you're cutting out silhouettes, they are nimble and skillful, but when you're supposed to be sewing they suddenly become clumsy and uncoordinated.' I've never been able to cook, either, and don't fuss much about food."[16] Describing herself as constitutionally incapable of performing gender in the ways she felt were expected, Eisner narrates her own coming of age in terms of the qualities she felt differentiated her from her peers: her creativity, her independence, and her antipathy for femininity.

The advent of her eighteenth year, the beginning of the war, and her brother's enlistment marked the end of Eisner's childhood. In her memoirs, she identifies the period of her enrollment at a boarding school for women in Karlsruhe with both academic and personal fulfillment, as well as a growing sense of independence from her parents, who, unlike Eisner, initially supported the war. The women's academy in Karlsruhe was the first German institution to offer a *Gymnasium* education—which prepared students to take university entrance exams—to female students, beginning in 1893.[17] Eisner states that she spent one year at Karlsruhe, passing her Abitur around the time she was twenty years old. She devotes the majority of her reflections on this period in the memoirs to a friendship formed while in school there with one Anneliese von Rohrscheidt, whom she describes as her first real friend.[18] Eisner would remember their relationship with deep affection, and she expresses in her memoirs the pain and surprise she and Anneliese experienced when their friendship was interrupted by Anneliese's father, who forbade them to see each other on the grounds that Eisner was Jewish. While she had somewhat limited firsthand experience prior to her late teens with anti-Semitism, the memoirs suggest that with her desire for independence dawned the recognition that the privileges of her childhood and upbringing would be insufficient to shield her from discrimination on the basis of her gender and Jewish identity, however tenuously connected to either she felt herself to be.

According to Freidenreich, Eisner would have been part of a significant minority of young women in secondary schools who were Jewish, some of whom had similarly ambivalent relationships to Jewish identity. A number of factors likely contributed to the high enrollment rates among Jewish young women in secondary education, including class status, the higher concentration of Jewish populations in urban areas where access to secondary and post-secondary institutions of higher learning was possible for students who continued to live in their childhood homes rather than boarding or living independently, and post-emancipation assimilation into German society and culture. As Freidenreich argues: "the secular Jewish culture developing in acculturated Jewish homes fostered the pursuit of higher education for both men and women as a means of more effective integration into the *Bildungsbürgertum*, the educated bourgeoisie."[19] While Eisner seems to have anticipated university study in her future from an early age, it is only explicit in retrospect that she understood that her education had provided her some means of economic independence from marriage or family, and of assimilation; during childhood, she saw it simply as a fulfilling pursuit that economic privilege and the support of her family made possible.[20]

FRAUENSTUDIUM: "DIE EISNERIN" AMONG THE GERMAN MANDARINS

Eisner was a member of the second generation of central European Jewish university women, born before the turn of the century and awarded their degrees before the end of the Weimar Republic in 1933. While they still represented a minuscule percentage of enrollments, this second cohort of university women was larger and more diverse than the prewar cohort, and they managed to complete their degrees—and in some cases find work using those degrees—before the expulsion of women and Jews from German universities and public service, beginning in the early thirties. By the time Eisner began studying at the University of Berlin in the winter semester of 1920, the enrollment of women at Prussian universities had been dramatically increasing for about a decade: in 1908–09, women made up 2.5 percent of university students, by 1911–12 they were 6.4 percent, and by the time Eisner received her degree in 1924, women represented 11.5 percent of enrollments in central European universities.[21]

Of these students, Jewish women were a shrinking minority, in spite of the fact that their enrollment numbers consistently rose: 102 women total in 1908–09 (17.9% of the total female university enrollment), 189 in 1911–12 (11.2%), and 389 by 1924–25 (12.2%).[22] Among these women, many pursued professional degrees in medicine, social work, and education. A number of women pursued doctorates in law, sciences, and the humanities, but according to Freidenreich's assessment, "Law and academia offered the least promise as professional fields for women and for Jews," given the insularity, conservatism, and homogeneity resulting from (and reinforcing, in turn) the self-replicating gatekeeping norms of these fields.[23] In fact, as Freidenreich argues, in the late nineteenth-century debates about admitting women to German institutions of higher education, many advocates focused on women in medicine, arguing that while it could be considered a given that women were not suited to academic pursuits per se, their innate feminine capacity for nurturing might be a strength in the context of medicine. Questions about the suitability of university life for women, and vice versa, attracted significant public attention on the part of the professoriate and other interested parties, and contestation abounded in the popular and academic press. In her authoritative study of this discourse, Patricia Mazón emphasizes the degree to which it was a public negotiation of norms:

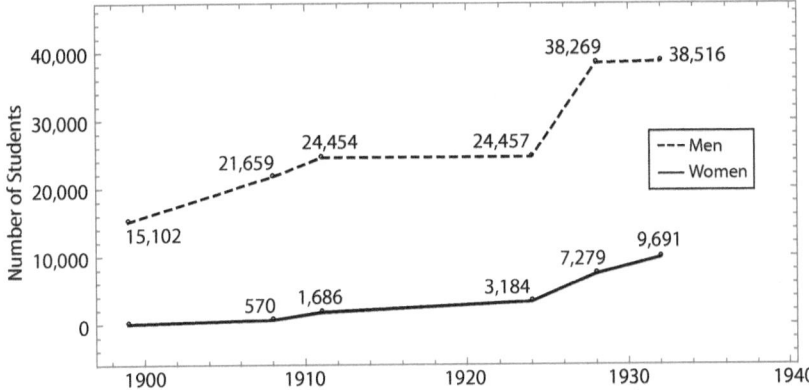

FIGURE 3. Enrollment data reported by Harriet Pass Freidenreich, *Female, Jewish, and Educated: The Lives of Central European University Women* (Bloomington: Indiana University Press, 2002). Chart by the author.

The fact that German universities were all-male was intrinsic to the shared vision of the institution. In educating the young man, the university prepared him for his future place in society and also sought to instill in him a certain kind of bourgeois masculine identity. Female students would have no place in this project. In the clash between the rhetoric of the woman question and academic citizenship that ensued, two main questions emerged. The more central of these was simply whether women should be admitted to the university. Yet the decisive factor in whether they would be allowed to pursue higher education at all would prove to be the subjects that women were expected to study and the careers they were expected to pursue.[24]

By the time Eisner began her studies in Berlin, it would have been uncommon but not unprecedented for women to enroll in art history or archaeology seminars, as she did; while she glosses over much of her experience at university in her memoirs, she seems to have felt neither singularly excluded nor specially encouraged by her peers and professors. Instead, the bulk of what she recounts in her memoirs about this period relates to what she was doing outside the lecture hall or library: going to the theater, seeing, and being seen at the right cafés in Berlin, earning from Bertolt Brecht the nickname "Die Eisnerin," hiking and traveling: in short, the experiences and anecdotes that would come to dominate her later retellings of the interwar period. Eisner describes her peripatetic studies—not unusual among German university students at the time—in Berlin, Freiburg, Munich, and finally Rostock as being dictated primarily by her interest in studying with particular professors or living in cities that offered notable amenities. Overwhelmed by the social calendar in Berlin, and feeling that her studies were slipping as a result, after several semesters Eisner relocated to Freiburg to study with archaeologist Ludwig von Curtius. In her memoirs, Eisner describes boarding in Freiburg with a doctor's family and the havoc extreme inflation caused her monthly budget. Purchasing books at the beginning of each month as soon as her allowance arrived, she found that the money left at the end of the month had devalued so precipitously that she could not afford to buy food, a situation she says forced her into the position of providing childcare for the doctor's family in exchange for a portion of the costs of room and board.[25]

Sometime in 1923, Eisner recalls, she expressed to Curtius a desire to enroll in the celebrated Swiss art historian Heinrich Wölfflin's final seminar, to be taught at Munich.[26] Wölfflin, at the peak of his career in the summer of 1923, had declared that he would be retiring from the profession and would therefore be giving a final seminar in the fall semester, resigning his chair in March 1924. The motivation for this abrupt and, to many of his colleagues, shocking decision has been much debated. Wölfflin himself gave several different rationales, including, most controversially, that the profession was at a dead end and he wanted to spend his time on more worthwhile pursuits.[27] Naturally, this line of reasoning caused consternation among fellow academics, and it may have influenced Curtius's response to Eisner's request, although Eisner offers no such context or clarification in her memoirs, and the press did not announce Wölfflin's intentions until September of 1923, which would have been very near the beginning of that fall semester.[28] According to Eisner, Curtius told her that if she left to enroll in Wölfflin's seminar, she wouldn't be welcome back in Freiburg and he would refuse to supervise her doctoral studies any longer. Nevertheless, Eisner chose to enroll in the Munich seminar, and in her memoirs she attributes Wölfflin's course with inspiring the methodology she would subsequently use in her dissertation. Once she had been cut loose by Curtius and completed the semester with Wölfflin, Eisner sought a quiet spot to write up her dissertation; she alighted at the University of Rostock, where a friend and colleague of hers from Berlin, Gottfried von Lücken, had recently secured his first teaching position. Among his peers, Lücken would have been young, only thirteen years Eisner's senior, and while she remarks relatively little about him in her memoirs, she does grant that she had followed his work since they parted ways and found it intriguing.²⁹ As we will see, it is unclear what exactly of Wölfflin's method Eisner might have applied to her dissertation, but Lücken's influence on the scope, methods, and rhetoric of her dissertation is apparent. Indeed, Eisner doesn't cite a word of Wölfflin's work in the text of her dissertation, and his name appears only once, without any special emphasis in the list of all professors with whom she studied over the course of her graduate career.

THE DISSERTATION

Written in a matter of months, according to the timeline recited in her memoirs, Eisner's PhD dissertation, "The Development of Composition in Greek Vase Paintings" ("Die Entwicklung der Komposition auf griechischen Vasenbildern"), traces the development of *Bildeinheit*—the image-unit, or picture plane—in black- and red-figure Greek pottery from roughly 570 to 440 BCE, relying on established attributions and methods of stylistic analysis to offer a novel four-part classification of this interstitial period of stylistic development. Although she describes having amassed a large research archive of images by the time she left for Munich, finalizing her methodology with the completion of that course, and finding in Rostock little more than a peaceful roost, a close reading of the dissertation suggests that several other key factors influenced its topic, sources, and methodology.³⁰

In order to understand how the project participated in contemporaneous art historical discourse, a few contextual notes are needed. The institutionalization of art history as an academic discipline in the mid-nineteenth century is often associated with German scholarship, in part because some of its first chairs were established at German universities. Before the turn of the century, the German and Austrian art historians who would come to dominate the field in the twentieth century—including Wölfflin, Alois Riegl, and Aby Warburg—had begun contributing their most important interventions.³¹ By the time Eisner began her graduate education, the discipline had been ensconced in the academy for almost a century and had weathered important debates about disciplinary boundaries, historiographical methodology, and stylistic analysis. Some of the major questions for early academic art historians dealt with the relationship between connoisseurship and scholarship and the epistemological differences between the two; for instance, what kinds of knowledge should art historians be concerned with, what role, if any, does taste have to play in that knowledge, and what is the proper relationship between aesthetic and historiographical analysis? Certain early German academic art historians were particularly concerned with formalizing quasi-scientific methodologies in order to firmly identify the field as a legitimate academic discipline. These scholars argued that the normative, thus innately subjective, mode of connoisseurship—for example, X work is of greater value than Y because of its stylistic or historical characteristics—was fundamentally incompatible with the mandate of academic study. The primacy of comprehensive studies advocating unified theory versus particularism had ebbed and flowed, and by Eisner's time there were respected partisans of each stripe. However, while developmental histories of art would have been relatively uncontroversial, there were lively disagreements about what kinds of arguments might be made about the directionality of development and the relationship of its constitutive stages to the economic, social, and political contexts in which particular works emerged. In her dissertation, Eisner subscribes to a fundamentally progressivist conception of art historical analysis, and she summarizes her methodology as a two-part process: first, she explains, a series of individual subjects were evaluated "for characteristic compositional features," and the prototypes thereby derived were then placed in chronological sequence. These were then compared with the chronologically organized oeuvres of certain "masters"—recognized artists or workshops—drawn from the Beazley and Hoppin catalogs, considered at the time to be among the premier field references.[32]

Accepting the argument made by contemporary scholars such as Emmanuel Loewy and, to an extent, Arnold von Salis, that Renaissance principles of realism (and the tropes of representation thereby solidified as naturalistic) find their roots in Attic red-figure pottery, Eisner sets out to trace the development of representation in the period immediately preceding. In her attention to the "painterly" and "Baroque," Eisner takes up a strand of contemporaneous art historical discourse seeking to unsettle the normative valuation of Classical style over Baroque and, perhaps less obviously, to dislodge the notion of Classical style as an inevitability, although it should be noted that she does not take her own argument quite so far. Naturalistic representation is characterized in her reading by *Bildeinheit*, attention to psychological and emotional dimensions of human expression (she singles out the way that the gaze is represented), and the introduction to painting style of a quality of mood, or *Stimmung*. Eisner takes it as a given that more naturalistic representation begins at the end stage of her period of interest, and the developments preceding this turn occupy the bulk of her analysis. Moreover, while she uses a chronological frame of reference for the four phases of development she identifies, Eisner is careful to emphasize the vagaries of stylistic development and the discontinuities in the stylistic trajectories at hand.

In spite of relying on the Beazley and Hoppin catalogs, as well as photographs of the MoMA catalog (provided to Eisner personally by the curator and eminent classicist Gisela Richter), Eisner's argument is largely unconcerned with questions of attribution, neither querying the assumptions embedded in the methodology of connoisseurship nor relying exclusively on purported authorship to substantiate or personify claims of stylistic development.[33] In fact, while Eisner remarks on the development of individual artistic style in some cases, the periodization of these works seems to serve as a more fundamental point of reference than authorship per se.[34] Within these parameters, Eisner's argument might best be described as a diachronic comparative formal analysis.

In broad strokes, the argument of her dissertation runs as follows: the development of *Bildeinheit* occurs in four phases, the first of which emerges in the sixth century out of the Orientalizing period and is characterized by what she calls "rhythmic composition," in which pictorial elements are set off from decorative elements, regularly interspaced, like "strings of pearls."[35] These compositions are characterized in the main, for Eisner, by their flat, uniform, graphic qualities: all human figures stand at the same height in these compositions, and their bodies appear, in Eisner's evocative turn of phrase, "as though they had been pressed into their robes," like herbs or flowers in a book. Here, too, the "germ" of *Bildeinheit* appears, in frieze-style composition, in which a central element guides the movement and interaction of figures, creating a sense of unified space among compositional elements.[36]

Following this phase, a profoundly "painterly" technique emerges, according to Eisner, and gradually the stiffer, more graphic elements of composition become softened and elastic.[37] Here she also identifies a quasi-Mannerist style and the introduction of diagonal composition, as opposed to either the horizontal composition of continuous decorative elements and friezes or the vertical composition of the metope, framed and set off by repetitive ornamentation. Her key point of reference is the rendering of the human figure, which she sees as increasingly prominent within the composition, depicted with greater fullness, yet "boneless" and mobile, characterized by a steadily more "painterly" interweaving of figures and their surroundings (i.e., depth of field). The progressivist strand of Eisner's argumentation comes to the fore in her analysis of the later works of this second phase; here she says that this tendency stands in direct contrast to the preceding stylistic development and ultimately bends back, in its overlarding of painterly details, to an even earlier stylistic point of origin: to the ornamental, decorative style, with the key difference being the addition of diagonal composition.

A third phase, beginning in late black-figure painting and carrying over to early red-figure painting, synthesizes the two previous phases, bringing both the rhythmic qualities of the first phase and the diagonal composition of the second to bear on familiar themes. As in the other chapters, Eisner performs evocative close analysis and description of the examples chosen, thereby fleshing out an argument for the unification of the image, which derives from the increasing "confidence" of certain key artists, Andokides and the Euthymides group serving as exemplars. Here, more pronouncedly than in previous chapters, Eisner relies on value-freighted descriptors to distinguish the period's stylistic features; the lines are increasingly "elegant," figures markedly more "lively."[38]

The final phase of development is distinguished by its rejection of diagonal composition—linked in Eisner's description to late-Renaissance compositions in the Mannerist school and to Baroque style—in favor of a new vertical composition style. Preserving the elasticity gained in earlier phases and presaging the "serenity" and "noble lines" of the classical period, this final phase is described as both the culmination of the previous developments and the key to the subsequent historical and stylistic developments.[39]

What fails to come through in a brief summary of the dissertation is the remarkably stylish package in which the arguments glossed above are conveyed. In addition to Eisner's zippy prose—and in common with the postwar scholarship she will begin publishing almost thirty years later—the dissertation makes use throughout of framing epigraphs that structure and pace the flow of her argument, each of them providing an important signal as to how she situates her work and in which contemporary discourses she sees her dissertation participating. After dedicating the work as a whole to her father, she prefaces her introduction and overview with a quotation from Arnold von Salis's influential *Die Kunst der Griechen*, which reads: "Think what you will about the worth and uses of image analysis, which directs contemplation to the cool spheres of geometric design: the classical Greek period does indeed work with such concepts, and for those who ignore its voice, the last and finest ideas of its works will remain enigmatic."[40] Salis's important volume would be issued in four successive editions in his lifetime, and at the time of Eisner's citation, it was considered a signal contribution to the field.[41] In it, Salis reprises the case, first made in his 1912 book on the Pergamon Altar, for applying art historical terms used to describe Renaissance art to what would be dubbed the "Hellenic Baroque" by Salis and others. Part of a wider discourse within the academy recuperating the Baroque, Salis flags his own usage with a note on the dangers of extending historically specific terms beyond their original period or point of reference, yet he proceeds to justify the application of the terms *Baroque, Rococo,* and *Mannerist* to Greek art on the basis of fundamental cyclical similarities and on the fact that, in this specific instance, the later period from which these terms originated drew quite explicitly on the earlier.[42] Two further quotations from Salis's book serve as the epigraphs for Eisner's first chapter; each is a description of certain stylistic hallmarks of the period directly leading up to that of Eisner's focus, and while it seems clear that the citation of Salis is meant to situate the work to follow, each passage could have been included as a footnote just as easily. By foregrounding these citations, Eisner emphasizes the influence of Salis's work on her own: sketching, in effect, the intellectual lineage within which she sees her dissertation. Interestingly, these short quotations of Salis—about rhythmic composition and repetition as a formal element—could have been attributed to other works, as this was by no means an observation made by Salis alone.

In actuality, it might have been more accurate to attribute these observations as influences on the analysis at hand had they been sourced from work by Eisner's advisor, Gottfried von Lücken, who had published in 1919 on the progressive development of Greek vase painting along representational lines and the decline in decorative logics of composition in style across both vase painting and sculpture from the sixth century through the fourth.[43] Eisner does introduce her final chapter with a peculiarly stylized citation of an article of Lücken's published in 1922: "Z.f.b.K. XXXIII."[44] In this article, titled "Toward the Emergence of the Image," Lücken traces the formal development of Greek vase painting from that of sixth-century, frieze-influenced, more decorative style to composition in the style of the metope, which he identifies as the point of origin of *Bildeinheit*. Eisner's somewhat unusual choice to identify this quotation's source with only the abbreviated title of the journal in which it appeared, rather than listing the author's name and the source's title, as in all of the dissertation's other epigraphs, may suggest that the dissertation was self-consciously addressed to a readership who well knew the source: Lücken himself.

In fact, Eisner's dissertation as a whole appears to have been shaped by the bounds of Lücken's areas of expertise and interest. It was normal to attend multiple universities over the course of one's doctoral degree in pursuit of coursework, but it would not have been uncommon for the PhD dissertation, the *Inaugural-Dissertation*, to be closely supervised by a single doctoral advisor.[45] In Eisner's case, it seems that the parameters of her dissertation corresponded directly to those of her advisor's publications and current work; Lücken's short 1922 article leaves off with the metope field, where Eisner's analysis begins, and her dissertation ends precisely where his next project began, with Phidias and the Parthenon, work that would have been on his desk at the moment she was writing her dissertation.[46] Moreover, in the piece he would go on to publish on the Parthenon, he employs precisely the same formalist progressivist stylistic analysis, arguing—in contrast to some contemporaries, including Jacob Burckhardt—that the differences in the north frieze should be attributed to stylistic shifts, rather than different artists. Interestingly, Lücken was awarded a patent around this time for a novel method of photographically reproducing the images painted on a curved surface onto a plane surface without distortion. As Lücken described in his patent filing, his method consisted of photographing the vase, thereby creating a photographic negative of the curved picture surface, then "winding a sensitized paper on a body having an evolvable surface as similar as possible to that of the surface to be copied and then projecting the negative onto the sensitized paper."[47] His method reduced the costs of reproducing the imagery on Greek pottery, a task that had typically been accomplished with sketches, incremental photographic series stitched together after the fact, or labor-intensive tracings, in the style of Beazley. There is about Lücken's patent something of the craftiness of the legendary German cinematographers and art directors (or *Architekten*) of the interwar period—Eugen Schüfftan, Karl Freund, Robert Herlth, Walter Röhrig—who devised ingenious methods of shooting, processing, and printing film, as well as building and lighting spaces in order to achieve particular aesthetics and effects. Eisner's dissertation took as its intellectual model the work of a scholar who shared a certain talent and way of thinking about film and representation—albeit in a rather different milieu—with the filmmakers whose work Eisner would spend a great deal of her later journalistic and scholarly careers studying, celebrating, and salvaging.

In addition to the classicists Salis and Lücken, Eisner's dissertation signals its affinities with Alois Riegl, the enormously influential nineteenth-century Viennese art historian. While he had been deceased for almost twenty years by the time Eisner began writing, Riegl's method of formal analysis and his theory of artistic value both informed her work.[48] Both the second and third sections of the dissertation are introduced with quotations from Riegl's 1901 work on the late Roman art industry, *Spätrömische Kunstindustrie*, in which he differentiates between ancient Greek and Egyptian composition and style, arguing that the interweaving of figures within the picture plane and diagonal composition are the two primary innovations of Greek art. Eisner's second and third chapters make nuanced arguments about composition and dwell at length on specific examples vividly described, but while these passages from Riegl's *Spätrömische Kunstindustrie* selected by Eisner provide tidy introductions and precedent for her own analysis, they may also have been chosen to signal an affinity with Riegl's larger argument in that volume for a progressivist, formalist analysis. Riegl's enormously influential concept of *Kunstwollen*, sometimes translated as "artistic will," or "will to style," is the major contribution of this work. While its precise definition has been the subject of much debate, the key aspects related to Eisner's usage are that it allows the art historian to discuss the individual artwork as a discrete object on a formal level and to place it within a historiographical narrative of style.[49] Crucially, and in contrast to the connoisseurship model, *Kunstwollen* allows the art historian to engage the project of periodizing style on less normative grounds; whereas nineteenth-century art historical doxa held that the art of late antiquity signified societal decline and degenerate style in contrast to high Classicism, Riegl's notion of *Kunstwollen* considers late style not in relation necessarily to the classical, but as the product of the materials, attitudes, and aspirations of the artist embedded in a specific place and time.[50] Not only is this model of art historiography more pliant—it is thus possible to draw a connection between Modernist style and the Baroque, an impulse described as "transhistorical" by Riegl interpreter Jas' Elsner—but it works to erode crusty strictures on what constitutes a worthy object of art historical contemplation. Perhaps as an outgrowth of her graduate work with Riegl's texts, Eisner's film journalism—particularly her work on documentary—in the late twenties and early thirties benefits from precisely this unsettling of taste cultures, and it advocates vociferously for the aesthetic and historiographical treatment of film as art.[51]

A second key intervention of Riegl's that Eisner engages throughout the dissertation is the notion of rhythmic composition, which is expounded in his 1893 *Stilfragen: Grundlegungen zu einer Geschichte der Ornamentik* (usually translated *Problems of Style: Foundations for a History of Ornament*). In this volume, Riegl makes the case that a continuous history of ancient decorative motifs can be traced across regional and temporal instances; Riegl scholar Margaret Olin argues that with *Stilfragen*, "[Riegl] came to see decorative motifs as representational tools with multilevel means for making a surface cohere visually and demonstrate flatness while maintaining visual interest."[52] Eisner engages the notion of rhythm and rhythmic composition throughout her analysis, but it is characteristic, for her, of the earlier stages of stylistic development traced in the dissertation; she sees plasticity of figures, an increasingly full and dynamic depth of field, and the earliest stages of *Bildeinheit* as superseding rhythmic composition by the final stages of development.

A third concept Eisner borrows—although it is unclear whether from Riegl, and if so, whether from Riegl alone—is that of *Stimmung*, variously translated as "mood," "voice," or "attunement."[53] In the final section of her dissertation, Eisner argues that the culmination of stylistic development in the mid-fourth century is the emergence of a cohesive image unit, defined by its lack of ornamentation and rhythmic elements as much as it is by its tendency toward a unified picture plane: "*Stimmung* and space: these are the two factors that hold the image together, the oblique connection of the motif is hardly necessary anymore, it recedes behind the others. From here the entire following epoch can be understood."[54] *Stimmung*'s use as a term of aesthetic theory is varied, long-standing, and much debated, and while Eisner would go on to develop a redefinition of the term in a cinematic context with *L'écran démoniaque*, in her dissertation she deploys it only a handful of times, never signaling an external point of reference or source for her own understanding or use of it. Michael Wedel, taking his lead from Eisner's memoirs, has claimed that Wölfflin's 1886 dissertation, titled *Prolegomena to a Psychology of Architecture*, "was to leave a permanent trace on Eisner's understanding of the term," but it is imperative to recall that she gives no such attribution in the text of her own dissertation and, more importantly, appears to have been relatively uninterested in defining her dissertation's uses of the terms *Stimmung* or *malerisch* with one or another interpretation in the larger contemporaneous discursive field.[55] Moreover, contrary to Wedel's further extrapolations, in her later works, Eisner is entirely forthright about the lineage from which her own use of *Stimmung* is descended: in *L'écran démoniaque* (1965) and *The Haunted Screen* (1969), Eisner cites Novalis, not Wölfflin.⁵⁶

Reading Eisner's dissertation together with the occasionally misleading reflections about it in her memoirs, it is unclear whether she hoped or expected to publish it and thus braid it into any larger discourse. It was not unheard of for the *Inaugural-Dissertation* to become a published work, or to be cited in the literature—Wölfflin's continues to be cited occasionally, and it is readily available online—but I have been unable to turn up any citations of Eisner's dissertation, except in her own memoirs, where they are quoted in order to demonstrate what she identifies as the influence of Expressionist poetry on her own prose. Emphasizing the continuities between her dissertation and later journalism on a stylistic level, it is possible that she hoped to clarify that the project's value lay not in the academic reception of her research, but the opportunity it afforded her to hone her craft as a writer and establish a rigorous vocabulary of aesthetics: "I tried, as I would later in my film and theater reviews, to recreate optical impressions and discoveries in words, to describe the inner movement of the images. In my style, I was greatly influenced by Expressionist authors. The words cluster and crowd together into sentences, parentheticals, exclamations, participles, and subordinate clauses, unusual adjectives popping out, the reader breathless by the climax."⁵⁷ It would have been extremely unusual for Eisner—both as a woman and as a Jew—to continue past doctoral study to pursue a *Habilitation* and academic career, and she seems not to have been encouraged in this direction by Lücken, or anyone else.

Following the award of her doctorate, Eisner embarked on what she hoped would be an extended period of travel, beginning in Italy. Several months in, however, she was summoned home to her father's deathbed. After a period of grieving at home, and without any work, she returned to Italy to participate in an archaeological dig. She would often say later, dismissively, that her colleagues were obsessed with questions that bored her, such as "whether the wall went this way or that" in a given excavation, and that she found herself sneaking away to look at art. Finding the work unsatisfying, she set out again for what would end up being a year of travel in the Canary Islands, Spain, and Switzerland. Returning home to Berlin, she seems to have been somewhat at a loss as to what she might do next, and so she visited Lücken at Rostock for advice. His counsel, as reported by Eisner, was that she was unsuited to museum work, didn't have the financial sense for curatorial work at an art gallery, and had demonstrated a knack for writing in her dissertation; why not make her way professionally as a writer?

TWO

A Reluctant Bellwether

DR. L. H. EISNER AND FLAPPER
AT THE *FILM-KURIER*, 1927–1933

LIVING AT HOME with her mother and sister, freelancing art and literary reviews for *Literarische Welt* and interviews for the *Berliner Tageblatt*, the first years of Eisner's homecoming to Berlin were a period of intense activity, both socially and professionally. In her memoirs and in interviews, Eisner described her transition from the *Berliner Tageblatt* to the *Film-Kurier* as a product of the vibrant Berlin arts social scene. While she represented the exact sequence of events leading to her employment at *Film-Kurier* differently on various occasions, the unvarying essentials were that she met a staff writer socially, and he suggested she write film criticism for the paper. In one version, after introducing herself to Hans Feld at a party as a journalist for the *Berliner Tageblatt*, the *Film-Kurier* editor and critic said he'd never read her byline and asked for which section of the paper she wrote. When she answered that she conducted interviews for Walter Zadek's column, Feld replied by insulting her boss: "Aha, Zadek . . ., that pig: he lets others do the work and takes all the glory for himself. And he pays you a pittance! How would you like to work as a salaried film critic for us?"[1] As with other interactions reported in her memoirs and interviews given later in her life, Eisner's use of quotation marks may have been liberal and figurative, but the uninhibited style of the *Film-Kurier*'s Feld was true to life.[2]

Six years her junior, Feld filed his doctoral dissertation in law the same year as Eisner filed hers in art history, and after a brief period of employment as a salesman, he joined the staff of the *Film-Kurier* in 1926.[3] His prolific and distinctive contributions to the paper included theater and film criticism written in an informal, emphatic style marked by its proximity to the spoken word, bristling with exclamation points, question marks (often rhetorical), dashes, ellipses, fragments, and onomatopoeic outbursts. His film critical approach was less concerned with an epistemological or ontological analysis of the medium than it was with reactive advocacy for the kind of filmmaking he found most interesting. According to Rolf Aurich and Wolfgang Jacobsen, Feld's style of criticism was deeply interactive; offering "open-ended—perhaps even ultimately incomplete—perceptions of a person or a film, a gesture or a scene, based on momentary impressions." The critical voice adopted by Feld was a provocation to the reader, "soliciting a spontaneous reaction, whether assenting or dissenting." Moreover, they argue, Feld's primary critical rubric for film aesthetics stipulated that film form ought to flow directly from its content.[4] As we shall see, while this approach differed along many registers from Eisner's, the effect of sharing certain areas of coverage was generative, at times even harmonious, perhaps for the same reasons the two were able to share a close friendship and mutual esteem throughout their lives.

As a group, however, the distinctive and variegated writing styles adopted by each of the paper's regular contributors resulted in neither a coherent editorial voice nor a congenial work environment.[5] According to Werner Sudendorf's profile of the *Film-Kurier*, its editorial staff rotated in and out, and the head editor position was occupied on and off during this period by a particularly volatile character, one Ernst Jäger. Jäger's biographical details are sketchy, but researchers place his birth in Dessau around 1895 or 1898. Sudendorf states that Jäger spent the early 1920s writing for a variety of different publications and organizations in Dessau; upon his 1923 arrival in Berlin he began work as a journalist at *Der Film*, and later at National-Film as a press officer. After contributing articles on an occasional basis to the *Film-Kurier*, he was appointed its chief editor in 1924, a post he held with intermittent breaks until 1935. This was a period of enormous growth for the paper, during which its circulation increased almost tenfold.[6]

Feld and Eisner both recalled that Jäger styled himself as an avowed leftist in the mid- to late twenties, yet each would later cast a jaundiced eye on Jäger's leadership of the *Film-Kurier*, arguing that his allegiances shifted with the political wind. After the March 1933 purge of the paper's editorial board, it is clear that Jäger cultivated a cozy relationship with various Nazi Party members and their associates. Under Jäger's stewardship the paper listed decidedly to the right, but he left his post as chief editor in 1935 and emigrated to the United States in 1939. In a biographical sketch reviewing Jäger's work in Germany and the United States, Sudendorf argues that Jäger was essentially an opportunist and that the rightward turn of the *Film-Kurier* was perceptible, even imminent, before 1933. Other scholars have concurred with this assessment of Jäger's ideological ambivalence and careerism.[7]

THE *FILM-KURIER*, 1927–1933

In spite of these eventual difficulties, during the bulk of Eisner's tenure at the *Film-Kurier* it was a successful and influential left-leaning daily trade publication that concerned itself with the aesthetic, technical, economic, and political issues of the day: international in scope yet emphatically German, and boasting the widest domestic circulation of any of its peer publications.[8] Throughout the late twenties and early thirties, the front page of the *Film-Kurier* was devoted to coverage of the German industry association conferences and meetings, international and domestic regulation (import and export quotas, censorship, advertising, production, distribution, and exhibition regulation), the advent of sound film technology, and inter- and transnational film industries. Beginning in September 1928, the *Film-Kurier* also served as the official organ of the German exhibitors union (the *Reichsverbandes Deutsches Lichtpieltheaterbesitzer*).[9] While the paper tended to focus on US, British, and French—and to a lesser extent, Czech and Italian—industries in terms of quotas, advertising, and their respective regulation of production, distribution, and exhibition, the US industry was generally reported in greatest depth. Specific US markets such as New York and San Francisco were part of regular coverage of the distribution, exhibition, and reception of German films, and Hollywood enjoyed regular, highly detailed social and industrial coverage, as well as frequent reports on the exchange of German and American personnel.

Below the paper's iconic masthead, pride of place was devoted to domestic and foreign industry coverage, these columns sprinkled with thumbnail advertisements for recent releases, turning over roughly every two weeks. A handful of brief notes covered news items concerning personnel—their deaths, new or expiring contracts, travel, awards, marriages and divorces—and notices regarding professional associations: usually current and upcoming conferences and meetings or public lectures. The second and third pages of the daily edition were most often reserved for three to four film reviews, one or two theater reviews, a book review, coverage of public lectures or exhibitions, reporting on foreign and domestic industry news, and commentaries, which ranged in terms of their subject matter, delivery, and length.

Among the editorial staff, Willy Haas, Ernst Jäger, Hans Feld, Georg Herzberg, and Eisner tended to cover Berlin, with correspondents Leo Weiß in Frankfurt, Paul Medina in Paris, and "Ernst Chaparral" in Hollywood.[10] A portion of the third page and the entirety of the last page were given over to advertisements for films, theater seats, lightbulbs, fans, projectors, bookers, clerks, and typists. Decorous personals ads soliciting or publicizing marriageable readers of the *Film-Kurier* appeared from time to time amid the furniture and employment on offer.

The extended Thursday and Saturday evening editions of the paper typically included special review inserts and supplements devoted to genres of domestic film production (e.g., *Tonfilm*, *Kulturfilm*), film music, and debate over specific technical or aesthetic issues. The technical review insert, *Kinotechnische Rundschau*, most often offered a comparative overview of a single technical development: for example, improvements in theater design and cooling systems, screen design (aspect ratio, curvature, stereoscopic projection), innovative projectors, new lightbulb designs, and sound-on-film technology. With less frequency, but often enough to constitute a pattern, the special editions of the paper ran columns of opinion, advice, or review by notable filmmakers: Béla Balázs on screenwriting, Guido Seeber on camera design, Carl Hoffmann on transnational technical and aesthetic trends, Erich Pommer on international competition and quotas.

Among coeval US trades, the *Film-Kurier* most closely resembled *Variety* in terms of its breadth and its attitude toward various industry interests, but with the important distinction—both from *Variety* and peer German trades—that it spoke in a single, unambiguously critical voice regarding censorship. As Sudendorf has argued, "The unique quality of the newspaper consisted in its extensive news section and in its openness to views of any political color. If the paper represented a political point of view, it was the struggle against the narrow-mindedness and arbitrariness of censorship. Since the prohibition of a film for production and rental also meant financial losses, the industry was largely behind the *Film-Kurier* on this issue."[11] Moreover, in the realm of avant-garde theater, film, literary, and art criticism, and in their reviews of actors, according to Hans Feld, he and his fellow critics were able to write with great candor, although not without certain limitations.[12] In her memoirs, Eisner recalls with amusement a meeting with Alfred Weiner, then the *Film-Kurier*'s publisher, in which she was scolded for panning a film. Because the *Film-Kurier* depended in part on the placement of advertising by film producers, Weiner cautioned her, it wasn't good business to run negative reviews. He advised Eisner to stick to reviewing films she would be able to praise, however faint such praise might be.[13]

In her memoirs, Eisner leads the chapter on her years at the *Film-Kurier* by describing herself as the first professional female German film critic, assigned to the table scraps beat: "I rushed from one deadline to the next, and initially got the unpleasant tasks that no one else wanted to do—all manner of undesirable editorial duties, first among them covering the Ufa *Kulturfilme*. You cannot imagine something more boring and odious." She goes on to disparage the unsigned puff pieces she contributed, reproducing in its entirety a confection verging on parody, supposedly written by a contemporary star about what types of hats she prefers for the present weather and various occasions.[14]

While some of her sense of being passed over may have been purely routine—she was the newest writer on staff for a time, and at the bottom of the hierarchy—Eisner's perception was that a measure of this unequal treatment stemmed from her gender; at the time, she was the only female journalist on the editorial staff at the paper, although there were other women who published in the *Film-Kurier*, and who published on film for other publications. In her memoirs, Eisner remarks that she was paid less for the same amount of work her male peers were doing, and even her most sympathetic colleague tended to infantilize her and trivialize her work:

> The collaboration with Hans Feld—who gave me free rein in my area of expertise, the theater—was ideal. He says today that I was a "gushing teen" when I began at the *Film-Kurier*, but my emotionality had been restrained by academic training, and my knack for spotting talent was unmistakable. An enthusiastic and sentimental style marked by proclamations, question marks and dashes, adjectives of rapture and repulsion was standard. We all write this way, but to refer to a woman of thirty-one years as a "teen"; of that I'm less certain.[15]

Indeed, this might have served as a fair characterization of Feld's own style, yet it would be at best a stretch to describe Eisner's work at the *Film-Kurier* this way.[16] It bears emphasizing that during this period Eisner and Feld were among only a few journalists on the editorial staff to have doctoral degrees. While Eisner was older than Feld and her training much more directly related to aesthetic analysis and evaluation, he had been at the paper—during a critical period of its growth, no less—for a full two years before he recruited Eisner.

Tellingly, although they worked together closely for over three years and remained close friends for decades after, Feld would later recall Eisner at the *Film-Kurier* as "a newcomer with her own contribution ... down from university."[17] Two readings of this rather prim remark—offered, it is important to stress, in the context of a warm and respectful characterization—suggest themselves: Feld may have felt proprietary about the paper or intimidated by her training and extensive frame of literary, historical, and artistic reference, hence the emphasis on her originality and her doctorate. He would not have been the only one, either; during her time at the *Berliner Tageblatt* and in the early years of her exile in Paris, she was asked to write on topics well outside the ambit of her training. According to Eisner, she was often asked to conduct interviews on physics, medicine, and the history of science, among other things, simply because her byline could truthfully read "Dr. Eisner."[18] The second, complementary reading might detect a whiff of class privilege (and his British exile) in Feld's phrase, "down from university." Eisner would be the first to admit that her exposure to contemporary film prior to the *Film-Kurier* gig had been limited to the occasional Rin-Tin-Tin or Chaplin picture; such outings were chaperoned by her father, as befitting a young, single woman of her upbringing. Yet the early period of her employment at the *Film-Kurier* marked a bid for independence from the prohibitions her late father had enforced on her theatergoing, moviegoing, and socializing. She would recall in her memoirs that the greatest benefit of the job was that it paid her enough to afford a little flat of her own in the bohemian district and the services of a maid.[19]

Given her own ambivalence, it is hardly surprising that subsequent studies of the late Weimar popular and trade press discourse on film have tended to overlook Eisner's contributions to the *Film-Kurier*; when this work is mentioned in the secondary literature, it is usually described as being limited to film reviews. Eisner herself would later characterize it, somewhat more broadly, as film journalism, but during certain periods of her tenure at the paper, she actually published far less about film than about the theater.[20] One of the more intriguing aspects of Eisner's body of work at the *Film-Kurier* is that it troubles hard-and-fast delineations between reportage, criticism, theory, and commentary, and, much in the spirit of the era, it sprawls across disciplinary boundaries between the arts. Eisner's later reminiscences of her early days at the paper—in particular, admitting to having thought of film, disparagingly, as *so populo* ("rather lowbrow")—belie the seriousness and rigor with which she approached criticism across media and genres.[21]

Equal care is taken in her reviews of popular fiction, educational documentary, classical drama, avant-garde cabaret, and variety shows, and a clear explication of the standards by which she measures a work is always provided.

During her five and a half years at the *Film-Kurier*, Eisner published a variety of pieces under a handful of bylines.[22] It was common at the *Film-Kurier*—increasingly so into the thirties—for articles and commentary to run unsigned, and areas of coverage were often shared among several editors. Nevertheless, the distinctive style and characteristic interests and approaches of each of the regular contributors make a few generalizations possible. First, the signed contributions between August 1927 and March 1933 attributed to Eisner number around 860, and save for several periods of travel or vacation, Eisner contributed several pieces each week to the paper throughout her tenure. Second, although she appears never to have contributed to the technical review insert—run during these years by Georg Otto Stindt, and later, Günther Herkt—and certain columns ran under only one editor's name ("Wochenschau" and "Tagesschau" were reserved for editor in chief Ernst Jäger, later Walter Jerven), apart from these exceptions, Eisner contributed to all other areas in the paper's regular editorial purview. These included: reviews and coverage of music, dance, opera, theater, variety and cabaret, literature, salons and public lectures, art, architecture, design, fashion, news coverage and opinion on politics and economics in the theater and film worlds of Berlin, on-set reportage and commentary, film industry conference and trade association meeting coverage, travel writing, interviews, cultural criticism, and sketches of Berlin city life.

Surveying this diverse body of work, several overarching themes and trends emerge.[23] Perhaps most striking among them is that even at its peak share in 1930, film-related coverage—including reviews, industry news and reporting, criticism, and commentary—only accounted for half of her signed contributions. Over the course of her first months at the *Film-Kurier*, while Eisner wrote on a number of different topics, the bulk of what she published is most accurately described as commentary: short pieces offering witty observations, anecdotes, and cultural criticism, and amusing vignettes on the periphery of film sets and theater rehearsals. While this vein of her work rarely predominates, it persists until the final months of her time with the paper, when her byline is only attached to film and theater reviews and, overall, appears far less regularly.

In her first full year at the paper (August 1927 through August 1928), Eisner contributed roughly two hundred signed articles, most of which

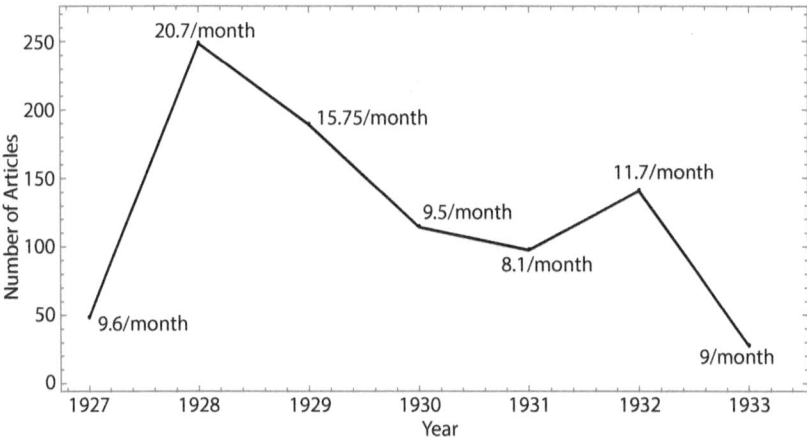

FIGURE 4. Yearly totals of Eisner's signed publications, with monthly averages noted. Data collected and chart drawn by the author.

were devoted to theater coverage: reviews; interviews; and reporting on political, economic, and aesthetic developments. Coverage of the German film industry—production, on-set reporting, industry regulation, and international industrial cooperation—was the next significant area of her output in this period, but the number of pieces under this rubric come to less than half of the count for her theater coverage. These articles roughly equal in number her reporting on lectures, salons, and public events related to literature, architecture, and art. Film reviews made up barely a tenth of her contributions, squeaking in just above the share of book reviews and cultural criticism she published in the paper between August 1927 and October 1928. In 1929, however—perhaps as a result of her increasing interest in covering film and having earned the right to advocate for choicer assignments—the emphasis of her coverage shifted to a roughly sixty/forty split between film and theater topics. In 1932–33, Eisner's last year at the paper, the balance shifted again and came closer into line with her earliest months; her signed theater-related coverage again roughly doubled that of film.

Several factors may account for this variation in the types and topics of her coverage. Consistent features of the commentary Eisner penned her first several months include the rather elegant style—slightly more formal than the voices of other regular columnists—in which these pieces were couched, and the cultural fluency evinced by the references, comparisons, and standards of evaluation she invokes. An arch, quippy sense of humor, sharp eye for detail, and, tellingly, a penchant for the word *persiflage* distinguished

Eisner's writing style. Less glib than Jäger, less dry than Weiß, and less freewheeling than Feld, Eisner's strengths and qualifications in the first months of her time at the paper likely contributed to the types of pieces she was assigned: she was a good writer, she was knowledgeable about history, politics, art, and culture, and she had the credentials to offer authoritative, compelling critiques of art, literature, architecture, design, fashion, and theater.

Because of her initially anemic movie-going habits and lack of experience in covering the industry, Eisner devoted a great deal of time during her first months at the *Film-Kurier* to absorbing all she could about the technical, artistic, and industrial aspects of film production, distribution, exhibition, and reception. The time she spent during those first months on film sets and in movie theaters, interviewing filmmakers and covering industry news resulted in dozens of vivid sketches of film production, and a number of opinion pieces that offered suggestions for premises, themes, or single scenes she deemed particularly filmic.

In one exemplary mid-September 1927 column, Eisner offers "to the director" a scene in which a frustrated professor—she invokes Mann's Unrat—grades a stack of notebooks on a sultry late summer evening, with increasingly profuse eruptions of corrective red ink. It's a pity, she says, that the red ink won't translate to the screen, but she hopes the director may find they can "make something of it."[24] Most of these sketches are brief, running between two and three hundred words each. In a characteristic piece from late 1927, titled "Jobs," Eisner proposes a film about a human billboard.[25] She begins the piece by recalling several recent news items involving splashy advertising campaigns that used human billboards: one about a man who was paid to advertise a local business by wearing an oversized pencil costume, and another who at the height of summer was paid by a local furrier to dance in the streets of Leipzig in a sweltering full-body outfit—suit, hat, and boots—of fur. Eisner proposes that in the film, the man's wife ought to be sleeping with their lodger, because the resultant constellation of commerce, tragedy, and comedy would make for a deeply filmic subject, symbolic, yet not broadly so, or in an infelicitously literary fashion.

CRITICAL PERSONAE

Among the ten bylines Eisner used, two distinct subgroups tended to consistently tag a specific writing style and area of coverage, functioning in this way almost as personae. The first set—variations on Dr. Lotte H. Eisner—tends to accompany her coverage of documentary and is distinct in that it cites her degree. The articles and special inserts signed by these bylines typically comment on the state of documentary production and distribution, and they often advocate a particular policy or strategy. Presumably, the gender-neutral and authoritative Dr. L. H. Eisner, used in the first several issues of her special insert, titled "Der Kulturfilm," lent a certain credibility to both the reportage and opinions it undersigned. A second, more complex case is that of the bylines Flapper and Lolott, which Eisner adopted in coverage and commentary about fashion and gender.

Flapper is the most distinctive of the various voices Eisner adopted (not least for its self-consciously referential, foreign, and modern ring), and it stands apart from the bulk of what she wrote in terms its areas of interest and its tone. It also brings a few of the thorniest aspects of Eisner's commentary about gender and class to the surface and serves as an important point of reference for the not infrequent—and, for many of her later interlocutors, puzzling—instances of her self-identification as a "misogynist."[26] Lynne Frame has shown that cultural commentary about women and gender performance forms a kind of minor genre of period discourse:

> Weimar culture was obsessed with taxonomies. Without hesitation, journalists, social critics of all hues, and scientists alike constructed human typologies and made pronouncements on their relative social "worth." . . . Such typologies often shared the anthropological project of appraising the German population, especially in terms of its relationship to metropolitan modernity. Women often stood at the center of these analyses, as many writers treated the seemingly drastic changes they were undergoing—in lifestyle and appearance—as a barometer of modern society[,] its progress and its discontents. . . . [These articles] invited women readers to "measure" themselves against a given typology, or rather, to place themselves in it. [They] encouraged [women readers] to construct an image of themselves and their identity, and to consider their own contributions to the promotion or impairment of modernity and progress.[27]

Eisner offered an intriguing variation on the genre, ventriloquizing some of the harshest strains of the period typologies that Frame identifies with the popular press and women's publications under her alternate bylines. Almost always, the articles signed by Flapper are about women, although they rarely address women as readers; they are also marked by their snide, mocking tone, at once condescending and playful. Occasionally, Flapper verges on bald misogyny, leaning hard into vicious caricature and stereotype. In a piece titled "Springtime Struggles," Flapper describes the difficulties a change in the weather pose for the young lady anxious to make a fashionable impression.[28] After lamenting that, come spring, a man need merely check the barometer and swap in his winter coat for a summer jacket, by their nature, young women are compelled with the change of the seasons to fret about their outfits. After mulling whether a tailor might be able to update the previous spring's fashions suitably for reuse this year, the narrator resolves to instead prevail upon the largesse of a husband or sugar daddy: "But the damage isn't terrible: for spring I barely need anything—it's winter shopping that will really set you back." Can it be true, she wonders, that this crock of a hat is the same sweet little number I splurged on last spring? "Thus the annual routine commences, and with it the customary cycle: shop, splurge, regret.... And on the first nice sunny day, as always, you'll sigh and say, 'I don't have a thing to wear.'"[29] The shifting modes of address ("I" versus the impersonal second-person generalization) notwithstanding, this piece takes a dim view of young women and fashion; Flapper betrays no interest in exploring how self-presentation refracts class, gender politics, or creative expression. Instead, the portrait of a feckless clothes horse invites the reader to wag a finger at women's frivolity and susceptibility to suggestion.

In a more venomous sketch published two weeks later, titled "A Short Natural History of the 'Woman of the World,'" Flapper invites outright ridicule of the so-called *Dame vulgaris*. After describing the laziness and indulgence of this "species," Flapper launches into a description of a day in the life of one "specimen": late to rise, she spends her morning in bed on the telephone cranking the rumor mill, later going out for shopping and socializing. When she shops, Flapper snarks, "she is a milliner's nightmare": she tries on twenty-seven hats only to reject the twenty-eighth. After a dishy tea with the friend she was gossiping about that morning, she will go dancing; she prefers gigolos and taxi dancers, and by the end of the evening, she will pick up a man who's "seen better days." If she doesn't go dancing, perhaps she will see a Freudian for some analysis, or attend a lecture on psychoanalysis: "She never misses a lecture by Magnus Hirschfeld. After all, theorizing kinky sex is very *up to date*" (in English).[30] She beguiles innocent young men with her demonic appearance, enhanced with red lipstick, thin eyebrow pencil, and blue eyeshadow. Occasionally, Flapper remarks, one of the species will die. This is of no consequence because one of many more just like her will move in to replace her.

The nastiness of this caricature, its flip delivery and stylized structure—particularly the repetition of its bookends, "The species 'Woman of the World' (*Dame vulgaris*) can be found across the climes of popular novels, films, and real life"—leave a strange impression.[31] Flapper's emphasis on observations of particular behaviors, especially the lecture attendance, suggests the piece was less a critique of stereotyped representation on screen than a screed against a person or clique in particular. This piece sits cheek by jowl with a second typological profile, the "Young Woman of Today," signed with Eisner's other fashion-and-gender byline: Lolott. In this second piece, the ideal independent woman of the day is described. She is smart, cool, and not at all frumpy: "She has nothing in common with the suffragettes of yesterday. . . . She's less a Bluestocking than a Silkstocking."[32] Employed outside the sphere of traditionally female-gendered labor, and untainted by the "misandry and resentments of the old maid," she is a peer among men: "in front of this young woman of today, one can say anything, even risking a coarse word from time to time." Neither a naive romantic nor a callous skeptic, she holds out hope of finding a partnership that is unconventional and that would allow her to take equal joy in her intellect and femininity: "This young woman of today doesn't have it easy, because she seeks to unite all possibilities. She looks forward to a new spring hat as much as a cerebral book. . . . The young woman of today, for the time being, stands between two worlds. Small wonder, then, that here and there she missteps in her search for balance. But balance she will find!"

The juxtaposition of the two profiles may have been intended simply as a provocation. However, in the context of Eisner's later remarks, they suggest a complicated relationship to gender mediated by class. The *Dame vulgaris* is disparaged largely on the basis of her self-presentation and her social world: she is crass, tacky, overtly sexual, gossipy, fad-obsessed, and she fraternizes with gigolos and students. In the body of the article, every appearance of the name *Dame vulgaris* is offset in Latin script rather than Fraktur, following the convention of binomial nomenclature. In the natural sciences the epithet "vulgaris" indicates, roughly, the garden-variety or most widespread, yet the Latin adjective from which it is derived, *Vulgaris*, refers to the commons or to the common people. Thus, *Dame vulgaris* invokes both a weed and a person of low- or working-class status; indeed, in Flapper's view, these qualities are fundamentally inextricable, perhaps even identical. The Young Woman, conversely, is celebrated for her ability to hang with the guys, to assert her intellectual and financial independence without being prudish, shrill, or stridently feminist. She is economically independent, and her taste for expensive, conventionally feminine clothing is identified as a prime virtue.

In her memoirs and interviews, Eisner offered a number of anecdotes about this period in her life suggesting that she was deeply ambivalent, if not conflicted, about how her gender affected her work and social life. She describes patterns of unequal treatment in the workplace: marked disparity in pay for equal work, sexual harassment by editor in chief Jäger, facing retaliation for rejecting his advances.[33] Yet Eisner's reflections on her own performance of gender and sexuality are roundabout, suggesting that public disclosure, if not her lived experience of her own sexuality, was an uneasy topic. Alternately ambiguous and bracingly candid, often phrased in peculiarly cliché or stereotyped language, Eisner's remarks are clear on only several points: she was uninterested in marriage; ambivalent about sex; fearful of becoming pregnant out of wedlock; and later, during her years as a fugitive, grateful to be single and unattached.[34] Perhaps as a function of the way her memoirs were recorded, these garbled remarks indicate that Eisner grappled with a fundamental conflict between gender performance and her intellectual and professional ambitions. It seems clear that whether the relationship between Eisner's career and her decision to be single was strictly causal or not, she perceived herself as different from most women, if not more similar to men. This complex, and perhaps not entirely conscious, struggle with identification and gender may explain the bile with which Eisner execrated certain exemplars of modern femininity. For Eisner, who conceived of her own independence, at least retrospectively, as being hard-won (and perhaps more precarious than she could afford to acknowledge at the time), the popular celebration of a diametrically opposed model of female independence might have been intolerable. Perhaps, too, the caustic language about women functioned as currency among her male peers, allowing her to signal her affinity with them via disavowal of other women.

Indeed, later in life Eisner not only repeatedly identified herself as a misogynist, but specifically called out certain examples of her own film criticism in the *Film-Kurier*, arguing that at no point did she find common cause with women, peers or not.[35] She believed she had often been sabotaged by women who were jealous of her, whereas she felt proud of impressing her male colleagues and acknowledged no barriers to her own acceptance within their social world.[36] Rejecting what she sees as an effort to lump her own unique struggle in with a collective narrative, Eisner attests—in an interview with the feminist film journal *Frauen und Film*, no less—that she had no need of feminism at any point, because her work was of equal quality to that of her male colleagues, and this allowed her to move as freely as any man in her professional life.[37]

To complicate matters further, a number of the interviews and sketches Eisner published at the *Film-Kurier* imply an understanding of the concerns addressed by feminism, in spite of her stated antipathy to feminism per se. In one particularly striking example, published less than a month later, Lolott offered a deft, funny morsel of cultural criticism taking aim at the objectification of women by way of a sketch about people on the public bus. In it, she describes the commotion caused by a group of seven pretty young women, described as having darling "postcard" or "pin-up girl" faces (*niedliche Poskartengesichter*) beneath colorful felt hats, accompanied by an unmarried older woman with "an old man's face." Chattering among themselves in "the broad, throaty English of the USA," the young women are judged to be dancers, probably Tiller Girls, per a knowing fellow passenger. The description, repeated rhythmically throughout the short piece, of the seven women in colorful hats suggests an idealized femininity, something like the so-called "Vargas Girls" pin-up images; indeed, their creator, Alberto Vargas, illustrated some of the iconic Ziegfeld Follies publicity pin-ups in the 1910s. A literary type in horn-rims—possibly a dig at Siegfried Kracauer and his 1927 *Frankfurter Zeitung* piece on the Tiller Girls, which went on to be anthologized and parsed at great length—gushes to a pudgy, briefcase-toting bourgeois sitting nearby: "You see . . . one can hardly distinguish among them. Seven, each one like the other. The *Girl* [English] as a prototype of the collective man!" In response, the bourgeois "smiles courteously in helpless incomprehension, and cranes to catch a bigger eyeful of the darling pin-up girls than the passengers behind him." The passengers speculate as to whether the women are Tiller Girls, or perhaps,

> some newly-imported troupe from America? The words "Ziegfield [*sic*] Revue" are overheard, and all the men stare, fascinated, at the seven darling pin-up girl faces beneath their felt caps of every color. *Ziegfield*! — — —
>
> At some point, their scrawny chaperone rises, and the seven darling pin-up girls rise: Here's our stop! All the men goggle after them. To peep at those seven darling pin-up girls on the sidewalk, with their unbelievably impossible legs.
>
> "So, not dancers after all," says a lady to her companion, a little triumph in her voice.
>
> "So, not dancers after all," murmur all the men to themselves, crestfallen.
>
> "Boarding-house girls," sighs the fat man with the briefcase.

The literary fellow with the horn-rimmed spectacles peers censoriously; "A first pass at the collective man, at any rate," he concludes.

The bus gets on its way. Somewhere in the distance, seven darling pin-up girls stride along down the street on their impossible legs.[38]

Clearly, Lolott makes no attempt here to inhabit or portray the point of view of these women as they are being ogled, unwittingly (as far as we are told) mobilized in a critique of capitalism and visual culture, and assessed by their fellow passengers. Lolott caricatures the process by which these women are objectified by everyone else on the bus; each passenger flattens the seven dancers and projects onto the women wistful, fearful images of their meaning and their power. They are the fat man's fragrant madeleine, redolent of youth. The lady takes comfort in her ignorance, thinking that since they aren't part of a dance troupe whose name she recognizes, they don't pose the moral or sexual threat she had initially feared.

The conceit, of course, is that each of these passengers is mistaken. Brief as it is, the sketch suggests a biting critique of the patriarchal optics within which each of these passengers is operating as they assess the power and status of all eight women in the party. At an oblique angle, Eisner's observations suggest how imbricated the Frankfurt School's lineage of critical theory was with the society from which its most prominent proponents emerged, marked by prejudices that ultimately eluded their considerable powers of insight and rhetoric.[39] Kracauer famously called the Tiller Girls "products of American distraction factories[,] no longer individual girls, but indissoluble girl clusters whose movements are demonstrations of mathematics."[40] Per Patrice Petro's apt summary, "Kracauer's description of the abstraction and fragmentation of the female body in the service of capitalist expansion attests to his awareness of the construction of woman in mass culture as spectacle, as object of desire and endless exchange."[41] Indeed, he claimed that his critique, "The Little Shopgirls Go to the Movies," simply listened carefully to hear the "rude secret" burping forth from seemingly innocuous fare, the recurring tropes of which reveal "how society wants to see itself."[42] And Kracauer does tally the precise variations of reactionary pablum in the films under review, but the butt of the joke every time is female spectators: the final sentence of every single one of these pieces caricatures the shopgirls. Patronized, infantilized, and ultimately blamed for the retrograde politics of the films, the figure of the ingenuous woman in the movie theater is a trope of critical theory that follows a long tradition of misogynist contemplation within continental philosophy.[43] As a champion of the everyday and a critic of ideology, but also as a ridiculer of women, Kracauer is worth reading with fresh eyes for what he says and for what his work says about his milieu. As Lolott pointed out contemporaneously with the original publication of Kracauer's pieces on the Tiller Girls and women at the movies, such critiques of the constitutive role of the fetishized female form in industrial capitalist aesthetics rest, ironically, on a doubled objectification of women.[44] Lolott's caricature strikes me as particularly apposite in another regard: the women on the bus, just like the little shopgirls, appear to be minding their own business in public. Lolott's caricature teases out the underlying assumption that Kracauer's cultural criticism and the passengers on the bus share in common: young women are conspicuous, provocative, and distracting because they don't belong in these spaces, and on some level, their anomalousness (their "unbelievably impossible" embodiment) excuses any thirsty, dehumanizing excesses to which onlookers might be led. As Heide Schlüpmann has argued, it was never unremarkable how preoccupied some men at the movies seemed to be with the women they noticed in the audience; Emilie Altenloh observed it in 1914, noting that these men appeared to be more interested in watching the women than the movies.[45] To turn Kracauer on his head: as we read about him through his little shopgirls, we "gain unexpected insights into the misery of mankind and the goodness from above," which is to say that we appreciate precisely how contingent upon the diminishment of women his identification with power—for the position of a cultural critic is a position of power—was.[46] But it may take one to know one: as I have argued, the same can be said of Eisner, especially when she wrote as Flapper and Lolott.

Most of the time, Eisner's more sympathetic observations about women are folded into larger critiques, such as when, in coverage of a lecture presented to the Society for Psychology and Characterology on the topic of "The Actress" throughout history, she observes that the speaker's problematic reliance on "antiquated prejudices" about women isn't even the biggest problem with the talk: it's that the misguided Dr. Johannes Günther bit off more than he could chew.[47] Similarly, she remarks in a conversation with silent film actress Barbara Dju about typecasting that there is a well-known tendency in the industry to fetishize the so-called exotic, and that women in particular face extraordinary difficulty in developing a body of work that reflects their artistic inclinations within an industry and a representational regime that relies so heavily on the stereotyping and racialization of women and foreigners.[48]

Equivocal on gender, Eisner appears to have considered her own class and privilege only indirectly in terms of her success. While she was quick to point out that her education and her taste were advantages, she seems never to have explored how each of these things—let alone a preference for expensive clothing and distaste for makeup and taxi dancers—might be bound up in class. Eisner jokes in her memoirs that in spite of being raised a Princess of the Tiergartenviertel with vague notions of one day being swept off her feet, she instead became a Fräulein Doktor. For her, the key distinction between how she was raised and how she chose to live as an adult came down to electing not to marry, insofar as it was a mark of her intellectual independence. That the means to an education and the freedom from marriage were also material is never acknowledged. In a sketch by Flapper on an open call to fill a chorus line, titled "Wanted: A Thousand Gams," the nervous energy of the young women auditioning is described—in what seems an either hopelessly quaint or willfully evasive effort to ignore the economic stakes at hand—in terms of a fairytale Prince choosing the lucky damsel for a dance.[49]

OUT AND ABOUT: A CRITIC AT LARGE

One important area of coverage that depended on Eisner's economic independence qua social independence was travel coverage. In a handful of striking observational commentaries, Eisner reports vividly on the postrevolutionary festivities—and, two months later, on a bullfight—in Barcelona, on cinema-going and public space in Amsterdam, and a night at the movies in Mussolini's Italy. In these pieces, Eisner narrates as a flâneuse: eavesdropping, perambulating, people-watching. Evocative description and wry commentary are interwoven with deft observational criticism; in a piece on the Cinema Verdi in Nervi, she remarks that in the dangerous political climate of fascist Italy, all small talk among men in public spaces has been reduced to remarking on the weather. In Amsterdam, Eisner tours the city's cinemas, commenting on their architecture, environs, clientele, projection speeds, subtitling, ticket prices, and her impressions of the stylistic finesse of an American newsreel, which she compares to Ruttmann's stylistics and Soviet cinema.[50]

Other similar sketches observe Berlin city life. One striking piece recounts an incident in which a street vendor along the Kurfürstendamm chases after his runaway balloons, caught like "a cluster of colorful, alien fruit" in a tree.

As in many of these early sketches, Eisner remarks on the cinematic quality of the scene. The conceit of this particular sketch is that happenstance has a wonderful eye for the cinematic; she closes with the remark that chance is the best advertiser, and the best director. Shame, she says, that said director didn't bring a camera along to capture the moment.[51] One way to read these sketches, and to understand the emphasis placed on seeing things cinematically, is in the context of Eisner's retrospective self-identification as a dabbler, at best, in film prior to working at the *Film-Kurier*. These remarks on the cinematic everyday may have emerged from an effort to immerse herself in a medium-specific aesthetics, to approach the task of criticism informed not only by an understanding of the industrial, social, and political context proper to film, but of its tropes, codes, and unique means of expression.

Another area of writing that emerged from this ongoing project of self-education is the series of on-set reports Eisner filed: observational narratives of in-between moments during shooting that came out of the hours Eisner spent hanging around film sets watching and learning; later in life, Eisner would describe her awakening to the medium as a direct result of her visits to the studios:

> Slowly, I understood what film was about. I went to studios a lot to get to know the camera, because I was truly an idiot in terms of the technical aspects. I had to actually learn everything about filmmaking first. I didn't know then who Friedrich Wilhelm Murnau was. I met Fritz Lang then, and found his *Nibelungen* very Teutonic. I didn't see the architectural rigor of the film; I recognized it only later. And I saw Murnau's *Last Laugh* and found Jannings terribly sentimental; I didn't understand the technical camera work at all. I went to the studios a lot, so I saw people shooting, editing, and all that. In truth, I got my education in the studio, and I think it's a pity today that most film critics hardly ever go to the studio.[52]

The short, evocative vignettes she published speak to the iterative process, the somewhat unruly atmosphere around the edges of the shot, and the frustrations and improvisations as the cast and crew attempt to create and capture certain effects. In the earliest of these pieces, the continuities with her interest in the theater are apparent: she zeroes in on the cast wisecracking around the portable heaters on the set of Jacques Feyder's *Thérèse Raquin* (1928) during take after take of the lake scene in a frigid former zeppelin hangar in Staaken, or the herding of clueless dozens of extras playing gussied-up theatergoers in a scene from *Mädchen, hütet Euch!* (Valy Arnheim, 1928).[53]

As she became more familiar with the technical aspects of filmmaking, her commentary more often highlighted the work of set designers and camera operators. Recalling for her readers an early December 1927 visit to the set of *Schinderhannes* (*The Prince of Rogues*, Curt Bernhardt, 1928), Eisner remarks that she chatted during the lunch hour with art director Heinrich Richter about his decision to use genuine loam in favor of the usual sand for the construction of a more authentic ravine in the pine scrub landscape for that day's shoot. Before work begins again, Eisner spots "A great-looking firefighter—a Gulbransson type with a tiny stork-like head, colossal helmet and a tremendous mustache—stealthily, cleverly slinking off like a dime novel detective to sneak a forbidden cigarette at a distance from the unsuspecting. How he relishes his power!"[54] Passing the time, actor Ivan Kowal-Samborski juggles a pistol. Cast and crew are reassembled, rehearse over and over a complicated crowd scene, and get what they think is a clean take, until someone realizes a crew member may have been visible in a corner of the shot, and they begin to reshoot, as Eisner makes her way to the exit. Comical, wry, and sharply observed, these sketches suggest a progressively detailed interest on Eisner's part in the nature of profilmic mimesis, trickery, and craft. On the set of *Haus Nummer 17* (*Number 17*, Géza von Bolváry, 1928), Eisner discusses special effects used to produce the creepy ambience of a rooftop scene, laboriously fabricated from roofing tiles pilfered from Berlin slum housing and a hidden incense burner. Over the course of the sketch, cinematographer Eduard Hoesch becomes increasingly fussy, grousing about an insufficiently dirty-looking patch of the set, and Eisner closes with the remark: "Is it due to the latent perfidy of objects that only now, after the end of the take, the chimney smokes in a very picturesque way?"[55] One of the most striking and stylish of these early columns was reported several days later from a night shoot for the 1928 release *Vom Täter fehlt jede Spur* (*Berlin After Dark*, Constantin J. David, 1928). In it, Eisner observes,

> On the ruins of the *Metropolis* set at Ufa, Jacek Rotmil built the big city street set for the big-deal crime picture, *Berlin After Dark*. The night sky and a chill set the scene. The asphalt is mirror-like, having just been sprayed down. Cars and people wait for the liberating cue that will call the movie to life. . . . Posters, lights. Porters and elevator operators in fancy livery in front of the wide glass doors. In a corner with wooden scaffolding and crates, the upper half of the establishment in subtle miniature, a subway entrance with reverse script, to be reflected by the Schüfftan process. A genuine cop is standing in front of C. J. David, the director, painstakingly giving his report

on traffic and vehicle choreography. The signal: "Attention—High Beam Lights On—Action!"—and the city's bustle begins.[56]

Eisner watches as the traffic ballet haltingly and with a few missteps comes to life, and notes that in the frigid night air, the wet asphalt has developed a treacherous coating of black ice, on which the crew sprinkles sand. A bottle of cognac is passed around. Off to the side, the consultants from the homicide squad are dispensing their counsel, ensuring that the murder and its investigation occur true to life, avoiding the "cheesy, pat" style of those cigarette-ash diagnoses by Sherlock Holmes. She closes as the shoot wraps up, "The lights go out. Freezing extras stand in the dark. And the cars drive off the big city set out into the real big city." By this point, her interest in craft, effects, and style is no longer that of a novice, and references to specific techniques have been woven into Eisner's signature blend of puckish observation and elegant encapsulation.

Eisner did not review feature-length or fiction film until 1928, when she became one of the regular signed contributors to the paper's "Film-Kritik" column. Her style, by contrast to that of the other regular reviewers, is careful: her language is more ornate, her tone more measured, and unlike other reviewers, she declines to disparage the general moviegoing public. Her theater and film reviews proceed from a discussion of the context from which the work emerged and a few remarks on the director or writer to an assessment of its success or failure as a premise and in terms of its execution. Midway through film and theater reviews, Eisner will often evaluate the political import of the text—its tacit endorsements or the tendencies of its lines of argumentation—and to remark on its relationship to the contemporary social and political context. From there, she reserves several lines for the set design, cinematography (in the case of film), the actors, and a recommendation. Particularly for plays, variety, and cabaret, Eisner offers feedback: what could have been emphasized more strongly, what fell flat. In the context of opinion pieces and reporting outside her reviews, Eisner advances a philosophy of the critic's role as one of expert interlocutor, engaging the work of art and its audience with equal seriousness, and distinguished from the latter only by virtue of having a broader and deeper view of the history and potentialities of a form.

For Eisner, the critic, like the artist, is both a product of and influence on the culture of their time. Her theory of criticism was articulated in sharp contrast to, for example, Alfred Kerr's, which emphatically foregrounded the critic's subjectivity, individuality, and creativity, and which she found both "egocentric" and "out of touch."⁵⁷ The extent to which a critic might be a creative coproducer was explored indirectly in a few pieces, most cogently in an opinion piece Eisner wrote about the benefits to editors and directors of prescreening films. In it, she makes the case that whereas live theatrical performances can benefit from criticism and feedback in real time over the course of a production's run, in the German exhibition context by the time a film reaches critics and audiences it has been cooked, and those know-it-all viewers who walk out of the theater saying they might have made a fabulous film with a few cuts here and there do the picture no good. Why not, Eisner suggests, adopt the American custom of prescreening movies and taking the reactions of audience members back to the editing room; only, she says, don't invite the literati and West Berlin snobs: "Rather invite experts, and the butcher next door, and the green grocer across the way. You will find out right away what is essential."⁵⁸ And while her patience with distracted fellow audience members runs rather thin on occasion, by and large she advocates in reviews and reporting for more nuanced and frequent presentations of political and social issues.⁵⁹ In a review of *§173 St.G.B. Blutschande* (James Bauer, 1929)—a social-problem picture about state regulation of sexual mores—she remarks, "The miracle of film art is its ability to act directly, to promote a thought to the masses, to fight. [It is a t]ool for the truth that goes beyond pamphleteering and surpasses the best speeches." To illustrate the point, she describes the interactive, unruly atmosphere of the screening as inherently political and thus ripe with possibility: "The audience spontaneously clapped in the middle of the film [when a policeman defies an unjust order]. After the film there was thunderous, lasting applause. In the aisles [there were] debates, exclamations of indignation at the disgrace. [This is the] immediate, penetrating effect of a film idea. Show the film to a broad audience, for which it is conceived, in order that the public may demand an overhaul of the extortionist [Paragraph 175] and demand a revision of the neighboring paragraphs in a unified front."⁶⁰ Eisner also occasionally offered such cultural criticism outside the bounds of film reviews; in an early 1928 opinion piece, she weighs in on a preemptive public debate then raging about the treatment on film of the so-called "Steglitzer Tragedy," a high-profile contemporary criminal case involving an incompletely executed suicide pact among a group of privileged teenagers, in Carl Boese's *Geschminkte Jugend* (*Painted Youth*, 1929). In Eisner's view, debate about the moral propriety of representing on film a case that had been widely covered in the news was entirely misplaced. Indeed, Eisner argues, why should anyone assume that artistic representation is not, in fact, the most appropriate realm for such topics, pointing out that among Germany's proudest cultural moments exist many attempts to deal with affecting, tragic events like suicide, such as Goethe's *The Sorrows of Young Werther*.[61] Fed up with the terms of the public debate, Eisner suggests that the claims that a film on the subject might encourage further fraying of the social fabric are nonsensical, arguing that if anything, a film might encourage healthier and more open discussion of suicide: "Should film be oppressively limited to *happy endings* [English], prohibited from depicting real life? All this sermonizing about actuality, and the drawn-from-life. No medium can be as immediate as film. Film, the art of the masses, lives and dies by actuality. So why the ruckus?"[62]

Nor, in Eisner's view, was the medium's power to effect perception and social change limited to fiction film. In her extensive coverage of nonfiction film—consisting of scores of articles published largely between 1928 and 1932 that approach the topic from the standpoints of reportage, criticism, advocacy, and commentary—Eisner shaped a series of arguments about the properties, politics, and potentialities of documentary film writ large. These arguments, in the main, center the claim that in film's affinity for actuality and its ability to abstract from the quotidian, it is uniquely suited to nonfiction narration, particularly in an educational context.[63]

DOCUMENTARY AND AVANT-GARDE FILM: CRITICISM, ADVOCACY, AESTHETICS

By the late twenties when she began covering the genre for the *Film-Kurier*, a number of subgenres of nonfiction film were organized under the broader heading of the *Kulturfilm*, including promotional and advertising films (*Werbe-* and *Reklamefilme*), educational films (*Lehrfilme*), nature films (*Naturfilme*), industrial films (*Industriefilme*), travel and tourism films (*Expeditionsfilme, Landschaftsfilme,* and *Städtefilme*), short films exhibited alongside feature-length screenings (*Beiprogramme, Kurzfilme*), and newsreels (*Wochenschauen*). Many *Kulturfilme* shared the features of multiple subgenres, yet the sorting and regulation of genres was a contentious business; educational films deemed culturally or artistically significant qualified for a substantial tax break for exhibitors, thus incentivizing exhibition, distribution, and, indirectly, production of nonfiction films. The body in charge of granting this designation, headed by Professor Felix Lampe and organized under his directorship at the Central Institute for Education and Pedagogy, was staffed by educators who tended in Eisner's view to be too conservative in their pedagogical and aesthetic predilections. With an increasingly sharply worded series of articles on the committee and its judgments, Eisner outlined a critique of the committee's reluctance to grant certification to films that experimented with aesthetic and narrative strategies and the resulting stultification of production and exhibition. In an exemplary article penned in the later years of Eisner's coverage of the topic, "The Dilemma of the Kulturfilm Producer," she argues that the Lampe Committee's overbearing influence has actually harmed documentary film production and exhibition. The reliance on conservative definitions of what constitutes an "exhaustive" study on film, Eisner argues, reduces the possibilities for experimentation and results in dry films that she disparages as "illustrated textbooks." These being the only films awarded the coveted tax break by the Lampe Committee, no economic incentive remains for producers to experiment in terms of editing or narrative strategies, and in this way the arid standards of the Committee have starved the landscape; Eisner reports that one producer told her that while in recent years he used to print thirty copies of a certain genre of travel film, he now had need of only three distribution copies given the skittishness of exhibitors about paying the full entertainment film tax for short travel films, should the Committee end up not granting their seal of approval.[64]

One of the key areas Eisner focused on in both her regular special insert "Der Kulturfilm" and the occasional front-page article was the critical coverage of international industry conferences for advertising and educational film, convened by industry unions, which functioned in many ways as lobbies. As the *Film-Kurier*'s designated correspondent for these events, Eisner reported on the events, debates, and policy outcomes of these meetings, and she offered her own interpretation of the potential consequences and pitfalls of what she lambasted as the "anti-film bias" of the old guard.[65] Eisner's coverage in these instances pulled no punches: the delegates at the World Advertising Congress of 1929, for example, failed in her estimation to include adequate representation and discussion of developments in the advertising film not just because they and the industry press were woefully uninformed, but because of a failure of imagination.[66] Skewering several contemporaneous press reports that got basic facts about the few films that were featured at the conference wrong, Eisner argues that the enormous potential of advertising film has been largely misunderstood and thereby squandered by an altogether too narrow-minded approach to advertising filmmaking.

Although she advocated consistently for more widespread and creative use of film in these areas, Eisner maintained that the interests of various stakeholders, including the state, needed to be clearly understood and, in some cases, checked. Throughout her reporting on the educational film conferences, for instance, Eisner held that education, propaganda, and advertising were at risk of becoming hopelessly tangled by the nationalist and protectionist interests of the Union of Educational and Documentary Filmmakers [*Bund der Lehr- und Kulturfilmhersteller*].[67] The case of Hans Cürlis is illustrative in this respect: as the head of the Institute for Cultural Research, as well as the chairman of the Union of Educational and Documentary Filmmakers, he advocated for aesthetic experimentation in educational and advertising filmmaking. Like Eisner, Cürlis believed that cross-pollination among subgenres of Kulturfilm was a natural, beneficial feature of the entwinement of these modes of filmmaking on the level of personnel, declaring in the *Film-Kurier* in 1929, "Film is promotion par excellence."[68] However, prior to producing his celebrated *Schaffende Hände* series—a set of short films that documented the creative process of artists and artisans, beginning in 1923 with a film about the artist Lovis Corinth—Cürlis produced a battery of stridently nationalist propaganda films for the Foreign Office in the first years of the Weimar Republic, mostly concerning the injustice of the Treaty of Versailles and Germany's war debt.[69] In 1926, he directed *Die Weltgeschichte als Kolonialgeschichte* (*World History as Colonial History*), a film Cürlis argued served purely educational purposes, but which worked to burnish the German colonial project on spurious historical grounds as the privilege of great civilizations throughout history and as the means by which Germany might meet its World War I debts.[70] These propaganda films, as well as those he produced while serving as the director of the Institute for Cultural Research under the Nazi regime, were nakedly political and starkly revanchist. In spite of the fact that the *Schaffende Hände* films would remain among Eisner's critical touchstones into the postwar period, the tenor of Cürlis's nationalism and his cheerful endorsement of the medium's ability to blur commercial, pedagogical, and political interests was a recurring point of interest in Eisner's coverage. Unequivocally in favor of the aesthetic interchange and influence among the various Kulturfilm genres, Eisner maintained that clear delineation among these genres was of vital importance because the funding, taxation, distribution, and exhibition channels of any given film depended on how its content had been classified by regulators. Without clear, well-researched, and thoughtful guidelines, Eisner warned, films serving a purely commercial purpose and those in the public interest were in direct competition for the same resources.

Eisner also advanced arguments for increased state funding of educational film, expanded use of film in the classroom, and state support for amateur filmmaking via the education system.[71] As a rule, Eisner used every opportunity to critique industry practices that stifled experimentation, isolated educational and commercial films and filmmaking techniques, and walled the German film industry off from international and transnational production, distribution, and exhibition opportunities. In this way, her work stands apart from that of other early theorists of documentary who, like John Grierson, argued that the ethical and economic imperatives of documentary filmmaking were essentially those of a national cinema: film produced with the moral education of a citizenry in mind.[72] By contrast, Eisner's appetite and aspirations for documentary filmmaking were the ever-expanding experimentation with form, content, and exhibition practices: a less prescriptive vision that was altogether more tolerant of an omnivorous intermixing of taste cultures.

In spite of Eisner's dismissive attitude toward it in later recollections, this body of work from the late twenties in which she seriously engaged documentary rewards careful consideration, particularly in terms of how Eisner developed and extrapolated a theory of film with regard to aesthetics and culture. In a forceful 1930 article titled "The Cinema Needs the Kulturfilm," Eisner advocates for increased investment on the part of major studios in the production of sound and silent documentary, arguing that the feature-length documentary is a key component of production and exhibition on which sustainable, diverse, public cinema-going culture depends.[73] Not only, she argues, does the quality documentary serve as a bridge to the cinema for audiences disinclined toward standard narrative fare, but it performs a crucial role in cultural discourse and education.

Most often in reviews, but occasionally in opinion pieces, Eisner also offers notes toward an aesthetic theory of documentary film. This commentary unfolded steadily throughout her tenure at the *Film-Kurier* and was consistently articulated in the spirit of enthusiastic advocacy: celebrating examples of effective themes, content, narrative, and visual style, and pushing for the implementation of new techniques and modes of production she believed would be particularly fruitful. In the exemplary "More Montage in Documentary!," Eisner argues that while some documentary filmmakers and producers will claim to be well versed in Soviet montage theory and practice, what passes for montage in contemporary German documentary leaves both a great deal to be desired and, by the same token, a host of interesting formal and narrative possibilities on the table. Why not, she argues, take the opportunities presented by the large amount of footage gathered in shooting these documentaries to innovate? Rather than simply mimicking the ways montage is deployed in feature filmmaking, and with Soviet innovations serving as their model, documentarians will need to experiment with various adaptations in order to find a mode suited to nonfiction narrative.[74]

Beyond montage, Eisner advocated for the implementation of stylistic techniques borrowed from fiction film across all genres of documentary filmmaking, and she placed special emphasis in reviews on films that used innovative visual and narrative style, even when she deemed the films ultimately unsuccessful. In a 1928 review of a pair of short films about the tobacco industry straddling the (thin) line between industrial and advertising documentary, she praises the use of slow-motion and time-lapse, maintaining that animated sequences have become a crutch for the illustration of complex technical processes and should be substituted by "the things themselves[, which] can provide the best illustration of their own operations."[75] Instead, she advocated for the select use of animated intertitles in the style of Lotte Reiniger's work, arguing that landscape and travel films in particular would stand to benefit from this technique.[76] In fact, while she attended to all areas of documentary narration and often made a point to comment on the lectures that accompanied the presentation of scientific films, her most persistent gripe was with the intertitling of documentaries.[77] Intertitles too often, in her estimation, suffered from stilted, pedantic writing, a reluctance to experiment with visual and linguistic narrative techniques, and a fundamental underestimation of the audience's intelligence.[78]

Perhaps the most intriguing aspect of this subset of Eisner's writing at the *Film-Kurier* is that while she engaged the aesthetics of documentary in a sustained and nuanced way over years of regular coverage, it has yet to be addressed on its own terms in the secondary literature, although even a summary engagement with it suggests a number of productive potential inquiries.[79] The work of critics like Grierson, Kracauer, Rudolf Arnheim, Iris Barry, Béla Balázs, Harry Alan Potamkin, and Paul Rotha has been anthologized and collected, and all of it, importantly, was originally published in or later translated into English. Eisner's has not.

In accounting beyond the issues of language and accessibility for the fact that Eisner's work has not circulated in the same ways, however, we confront the fundamental issue that Eisner's areas of interest and critical rubric do not map readily onto the more familiar exemplars of early documentary criticism. The distinction between Eisner's angle of approach and that with which contemporary readers might be more acquainted is encapsulated by a fortuitous side-by-side publication of a review column by Eisner and a commentary by her colleague Hans Feld in early April 1928.[80] Eisner's column, titled "The Beautiful German Homeland," is a report from the press screening of a set of recent *Landschaftsfilme* ("landscape," usually travel films somewhat in the vein of a tourism campaign), a subset she describes as "still the most difficult chapter of the Kulturfilm endeavor." The tendency of these films, according to Eisner, is to string together beautiful yet unrelated scenes that neither cohere as a narrative nor place their subjects "in relation to the landscape"; as a result, they ultimately fail to "show these people in the rhythm of their real work." The final film of the screening—produced by a Silesian political advocacy group allied with the conservative National Agricultural League—Eisner praises for its lively opening sequence depicting the life of the big city. From there on, however, she finds the film wanting. Eisner is particularly troubled by the film's shortsighted economic and political analysis of the region's labor history, bent to what she describes as propagandistic ends. It overlooks, she points out, the political stakes large landowners have in the telling of the region's labor history, and it takes a retrograde stance on immigration as a result. She concludes: "All in all, a new way must be found for the *Heimatfilm*. We do not want flippant sketches, feuilletonistic variations on the theme of home, but a characteristic one-of-a-kind, an entity: land, people, work, life." In effect, the column offers an aesthetic critique of both the genre and a specific set of films based in textual analysis, ideological critique, and a broader view of the contemporary field of documentary production.

Hans Feld's companion piece, titled "The Documentary Task of the Kulturfilm," printed side by side with Eisner's, takes an entirely different approach. He leads with the demonstrably false, polemical claim that the Kulturfilm has received little attention to date, particularly with respect "to the area of its greatest potential, that of documentation." In his signature clipped, graphic style, Feld describes the creative process:

> A painter at work. In the characteristic attitude toward things. His way of tackling, priming, grasping the subject. The finished painting is the

completed work of art. Film allows the capturing of the creative process. Enables it even more clearly than actually watching the process might, and it also allows you to reproduce the creative process as often as you like. This has already been hinted at in films of the Institute for Cultural Research [Cürlis's *Schaffende Hände* series]. The task is important enough to be systematically addressed. The films of sculpture, painting, and arts and crafts need to be supplemented. But above all they require publicity. In addition to instructional films that are interesting on a purely technical basis, possessing specialized knowledge, popular editions must be created and the public must be primed for them. It will be the task of the competent Kulturfilm producer to create these films. The duty of the press is to advocate for their dissemination.

Feld's enthusiasm seems intended to provoke interest in the potentialities of the form, but he offers few specifics. Cürlis's *Schaffende Hände* series was already well underway at the moment of Feld's writing, and it had been reviewed enthusiastically by Eisner in the pages of the *Film-Kurier* several times already, as Feld was surely aware. Moreover, his plea is most directly addressed to critics, whom he flatters as having special knowledge and the power to advocate for the production of more of these films and to prepare audiences for them. In appealing to fellow critics as uniquely suited to translating the high-culture good of such films to an ill-equipped public, Feld engages documentary film in period discourse—one familiar to contemporary readers by virtue of having been represented so often in retrospective overviews of early film writing—that trades in terms of high versus low culture, moral and aesthetic education of the masses, and the role of the critic as intermediary and tastemaker.

Eisner's criticism, and the aesthetic theory of film it advances, is perhaps most akin among her peers to Rudolf Arnheim's: both employ specific and clearly delineated critical rubrics; both draw from an extensive frame of cultural reference, regularly citing literary, theatrical, and artistic texts, as well as a work's historical and political context, in support of their critique; and, importantly, both critics tended to deploy specific examples in the service of any broader arguments made.[81] In contrast to the method of critics like Iris Barry, Harry Alan Potamkin, or Hans Feld, who might use provocative or strategically overstated claims in the service of a point about the nature or significance of a film genre, the medium at large, or a certain artist's work, Eisner and Arnheim framed their reviews as arguments, used reproducible standards of judgment, and made frequent reference to works deemed comparable.[82] Indeed, in their critique of Lampe Committee standards, Eisner and Arnheim spoke in one voice.[83] Notwithstanding certain rhetorical and methodological similarities in their film criticism, as Richard Lowell MacDonald has argued, Arnheim's early work on film aesthetics was predicated on the assumption, set forth in his 1933 book *Film*, that an aesthetic experience of film was only possible for select, highly trained viewers: "Arnheim was committed to a conception of art that cannot be realised on anything other than a minority basis, yet he professed himself also committed to social change that would banish the conditions within which minority and majority capacities were formed."[84] Yet when Arnheim revisited *Film* for his 1957 *Film as Art*, almost nothing of this argument remained; in his introduction, titled "A Personal Note," he explains,

> It was the precarious encounter of reality and art that teased me into action. I undertook to show in detail how the very properties that make photography and film fall short of perfect reproduction can act as the necessary molds of an artistic medium. The simplicity of this thesis and the obstinate consistency of its demonstration explain, I believe, why a quarter of a century after the publication of *Film* the book is—still and again—consulted, asked for, and stolen from libraries. The first part of *Film*, which develops the thesis, has worn reasonably well and is reproduced here practically complete under the headings "Film and Reality" and "The Making of a Film." I have omitted much of the rest: some of the chapters tangled with tasks for which respectable techniques are now available, such as my sketchy "content analysis" of the standard movie ideology; others dealt with temporary questions—for example, the early fumblings of the sound film—now mercifully forgotten.[85]

By 1957, we can see that Arnheim had pivoted away from programmatic statements on the capacity of audiences for aesthetic appreciation as a function of training, and of the privilege such training entailed, asking his readers to indulge him in this departure and to forgive his early attempts at an aesthetic theory of film experience. Admitting that some of his youthful admonishments missed the mark—in his haste to describe his own, highly developed aesthetic experience, Arnheim arrived at a condescending attitude toward what the inexpert majority might or might not be able to experience—he finds, nevertheless, that the "simplicity" and "obstinate consistency" of his fundamental arguments bear redeeming. In some ways, the specificity and precision of Eisner's criticism could explain why it has not received as much attention in the secondary literature: it is less conducive than, for example, Kracauer's dense critiques, or Balázs's evocative, poetic meditations to finely wrought exegesis. Still, the most significant difference between Eisner's interwar journalism and that of her peers is that she did not have access to that same "obstinate consistency." She did not, that is to say, have the opportunity to collect, publish, or develop her film journalism any further while she was still in Berlin, and it did not serve as the calling card or bridge in her first years of exile, before the war. Whereas Arnheim's *Film* was a stepping stone to safety, and Kracauer and Feld parlayed their journalistic work into publishing contracts and steady work in Allied countries, Eisner's work was interrupted, and when she did begin writing about Weimar-era film again after the war, it was from scratch.[86]

The continuities between Eisner's analysis of educational film, avant-garde theater and film, as well as the cultural criticism she published addressed to avant-garde filmmakers and artists, reveal a shrewd yet latitudinarian attitude toward the self-fashioning of both leftist artists and bourgeois businesspeople in the film world at large. This approach, in the context of a contemporary canon of early German film writing that has been saturated with the early ideological critiques of Feld and Arnheim and Kracauer, is a tonic—sophisticated, canny, and refreshingly lacking in disdain for the inner lives of movie audiences comprised of green grocers and young women. While in 1928 she cautions against passive acquiescence to the co-optation and overuse of the term *avant-garde* in "Avantgarde—Watch Out!," which she attributes to the ignorance of an outdated, elderly class of critics who gratuitously apply the term to all youthful art (and particularly that which confuses them), she also admonishes avant-garde artists to avoid thinking of their work as necessarily rarified.[87]

In "Avantgarde of the Masses," published the following year, Eisner argues that narrative films borrow the techniques of abstraction and *typage* from the avant-garde and that this should be considered proof of concept, rather than selling out: "It is easy to work at a remove from the masses, and difficult to engage them. Ways of connecting must be sought out." While feature filmmaking has benefited from such cross-pollination, "Avant-garde film must not be driven to inbreeding. To avoid stagnation, it needs the masses and it needs to be employed in the industrial realm."[88] In this way, Eisner avoided the predicament of leftist cultural critics who denigrated popular culture across the board, or the tortuous argumentation of film critics like Arnheim and Iris Barry, who would end up having to walk back a good deal of early bluster about silent film being inherently more filmic than sound, and the awkwardly parochial notion that narrative film is more filmic than abstract film. Moreover, and in harmony with her later film historical work,

Eisner's criticism and reporting in the early thirties emphasizes the collaborative and collective nature of filmmaking, and she advocates early on for the serious consideration of actors, set designers, and cinematographers as critical "co-creators" alongside directors, screenwriters, and editors.[89]

To readers familiar with her later work, it is clear that many of these interests and approaches persisted throughout Eisner's career. One of the more surprising aspects of her work at the *Film-Kurier* is the keenly anti-racist conscience from which her political views and aesthetic theory sprang; although Eisner's anti-racism is complicated by the degree to which racism is analogized in her writing with anti-Semitism, as well as the colonialist rhetoric and tropes invoked in some of her early criticism and in later film historical scholarship. In most cases, Eisner's anti-racist commentary comes across in the context of criticism of American films. An exemplary review of *Aloma of the South Seas* (Maurice Tourneur, 1926), takes issue not only with what she sees as its stilted premise and poor execution, but the happy ending "demanded by the American attitude towards race" in which characters are re-segregated after a brief moment of integration, arguing that the ending "is nothing more than a sanitized answer to the so-called race question and eugenics."[90] Perhaps the most striking example of her thinking on these issues, and her understanding of the history of racism in the United States, is one of the earliest reviews she published at the paper. In it she describes a concert given by the Utica Jubilee Singers—whose performance she extols—that was marred for her by the ignorance and arrogance of some attendees.[91] Posing as a fly on the wall, Eisner reports that at intermission, chatter among the audience could be overheard about how regrettable it was that the singers retained so little of their African heritage and sang only American songs: a pointed observation on Eisner's part, possibly intended to suggest the age and class status of the audience members out of whose mouths the remarks purportedly came. According to Kira Thurman, such attitudes were common in the late nineteenth-century reception history of touring Black musical groups, whose performances were heard "with a 'civilizing' ear. . . . To German listeners, the African American spirituals that the musicians sang symbolized the triumphs and tribulations of the black diaspora. . . . The musical ensemble served as a test case by which Germans could see for themselves whether blacks were amenable to westernization and evangelization."[92] Remarking, tongue in cheek, that in fact some of the singers had such light skin they might have been able to pass Harvard's admission standards, Eisner lingers on the origins of the songs on the program in plantations and churches, reflecting on the bitter hypocrisy of segregated houses of worship and on the power of faith to uplift.

Eisner goes on to report that in the second half of the concert, a white audience member interrupted the performance to announce that, in protest of the recent Sacco and Vanzetti verdict, a boycott of all American art would shortly take effect. She asserts that the grace the performers showed ought to serve as a model and history lesson to all who witnessed it, charging that the concert was an inappropriate place to lodge such a complaint on two levels. Interrupting a live performance was selfish, she argues, but of all people with whom you might take up grievances about the American judicial system, the Utica singers and Black Americans more generally are least to blame, having themselves been systematically oppressed by it.

Eisner's sensitivity to what she imagined the Utica Jubilee Singers' experience of racism and colorism had been in the United States may have derived from a wider Weimar-era leftist discourse on US racism and capitalism, as her review of *Aloma of the South Seas* suggests, but it may also have been informed by the work of Jewish German-language writers, such as Viennese translator Anna Nussbaum, who were interested in contemporary Harlem Renaissance art and literature; many of these writers drew explicit parallels between Black experience, as they understood it, and their own. According to Jonathan O. Wipplinger, Nussbaum published throughout the twenties on Black musical groups who toured Europe, including in *Der Wiener Tag* on a performance by the Utica Jubilee Singers—a month after Eisner's article appeared in the *Film-Kurier*—in which Nussbaum offered a more detailed "history of ragtime and jazz, as well as African American spirituals via collections by Stephen Foster, James Weldon Johnson, and J. Rosamond Johnson, and present[ed] information about figures such as Ira Aldridge, George Bridgetower, Sissieretta Jones, Roland Hayes, and Paul Robeson."[93] Wipplinger isolates in the work of several Jewish German-language writers—including Nussbaum, Hans Goslar, and Arthur Rundt—a thematic preoccupation with the voice in their criticism and translation of Black writers and musicians; whether because she had read their work or not, the theme of the voice and of a shared suffering between Black and Jewish diasporas forms the central subject of Eisner's review of the 1929 German release of *The Jazz Singer*:

> No blasphemy in the title card reading, "A jazz singer—singing to his God"; one comprehends, as never before, the duality at the heart of jazz singing:

it is born of that melancholy, laugh-to-keep-from-crying humor of the Jewish diaspora, of the Pierrots of the ghetto, as much as from the longing of the enslaved Black people of the plantation. Al Jolson finds his calling: blackface singer, Jewish singer.[94] It doesn't matter that the film is already technologically outdated, or that *The Singing Fool* is better-written and better-directed. . . . Despite all the clichés, despite the mawkishness: it is the film of the ghetto world. Unlike the world of *The Singing Fool*, which is accessible to all, this film is of a strange, confined world that is interrupted by the present. This world is best comprehended by those who are linked to the blood of the same old, long-forgotten tradition. For outsiders, it remains but a strange spectacle, a glimpse inside an obscure cult. For this reason alone, the current run of the film won't have the broad appeal that *The Singing Fool* enjoyed. Al Jolson's voice must be the bridge for everyone. When it falls silent, you feel Alan Crosland's film fall apart and lose its interest. . . . Al Jolson seems himself to be a preliminary sketch of the singing fool; not quite relaxed in his movements, not quite natural in his shift from tragic to comic. But with his heart in his hand, and that famous tear in his voice. That tearful voice inspires emotion and applause time and again. You just can't help yourself. Unfortunately, the synchronized music is banal and lacks real phrasing; one has come to expect this of American sound films. The best of American music is in jazz, in grotesque. This is obvious in the accompanying short *Six Brown Brothers*, a really colorful and funny production.[95]

As perceptive as Eisner's critique of colorism (and of white privilege within the left) may have been, in her review of *The Jazz Singer*, Eisner resorts to an emphatic foregrounding of Jewish experience over and above Black experience, reenacting what Linda Williams has described as the film's own "apotheosis of the popular culture connection between these two sufferings," under which logic "racial suffering [becomes] a more diffuse pain—a generalized longing for a lost home. Blackface is a symbol of the triumph of assimilation as well as of its attendant loss. Uncoupled from the specific historical persecution of blacks and the specific persecution of Jews, it is a suffering that becomes embodied in the melodramatic performing persona of Al Jolson, the Jewish, blackface mammy singer."[96] Notwithstanding the fact that Eisner had yet to travel to the United States and that most likely she had gleaned her understanding of the historical context and specificity of the Utica Jubilee Singers and *The Jazz Singer* from the writings and criticism of fellow central European Jews, it is as a foil, mask, and analogy for Jewish identity that Black experience is troped in Eisner's interwar writing. Moreover, in the absence of a connection to Jewish identity, Eisner's emphatic if casual endorsement of *Six Brown Brothers* is troubling; likely, she refers to a now-lost 1927 short film featuring a performance by the eponymous band, a Canadian vaudeville saxophone sextet comprised of white musicians—family name Brown—who frequently performed in blackface.

In the German context, Eisner more often engaged questions of anti-Semitism and fascism in commentary on theater and literature. In an early book review of Wilhelm Hegeler's popular novel *Das Ärgernis*, described as "train reading," Eisner uses an act of vandalism depicted therein as a point of departure for a penetrating critique of repressive social policies and norms.[97] In the novel, a group of right-wing male students take it upon themselves to deface a statue in the public square of a small town, an act that Eisner sees as part and parcel of both the ignorance—the statue's stylized nudity, she argues, would read as entirely inoffensive and normalized to all but the most naive or malignant viewer—and the menace of fascist, particularly anti-Semitic, discourse fixated on physiognomy. She goes on to charge that these students are the perpetrators, but not the instigators, and that there is little substantive difference, and often a great deal of slippage, between the rhetoric that pathologizes opponents based on ideology or their physiognomy.

According to Eisner's memoirs, among the *Film-Kurier*'s Berlin-based editors and correspondents, she, Hans Feld, and for a time, Ernst Jäger led the left edge of the paper's direct and indirect political commentary in the first years of her time there. By 1931, however, Feld had run afoul of the increasingly reactionary head editor Jäger. Certain key films, in which both Feld and Eisner identified anti-war and anti-fascist messages, served as flash points, namely, Feld's positive review of *Der Weg ins Leben* (*Road to Life*, Nikolai Ekk, 1931) and Eisner's positive review of *Der Geheimagent* (*Secret Agent*, Harry Piel, 1932). Several sources report that Feld's review of *Der Weg ins Leben*—which celebrated the film on aesthetic, political, and technical levels—was objectionable to Jäger primarily on the grounds of the comparisons it drew between the plight of the youth featured in Ekk's film and the increasing precarity of German youth in the face of school closures, rising unemployment, and political volatility.[98] Eisner's account of the episode involves a dispute under pressure of deadline; in her recollection, Jäger insisted that Feld change the text of his review before it could be run in the paper, and Feld shot back that it could only be changed without his permission and run without his name. When Jäger protested that it was his own privilege as editor in chief to make such a change, Feld reportedly replied: "We'll see. We can take this up publicly in the pages of the *Weltbühne* or the *Berliner Tageblatt*." Jäger demurred, and the piece ran as written. However, before it went to press, Jäger added an unsigned comment in a column abutting the review, which repudiated Feld's comments and analysis and, according to Eisner and others, precipitated Feld's departure from the *Film-Kurier* within six months.[99]

Eisner would later claim that this incident marked the beginning of the end for her at the paper, and while she would stay on a year past Feld, the political climate both at the *Film-Kurier* and in Berlin was becoming increasingly hostile. From her earliest days at the paper, Eisner's criticism took a staunchly anti-war position, seen most pointedly in her reviews of work that directly represented war.[100] The signal moment of this larger shift occurred following Eisner's February 19, 1932 review of Piel's *Geheimagent*, which endorsed what Eisner read as the film's blatantly anti-war message. According to Eisner, her review provoked a hostile response from the regime mouthpiece, the *Völkischer Beobachter*, first to the *Film-Kurier* at large and later to Eisner herself.[101] For the following year, Eisner's last at the paper, her signed contributions were limited largely to theater and film reviews, and while she would recall feeling that the task of articulating a leftist perspective within the paper's broader editorial voice, insofar as this was possible under Jäger's leadership, had fallen to her alone, doing so exposed her to risk.

While in many cases, Eisner's recollections of the final months she spent in Berlin are virtually impossible to fact-check, they add up to a mood of increasing alarm. In her memoirs, she recalls having a conversation with her brother, Fritz, around this time in which they quarreled about whether it was necessary to leave, and that she stated it would be better to leave imminently with a full suitcase than to wait and end up lucky to leave with only his life. Eisner reports that she and Hans Feld left Berlin at the same time, he for Prague, and she for Paris, both motivated by the rapid escalation of tensions in late March leading up to the purge of the *Film-Kurier*'s editorial board. Eisner's last signed film review ran on March 21, 1933, and ten days later, the paper ran a front-page notice of its own takeover by the regime.

THREE

"La seule historienne"

EXILE, SALVAGE, AND COMMUNITY
AT THE CINÉMATHÈQUE FRANÇAISE

IN THE END, Eisner packed lightly, leaving her library, furniture, and valuables—including a number of good-quality corsets—in care of Fritz and his wife, Paula, in Berlin. She was received in Paris by her younger sister Steffi and brother-in-law Eugène, and while it is unclear whether she had planned from the outset to remain any longer than a fortnight, this living arrangement rapidly degenerated: "[Steffi] was even more loathsome than usual, because she was pregnant, and I told myself: I've got to get out of here, whatever the next opportunity that presents itself. . . . I couldn't and wouldn't count on my French family, even though [Eugène] was a director with Shell Oil and earned plenty."[1] While she would avail herself of Eugène's help at several key later junctures, Eisner's desire to avoid accruing any debts (financial or of gratitude) to Steffi, in concert with her pride and awkwardness in discussing money, resulted in a precarious and wounding experience of Paris in her first years of exile. In her search for lodging, Eisner found herself leaning hard on her friend, the poet and translator Edouard Roditi, an American citizen whose grandfather had been close with Eisner's family. Roditi would help Eisner a number of times during these early years in Paris, and their relationship remained affectionate into the postwar period, but his generosity proved to be exceptional in her experience of Parisians. Roditi was an observant Jew who was well connected with Parisian Sephardim, and Eisner expresses in her memoirs a distinct, painful impression of having been discriminated against by French Jews and gentiles alike: "In their view, we who came from Germany were considered Eastern Jews. We were treated by them as condescendingly as we had treated the Eastern Jews from Poland and Russia. In that moment, I felt firsthand what it means to belong to an 'inferior' race."[2] The professional success and personal independence Eisner, now thirty-seven, had grown to appreciate over the first decade of her journalistic career in Berlin all but evaporated, as her fond regard for French culture and history was rudely confronted with the realities of finding work, shelter, and sustenance in an inhospitable new home:

> The first years in Paris were very hard for me, especially mentally—hunger diminished me, but the country was totally unlike that of my dreams, of the French Revolution and the Rights of Man. Not only were we considered by our own people to be Eastern Jews, the French themselves treated us as hostile foreigners, as *métèques*. In the prefecture, we were treated like dirt, and many foreigners were sent back if they had no family or money in France. The public resistance to Hitler at first seemed strong among the people. For this reason, I was all the more shocked that during the Occupation there were so many collaborators. A year passed with odd jobs and a great deal of bitterness within.[3]

She kept her press cards for free theater and film entry courtesy of Hans Feld and the post he supplied her as Paris correspondent for *Die Kritik*, but Eisner was compelled to take on odd jobs wherever possible. Working as a nanny, administrative assistant, tutor, translator, and, briefly, as a research assistant to a bookseller who couldn't get time away from his shop long enough to research his doctoral dissertation, Eisner's recollections of these jobs are overlaid with what seems to have been an overpowering sense of distaste and injustice. Feeling ill- or under-used by each of these engagements, yet, in retrospect, amused by her own inability to advocate for herself, Eisner recalls her mortified desperation when the parents of a child she nannied neglected to pay her wages before departing on a ski trip, describing herself as *zu vornehm* (loosely, "too bougie") to ask for the money she had been counting on for weeks and that she needed to tide her over. Upon their return, a chary Eisner asked the mother of her charge whether it might be possible to receive her earnings to date. The woman, "piqued," asked Eisner whether they had not already paid her, to which Eisner indignantly replied that she would never have asked for it duplicitously; in truth, she was very nearly too proud to ask once.[4] Although Eisner declines to state outright that her privileged upbringing left her ill-equipped and disinclined to negotiate her pay, in the context of the remarks she attributed to Lücken and often repeated about being clueless about financial management, as well as a passage in the opening pages of her memoirs about her family not associating with tradespeople such as the Lubtisches, it seems clear that a substantial share of the difficulty she experienced in her first years of exile was in adjusting to a fresh, biting sense of having fallen down in the world.⁵ In an interview a little over a year before she died, Eisner reflected that struggling to secure housing and make a living were draining preoccupations, yet the most humiliating feature of her early years in exile was the loss of status she experienced: "in Germany I was finally well known, and [in France] I had to start from the beginning again."⁶

This experience was common to a number of German Jews exiled by the ascendant Nazi regime, among them fellow film critics Siegfried Kracauer and Rudolf Arnheim. Like Eisner, Kracauer fled to Paris in 1933, where he, too, found it exceedingly difficult to secure work. Eisner's memoirs convey her distress and frustration as she strung together part-time, poorly paid jobs to cover her rent and buy discounted vegetables. After years of scraping by, Eisner found work at a pharmaceutical firm as a copywriter, a job that was enervating, yet enabling: it paid enough to help her afford an apartment of her own in a new building near work, which she filled with her own books and furniture, shipped by Paula from Berlin. In an aside, Eisner recalls her fury upon discovering that Paula had discarded the corsets stored alongside her other precious belongings, joking sheepishly that it was a testament to the scarcity and thrift characterizing these years in Paris that she quarreled bitterly with her sister-in-law over the loss.⁷ The mental and physical toll of this prolonged period of instability may account for the fact that—save for two articles she was not paid to contribute to Langlois's short-lived *Cinématographe*, an adaptation of her *Film-Kurier* piece on *Das Testament des Dr. Mabuse* for the French publication *L'Intransigeant*, and a handful of contributions to *Internationale Filmschau*—she appears not to have continued to publish under her own name. By the mid-thirties, she would have had similar journalistic credentials to Kracauer and Arnheim, both of whom continued to seek out, and ultimately secure, steady work and safe passage out of continental Europe. Kracauer's lot was by no means an easy one, yet in his case, it seems that his connections to US-based scholars and writers, the success of his novel *Ginster* (1934) and "social biography" of Jacques Offenbach (1937), and the fact that his wife, Lili, was able to take on work during their time in Paris and later Marseille made continuing to write, and continuing to develop his theory of film, possible.⁸ Yet, as Miriam Hansen has argued, "Looking at the Marseille notebooks [1940–41], one cannot help being amazed by the fact that they were written at all, considering the uncertainty, poverty, and danger that confronted Jewish refugees stranded in Vichy France."⁹ Compounding the difficulties of producing work in the first place was the problem of transporting and storing it safely while on the run in the early forties. Eisner herself claims to have written two novels during these years in order to pass the time and keep her mother tongue from slipping.[10] The first, an unpublished manuscript titled *Das Verbrechen in Durville*, she began in 1935 after reading a sensational account in *Paris Soir* of a provincial man who murdered his wife: "I wrote that [novel] for three years, but it disappointed me. I knew well how to conjure images, as I did with my film historical books, but I couldn't write dialogue. My characters spoke words that were not my own. Every one of the three hundred pages I wrested from myself for that manuscript lacked bite."[11] A second manuscript was lost during her time in hiding in Montpellier: "My best novella, *Hedda*, was burned. It, along with precious Surrealist sketches and poems given to me by Henri Langlois, fell victim to the frenzy of a slow-witted French housewife, who, fearing a Nazi raid, thought she had to burn everything I had kept in writing."[12]

COLLECTORS INTO ARCHIVISTS

One bright spot during these trying pre-Occupation years was the budding, relatively soon after her arrival in Paris, of a friendship between Eisner and Henri Langlois. Although the importance of this relationship is undeniable, there has been a tendency in the literature and lore about Langlois and the Cinémathèque française—in no small part thanks to Eisner's own rhetoric—to describe Langlois as the key figure of the second half of Eisner's life, for better and for worse. She often recounted the story of their meeting as a turning point for her, as in the following rendition excerpted from her memoirs:

> In 1934 I had the decisive meeting of my life. I had read a note in *La Cinématographie française* on two young Frenchmen who were saving old silent films from being destroyed, and I thought this might make an interesting article for the *Internationale Filmschau*. So I contacted the two young men, Henri Langlois and Georges Franju, to arrange an interview. We met up at the Café Wepler, on Place Clichy, where the Gaumont Palace was later built. In order to recognize one another, we each had a copy of *La Cinématographie française* folded under our arms.[13]

Charmed by their enthusiastic reception of her stories about rubbing shoulders in Berlin with illustrious filmmakers of the silent period, and perhaps by their youthful energy—Langlois was eighteen years Eisner's junior and at the moment of their meeting was just reaching the tail end of a desultory, ultimately incomplete baccalaureate—Eisner soon found herself spending her free time with Langlois and Franju, who had recently begun amassing a large private collection of silent cinema artifacts: "With his pocket money, [Langlois] collected old films, because he found they were selling cheap. Sometimes he found them in basement apartments, sometimes even old exhibitors [sold them to him]. For 500 francs, which Paul[-]August[e] Harlé, the publisher of *La Cinématographie française*, gave him, he bought *Caligari* and *Siegfried* and a few other things."[14] Among the tasks Eisner and Langlois undertook together during this period was the continued acquisition and, crucially, the cataloging of early film ephemera, documentation, and elements.

These artifacts were destined from the beginning, Eisner would later swear, for a museum of cinema over which the twenty-two-year-old Langlois dreamed he would one day preside. Yet in consistently attributing the germinal archive's impetus and collections logic primarily to Langlois, as was her wont, Eisner was guilty of a curious omission; as early as 1928, she had been seriously engaged in film archival problems, ideas, and questions, and she had advocated vociferously for institutional space and resources, as well as industry cooperation and support for a dedicated public film archive in Berlin. In a medium-length article dating from her first year at the *Film-Kurier*, published in an early summer special insert to the weekend edition of the paper titled, waggishly, "From One Who Went Forth to Learn What 'Cinema' Was. What the Prussian Staatsbibliothek Knows about Film," she offers an evocative account of a trip to the Staatsbibliothek taken by the author in order to assess the state of the library's film research collections.[15] Caricaturing the library's chilly, officious staff and its scribbling patrons, the article features a charming narrator in the person of Dr. Lotte H. Eisner: the very same tenacious researcher and systematic thinker whose interest in the ethics and poetics of historiography and collection would later inform her scholarship and archival praxis. Dissatisfied with the reading room's disorganized, incomplete resources, Dr. Eisner is advised by a sympathetic librarian to consult one Professor X. currently preparing a fresh set of catalog volumes: "A friendly old gentleman with a full white beard receives you in the midst of a sea of books. He organizes and organizes. With his finely etched, scholarly penmanship, he labors painstakingly on a card index. When asked about film literature, he shakes his head sorrowfully." But he obliges the narrator by allowing her to peruse the volumes in progress. Paging through the Professor's five-volume card index, and finding it wanting, Dr. Eisner muses to herself first, then aloud to Professor X. in dialogue:

> Not altogether as bad as you feared. But neither as much as you had hoped.
> "And is there no collection of censorship certificates? Surely that would be worthwhile — —."
> Professor X. makes a vague gesture. "What do you expect? All of that will have to wait for some future film archive." — — —
> It's just a shame that the work will be so much more difficult for this film archive of the future. It is often pointed out that our institutions of higher education are in want of a film curriculum, and crucially, filmmaking facilities and laboratories. But are we really doing any better in the realm of the theoretical?
> What if, within the framework of the Staatsbibliothek, with the existing collections as a foundation, a systematic, comprehensive Film Library and the longed-for Film Archive were finally created, giving over to film the space that it deserves?

At several junctures throughout the article, Eisner admonishes her reader to consider the benefits to industry, scholarship, and the public offered by a robust, accessible repository for resources on film aesthetics, technology, law, regulation, and industrial practices. Why, she asks, does industry not support such a public good with deposits of studio records and screenplays; why does the regulation of film content, exhibition, and taxation happen behind closed doors, rarely under public scrutiny? While the article's tone is playful, the concluding remarks are pointed, recalling to her reader her own running commentary and reporting in the *Film-Kurier* on educational films and film pedagogy. To this, regular readers would know, could be added a growing body of industry coverage, reviews, commentary on film criticism, technical innovations in filmmaking, and her columns of advice addressed to directors in search of new adaptations, new ideas. Clearly, the Dr. Eisner of 1928, at least, had the well-considered opinions and the wealth of technical research experience to be guiding the acquisitions and early cataloging efforts of the association that would later become the Cinémathèque française. Indeed, she articulates the problems, the logistics, and the stakes of film archival praxis in this 1928 article with brisk economy and confidence. In retrospectively describing their 1934 encounter as "decisive" for her, Eisner has usually been interpreted to mean that she was brought along by Langlois, and that the key ideas were his; in context, it seems clear that she had worked many of these out in advance, and that what the then-informal partnership and the young Langlois were in a unique position to offer her was a degree of social stability—much yearned-for in her first years of exile—and sense of common purpose.

In the first days, Langlois, Franju, and Eisner were driven by an awareness of the larger economic and industrial trends; in the early thirties, many studios and exhibitors moved to shift off their archives of silent films and make way for the hundreds of new sound features being produced every year. Pathé, Gaumont, and the Lumière Brothers had not yet begun to implement this practice across the board, but Hollywood studios, including Universal and RKO had, and according to biographer Glenn Myrent, Langlois was alert to the urgency of acting quickly, given the likelihood that the situation in Hollywood might forecast transnational trends. During this period, Eisner later recalled, Langlois often riffled through wastepaper at the offices of trade publications and newspapers for discarded film stills and photos, but his primary concern was snapping up silent film elements being sold off to firms recycling film for various industrial applications.[16] She and Langlois would regularly trawl the regional flea markets in order to divert films that might otherwise fall into the wrong hands. Georges Langlois would later describe his brother, somewhat hyperbolically, as having been motivated as much by a desire to seize the fleeting moment of opportunity as by an abiding, self-aggrandizing sense of moral outrage:

> But throwing them away wasn't even sufficient; from their definitive and total destruction those who had already reaped the benefits from [these films] hoped to make one last profit. Whole productions were sold as scrap by the ton, priced by weight, to industrial chemists. The film was washed and melted. It served to produce nitrate or varnish. I witnessed [Henri's] efforts and the hatred he inspired in those whose habits he discouraged, to those who only looked at it as a way to extract a bribe, a commission, an extra profit, by sending off to be melted the negatives that had taken others months and millions to achieve. [Henri] faced down the incomprehension and cupidity of businessmen, the same types he would run up against his whole life.[17]

While their next move is often described as an organic result of Langlois and Franju's membership in a handful of ciné-clubs around Paris, and Langlois's principled, quasi-political stance that the goal of saving silent films was to share them, it is also possible to discern a financial incentive in their decision to begin showing their growing collection of silent films to the paying public. Langlois's vexed maxim, "a cinémathèque is not a cemetery"—often trotted out to disparage the archival praxis of rival Ernest Lindgren—would later be described as the inevitable fruition of this stance.[18] Their club, le Cercle du Cinéma, was initiated in October 1935, soon after the purchase by Langlois of a trove of silent films from resale agents Baudon Saint-Lô, Klein, Mueller, and Séfaire; according to Myrent, "The original negatives were long gone, but there were still prints in good condition."[19] This haul, their largest yet, was made possible by a gift from Henri's mother, Annie Langlois, but the Cercle du Cinéma would subsidize future purchases with the income generated by the compulsory annual membership fees and the admissions charges collected at each gathering.

The meetings of the Cercle du Cinéma were emceed by Henri Langlois, by all accounts an ebullient hype man whose commentary, provocative billings, and infectious zeal were among the club's greatest draws. According to Eisner, an early member and regular attendee, Langlois *Mère et Fils* might have been a small operation, but it attracted a glamorous and enthusiastic crowd: "On the fifth floor of the Marignan Building, on the Champs Elysées, Langlois got a room with seventy seats, which he turned into a small movie theater where he presented his old films. Each time, ninety people or so would squeeze in; this original Cercle du Cinéma was very popular: Cocteau, Sartre, Simone de Beauvoir, Simone Signoret, and friends of Langlois from abroad, such as Cavalcanti, Comencini, and Lattuada, were all regular visitors of the club. Langlois's mother sold tickets and ushered everyone to their seats."[20]

Encouraged by the success of the Cercle du Cinéma's screenings and bolstered by increased financial support from Harlé, Langlois and Franju moved to incorporate an organization that would allow them to expand and formalize their acquisitions. Paris had been home to only a handful of cinema archives in the preceding decades, and none had concerned themselves with feature film preservation: as Myrent points out, the Army Cinema Archive (founded 1914) was mandated to preserve newsreels and footage of military maneuvers; the Cinémathèque of the City of Paris (founded by Victor Perrot in 1925) was tasked with preserving educational films; and the short-lived Cinémathèque nationale (1933–1940), under photographer Laure Albin-Guillot, had only ever managed to accumulate several thousand feet of film about the Great War before it was dissolved.[21]

Internationally, there was some—if very recent—precedent for the kind of organization Langlois, Franju, and Harlé would create: in 1934, the German state had established the Reichsfilmarchiv, and in the following year both the Museum of Modern Art (MoMA) Film Library in New York City and the National Film Library of the British Film Institute (BFI) in London would be chartered. Thus, it was when Langlois and Franju filed the Cinémathèque française (CF) bylaws in September 1936 at police headquarters in Paris, registering the offices of Harlé's *La Cinématographie française* at 29 rue Marsoulan as its headquarters, that the first bloom of a transnational archival moment reached Paris. Langlois and Franju, with Harlé's financing, Jean Mitry's archival organization, and Eisner's expertise, began to accumulate and catalog as many films as they could get their hands on, famously storing many of them in the upstairs bathtub of the Langlois family apartment. Around this time, thanks to an introduction by Harlé, Langlois, and Franju met with Alexandre Kamenka, director of Films Albatros, who subsequently agreed to put the company's films on long-term deposit with the CF. This was a coup for the nascent organization, and it brought Langlois into contact with a number of future allies, including Jean Epstein, whose sister and collaborator Marie would later become the in-house film preservationist at the CF, and the fourth key partner at the CF in its postwar heyday, with Eisner, Langlois, and Mary Meerson. In 1937, yet another key foundational moment for the CF came to pass when Langlois and Franju secured authorization from Yves Chataigneau, director of the Ministry of Foreign Affairs, to use the diplomatic pouch for the postage-free transport of films, which fostered inter-archive exchanges, enabling a degree of programming flexibility that in turn raised the public profiles of all archives involved and led, in July 1938, to the founding of the Fédération internationale des archives du film (FIAF).

Yet as Laurent Mannoni has emphasized in his recuperation of Eisner—which counters the common tendency to center the narrative of the CF's early years exclusively about Langlois—for Eisner's part, this vital institution- and network-building work was done entirely pro bono.[22] And while the CF and Langlois would outlast the Occupation—by some accounts flourishing not just in spite of but because of the war, thanks to Langlois's relationship with Frank Hensel, head of the Reichsfilmarchiv—by the end of the decade, the tenuous sense of stability Eisner had achieved by the end of her first seven years of exile would yet again be uprooted. In May 1940, Eisner was summoned by the police prefecture to present herself at the Vélodrome d'Hiver with no more than a hand suitcase, for processing and, ultimately, internment at a camp detaining all foreign nationals and politically unreliable persons. A harrowing experience, which cost her several teeth and any faith in the French state's good intentions, Eisner's imprisonment at Gurs ended, according to her memoirs, with her escape on foot, aided by a sympathetic camp officer. The next morning, after reaching Pau, a town nearly fifty kilometers from the camp, she bought a third-class ticket for Montpellier, where she was to meet her brother-in-law Eugène, who was stationed there.[23] From this point forward, Eisner would move from one safe house to the next, under false papers and with an increasing sense of dread and fear.

The chapters in her memoirs on the years from 1940 to 1945 are imprecise about dates and certain names, and they are populated with a cast of villainous German soldiers, provincial anti-Semites, trusty members of the Resistance, and a "Gypsy" fortune-teller who informed Eisner that she would survive the war and the Occupation, predicting: "one day you will be famous."[24] In spite of the occasionally dubious dialogue and events recounted by Eisner about this period in the memoirs, it is important to give credence to her account of her own mental state and the enormous strain she experienced living under a false identity and the constant threat of apprehension. The chronology of certain events might have been compressed in retrospect—particularly in terms of what exactly she knew about the nature and ends of the deportations, and when she knew it—but these memories were acutely felt, and they became fundamental to Eisner's sense of identity and personal history in the postwar years. Shortly after receiving a more legitimate-looking second set of counterfeit identity papers and taking on her nom de guerre, "Louise Hélène Escoffier," Eisner spent a frigid winter in a decommissioned chateau in Figeac, guarding and inventorying reels upon reels of films cached there by Langlois in order to avoid their appropriation or confiscation by Hensel of the Reichsfilmarchiv, with whom Langlois maintained a cagey yet mutually beneficial relationship throughout the Occupation.[25] Wary of the highly flammable film, Eisner recalls working the entire winter without a fire, breaking her fingernails opening the canisters as she checked each reel entrusted to her care, and trekking seven kilometers in the snow to procure ink when she ran dry: "It was a hard winter, but it was harder still without the ability to write."[26]

Among the consistent features of Eisner's retrospective narratives about her time in hiding, perhaps none features more significantly than Henri Langlois's friendship and succor. Indeed, Eisner's loyalty to him in all that would transpire in the postwar period was tempered with her gratitude for his financial and emotional support while she was in hiding, and for insisting, after Liberation, that she return to Paris to work at the CF, which she credited with giving her a restorative sense of belonging. One of the more dramatic episodes in the story of her time as Louise Escoffier revolves around a document reproduced in the memoirs—dated March 7, 1944, on official French government letterhead, which Eisner claims he stole—in which Langlois declares that her presence in Figeac is required by the CF and that she is acting as its agent there. Eisner would say in her memoirs and elsewhere that in a Nazi raid on May 2, 1944, that resulted in the deportation of almost nine hundred other people from Figeac to Bergen-Belsen, she was only spared by virtue of this document.[27] According to Eisner, the end of the war and her life in hiding came without bringing her the scantest sense of direction or purpose, until Langlois told her, "Your place is here with us, now."[28] The first of Eisner's postwar research efforts was to find out what had happened to her mother, Margarethe, and in the accounts she gave of this process, she would take care to note both Langlois's insistence that she take any time she needed to do this before settling in to her new work, and that it was her friend and doctoral adviser Gottfried von Lücken who ultimately helped her find the records confirming that her mother had been transported to Theresienstadt, where she died in 1942.[29]

What most complicates an outsider's retrospective understanding of the relationship between Eisner and Langlois is exemplified in this story: stretched tightly over the frame of the organization they were building, the warp of their work in common and the weft of their long friendship are shot through with trauma. It is precisely this interweaving of the professional and the personal and the affective cast of Eisner's recollections of and reflections on her work with Langlois that troubles attempts to sort the fibs and fables from the facts. In spite of her conviction that Langlois saved her life during the Occupation and made it worth living after the end of the war, he was a notoriously difficult colleague and leader, and the steady stream of work he provided Eisner was not always compensated accordingly, either financially or with due respect. Mannoni has suggested that it was only after the initial publication of *L'écran démoniaque* in 1952 that Langlois acknowledged Eisner as a peer:

> Langlois completely changed his attitude toward Lotte Eisner upon [its] publication.... With sincere admiration, he finally understood that she—whom he began calling "Lolotte darling" then—was not only a friend and faithful ally to him through the most extreme tests, but a competent conservator, an internationally renowned film historian, and a formidable intellect, something that the Cinémathèque had sorely missed since the departures of Jean Mitry and Jean George Auriol. In 1952, Langlois explained to Yvonne

Dornès that, "with the exception of Miss Escoffier" and himself, "there are no other employees at the [CF] who have passed a certain level of general education and studies at university" (forgetting that he himself never passed his baccalaureate).[30]

Julia Eisner has put it more forcefully: "She was, in effect, a middle-aged woman not just doing several different jobs but crucially doing several different *types* of job, some of which were considerably beneath her intelligence and ability," a situation she attributes directly to Langlois's attitude toward Lotte Eisner, continuing, "This invisible, feminised labour of administration was something that she regarded as a necessary element of the collecting process. ... The labour was unrecognized by [Langlois] and therefore also remained unacknowledged by everyone else."[31] While a great deal of attention has been paid to the foibles of Langlois and the chaos these caused the CF, it should be pointed out that in some cases, intentionally uncharitable accounts have been construed as credible too readily on the basis of their proximity to events and that, on balance, peer organizations under the microscope have exhibited similar pathologies.[32] Indeed, Janet Bergstrom has disputed such arguments, asserting that Eisner has until recently lingered in the shadow of Langlois, although, "it is important to remember that Eisner could not have done what she most wanted to do on behalf of German silent cinema without being able to act as Langlois's spokesperson. And in a reciprocal fashion that has gone largely unrecognized, he could not have done many of the things that he did without her."[33] I would add that the received wisdom about Eisner's labor and her place in the intellectual history of film archives and film historiography is best viewed as the result not only of Langlois's ungenerous tendency to downplay the importance of his colleagues' achievements when the benefits of acknowledging those accomplishments failed to redound directly to him, but from Eisner's own autobiographical narratives and the ways these in turn were mobilized by filmmakers, archivists, historians, and film scholars. In the few statements Eisner did make over the years about the importance of her own work—in the interwar years, at the CF, as a scholar, and as a mentor—she was often reluctant to claim credit for great achievements, instead, as we've seen, emphasizing that her unique capabilities and talents were in the realm of research, writing style, taste, and tenacity.

Nevertheless, Eisner mentions in her memoirs—placing only gentle emphasis on this fact—that for years following her return to Paris and engagement full-time at the CF, she was paid sometimes part and sometimes none of what she was owed. Consequently, she devoted her CF lunch hour to earning her basic living expenses, returning to the pharmaceutical company for which she had worked in the late thirties prior to going into hiding, this time moonlighting as a ghostwriter and researcher.[34] While he cut a charismatic figure at the head of the CF's charge to legitimize and bolster public-facing film archival work, Langlois's grandiosity, disorganization, and his tendency to interpret criticism and adversity as unjust victimization contributed to what was, by all accounts, a dysfunctional workplace periodically convulsed by existential crises. According to Mannoni, the situation reached its nadir in 1970–72, during the final stages of creating his Musée du Cinéma at the Palais de Chaillot, when the "tyrannical and dictatorial Langlois neglected day-to-day business. The organisation was extremely chaotic.... The abandoned staff complained that they no longer had any management."[35] Eisner attests in her memoirs to the habitual back-burnering of his staff's needs by Langlois and notes that his tendency to ignore urgent requests on her part for his signature or attention was enormously frustrating, saying that friends and colleagues at other institutions became accustomed to her dissatisfaction and inured to her periodic threats to leave the CF for greener pastures.[36] Yet Eisner's frustration with Langlois flared up occasionally in internal communications, in notes on the translations of important correspondence she provided to him, and in her reports on ongoing work. Long before the dark days of the late sixties and the Langlois Affair, Langlois's practice was to have potential acquisitions sent to the CF for his personal review, sending back to their owners only the items he was not interested in purchasing. Langlois tended to delay the return of materials as long as possible and drag out the processing of payment, or suggest that the items remain on long-term deposit, insured by the CF but never actually bought from their owners.[37] This process exasperated many, and Eisner was often on the front lines of conflict, negotiating between the filmmakers and Langlois. In a typical note, Eisner presses Langlois: "I entreat you to look with me at the photos belonging to [Otto] Hunte to tell me if there are some that you want to keep, because I want to send the others back to Neurohr [a broker] with the sketches not selected as soon as possible after the holidays. Answer.... I am very worried because Mary [Meerson] couldn't find the [Karl] Vollbrecht photos he had entrusted to me for reproduction. Please tell me where the ones you want to have copied are and which ones I can already send back. <u>Answer, please</u>."[38] The disorganization and poor communication that characterized Langlois's modus operandi were, it seems in some cases, less a result of underfunding or overwork than a calculated strategy on his part to muddy negotiations and perhaps benefit from confusion over where exactly a film or an artifact was, and to whom it belonged.

Occasionally, however, Langlois chanced upon an equally stubborn sparring partner, such as the notoriously peevish and changeable Josef von Sternberg, whom Langlois offended in 1961. Having tarried in depositing a token payment for the first chapter of Sternberg's memoirs—which had been sent to the CF on the promise that Langlois would review it and plug the forthcoming publication of *Fun in a Chinese Laundry* (1965)—Langlois provoked an angry letter rebuking his intentions and demanding the return of the manuscript. In her translation of Sternberg's letter from English, Eisner closes with the following stern note to Langlois: "Henri, I told you to pay him, like with so many others (the Germans, for example, for their set designs. You give us a bad reputation, and we will have nothing left.)"[39] The Germans being referred to here could be any number of filmmakers Langlois's lax attitude toward payment had irritated, including Peter Röhrig (son of Walter, and a production designer in his own right), Hermann Warm, Otto Hunte, or Rochus Gliese. The last wrote to Eisner in 1956, distressed about the delay of a payment he had depended upon having on time: "As my bank assured me, such a transfer takes no more than five to six days, so there must have been some mistake in Paris. I've been clear enough about my situation, you know it. What is to be done? I urge you to clear this up. Excuse my agitation, but I'm at the end of my rope."[40] Reading through even a partial record of the correspondence between these filmmakers and the CF, one cringes at the frequency and distress with which they admonish Eisner and Langlois to provide payment in full, the return of their work, or a firm date by which they can expect either.

It can be inferred in several cases, such as that of Peter Röhrig, that there were discrepancies between the expectations set by their initial encounter and negotiations with Eisner and the extended period of waiting that often resulted from Langlois's deliberative process and creative accounting. Poignant letters between Ewald Junge and Eisner indicate one of the stickier points of the extended acquisitions process: having deposited hundreds of his father Alfred Junge's sketches with the CF prior to encountering his own financial difficulties, he begs Eisner to inquire whether funds for a formal purchase might be made available,

> My circumstances have changed so much since the "gift" I made you in 1965 that I hope the position can be reconsidered. . . . Do you really need them

all? Can you even ever show them all? ... If you do want to keep everything, can you make some kind of payment (not necessarily on the American scale, which I know you can't afford, but on a reasonable valuation: say £5 per design)? I did in fact (at the time of the Cinémathèque "bust-up"), at your request, send you a letter specifying that all material was on loan to Cinémathèque. This was to prevent anyone grabbing it to pay debts or for other nefarious purposes. But, if you think it would help, you might mention this to Henri now. I am sure you will do your best.[41]

Eisner replied rapidly and with compassion, sketching out her plan for approaching Langlois with this request and her best guess as to the timeline for an answer, closing her letter with a tender note of affection for Junge's ailing wife, Sylvia. Emphasizing the difficulty of getting Langlois's attention between his trips to Montreal and the upcoming Palais de Chaillot exhibition, she makes it clear that she is sympathetic to the Junges and sees the possibility of a favorable resolution on the horizon.[42]

If not being paid and getting hung out to dry from time to time in delicate acquisitions negotiations by Langlois were the worst of Eisner's problems at the CF, the lack of competent oversight did grant her a greater degree of freedom in directing her research and writing and in articulating and carrying out her own distinctive archival praxis. Looking back on the early years of her postwar work, Eisner would remark, with amusement: "The first fifteen years of my work at the [CF] were truly the best. ... I threw myself into things, I flourished. My official title at the [CF] was 'Conservatrice en Chef' [Chief Curator] but in practice I was the dogsbody. I made acquisitions, I archived, I corresponded, I represented the organization if Henri wasn't available. I watched films, gave introductions, gave lectures, helped with the exhibitions and attended the FIAF meetings with Henri. Time flew."[43] As Marie Epstein would recall in her oral history of the CF, Eisner was the originator of the CF's efforts to establish a collection of interwar German cinema artifacts and film elements, leading both the CF's acquisitions efforts and the public exhibitions: "Henri Langlois himself said that two-thirds of the riches of the Musée [du Cinéma] were due to [Eisner's] investigations and acquisitions. She was his right hand during all those feverish days and sleepless nights of preparation for the big exhibitions, both in France and abroad."[44] Langlois had considerably less expertise in the work of the interwar German filmmakers than Eisner did, could not correspond in German—he required translations by Eisner of all letters and paperwork in German and English—and left it to Eisner to negotiate acquisitions and longer-term relationships with the surviving artists to whom she had established connections through tenacious research and unfaltering charm.[45]

In describing Eisner's methods as an exemplar, Langlois counseled Marion Michelle, about to depart on a July 1957 acquisitions mission to Los Angeles, "Be very enthusiastic, very solicitous, and very insistent, like Lotte Eisner, who won't leave them without getting what she came for—do not give them time to mull it over and think better of it," and later, with reference to the particularly ticklish case of Sternberg, "In any case, if you feel the whole thing is too difficult, do not force your hand as you will get nothing and it will be Lotte['s job] to come in to give a dose of her Berliner's charm." He instructs Michelle to check with Eisner about any other requests and visits that should be made, to consult her about planning to visit the widows of E. A. Dupont and Karl Grune, as well as the "very important" matter of the maquettes by various art directors. Langlois also warns Michelle to stay away from Mary Pickford and Pola Negri, so as to avoid interrupting Eisner's "marvelous" ongoing progress on these cases.[46]

If Langlois deferred to Eisner's expertise in 1957, it may also have been due to her track record; beginning in 1945, she worked to establish the whereabouts of the interwar German filmmakers scattered to the winds, building a network of relationships with the interwar cohort, many of whom she had first met in her *Film-Kurier* years, including Fern Andra, André Andrejew, Ludwig Berger, Bertolt Brecht, Louise Brooks, Hans Cürlis, Otto Erdmann, Paul Falkenberg, Oskar Fischinger (via his wife, Elfriede), Karl Freund, Valeska Gert, Rochus Gliese, Emil Hasler, Thea von Harbou, Robert Herlth, Otto Hunte, Alfred Junge (via his son, Ewald), Erich Kettelhut, Gerhardt Lamprecht, Fritz Lang, F. W. Murnau (via his collaborators, his brother Robert Plumpe-Murnau, and his cousin Hans Plumpe), G. W. Pabst, Julius Pinschewer, Walter Röhrig (via his widow, Ludmilla, and son, Peter), Margarethe Schön, Eugen Schüfftan, Walter Schultze-Mittendorff, Robert Siodmak, Josef von Sternberg, Karl Vollbrecht, Fritz Arno Wagner, and Hermann Warm. In virtually all cases, Eisner initiated contact with these filmmakers with the intent, not merely of extracting artifacts and treasures, but of recovering the wreckage of what she considered the most vital years of the German industry; throwing lifelines to the aging and infirm filmmakers themselves, their widows and children, Eisner would offer not only to purchase their work, but to redeem it as the object of serious aesthetic and historiographical contemplation. Soliciting oral histories of the period and productions in particular, Eisner also encouraged them to share any memories, addresses, and contacts they might have, which she would then use to further build out her network. In the case of filmmakers Gerhardt Lamprecht and Julius Pinschewer, who both made efforts to establish archives of their own work—and in Lamprecht's case, much more than his own, both as a private collector and later as head of the Deutsche Kinemathek—Eisner was collegial and supportive. As Eisner herself put it in a letter to Fritz Lang, to do good archival work, "one must follow up on every trace."[47]

Leaving aside their acquisitions of film elements, a key feature of Eisner's archival praxis, sharply distinguished from Langlois's, was its self-reflexively historiographical impetus. Whereas Langlois—often described as a collector, rather than as an archivist—betrayed a quasi-fetishistic preoccupation with film costumes and totems, Eisner seems to have been singularly focused on soliciting materials that might shed light on the filmmaking process and testimony that might help establish the working relationships and conditions under which films were produced.[48] Mannoni's accounts of the CF's climate during the fifties and sixties, which are inflected with his own experiences at the archive and Eisner's mentorship, emphasize Eisner's differences as fundamentally tied up in her status as the "most intellectual" among the quartet at the center of CF operations.[49] For her own part, Eisner identified as an art historian and archaeologist, intent on establishing both an archive and a body of scholarship; rather than fixating on the material traces of fictional worlds, as Langlois tended to, she hoped to safeguard documentation and testimonies that might allow scholars to better understand the films and the filmmaking process of what she called "classical German cinema."[50] From the outset of her correspondence with the interwar German filmmakers, Eisner explains that with these archival acquisitions she hopes to foster public interest and appreciation, as well as develop her own scholarship on the period; for years, across correspondence with Herlth, Hunte, Röhrig, and others, Eisner mentions a planned volume devoted specifically to the work of set designers that will emphasize the collaborative nature of the filmmaking process.[51] Eisner's interest in filmmaking teams dated back to the early 1930s; it would also form the basis for her analysis of Murnau's work in her monograph on his oeuvre.[52] If Eisner's focus on the filmmaking team as a creative unit emerged from her observations on the ground in the early thirties, then it took on a more emphatic inflection in the postwar French context. Eisner differed with the model of auteur theory advanced by some of the younger critics at *Cahiers du cinéma* on certain key points, referring to them as "the Cahiers snobs."⁵³ In an exemplary 1958 letter to Robert Herlth, Eisner frames this assertion in the negative: "And the films that come to us from Germany [today] are the proof of my theory that the lack of a real collective is probably the main cause of the decline of German film art."⁵⁴

SALVAGE AS ARCHIVAL PRAXIS

The traces of Eisner's archival praxis that have been preserved in the administrative archives of the CF, along with commentary she offered on her own methodology in interviews and in her published scholarship, suggest that, more than simply collecting and analyzing interwar German cinema, Eisner was engaged in a multipronged, affectively charged effort to salvage the work, support its living authors, and submit robust scholarly engagement of the period to a contemporary audience.⁵⁵ In using "salvage" here, I'm invoking its nimbus of associations with wreckage, trauma, and redemption, as well as the temporal relationship between disaster and salvage; Eisner's sense of her own narrow escape from the cataclysm—which she described ambivalently in terms of her own agency: it was a fated survival, yet one contingent upon her own grit—imbued her postwar work with a sense of urgency on two counts.⁵⁶ The Nazi program of cultural annihilation was exemplified by the 1937 *Entartete Kunst* exhibition in Munich, which worked to conflate art and artists that the regime found problematic, threatening, or hostile and to exclude them from the body politic. This regime left a gaping hole in the cultural fabric of central Europe, into which even those vital traces of the interwar period that managed to survive the end of the war were inexorably drawn as their authors and caretakers began to die off, lose track of hidden caches, or lose hope of ever finding an audience or home for their work. The correspondence between Eisner and Robert Plumpe-Murnau, for instance, points to the ways even the work of filmmakers who predated the Nazis became entangled with its project of wholesale destruction. In a letter dating from the beginning of their correspondence, Plumpe-Murnau recites the litany of calamities that have plagued his attempts to safeguard his brother's work:

> Thank you for your attention to my brother's memory and his art. I considered it my duty to watch over his filmic and literary heritage, because I was convinced of the documentary value of his screenplays, shooting scripts, and correspondence with famous contemporaries of theater, cinema, and literature. During the war, I sheltered this archive in different places. Immediately

after the collapse, I tried, from Kitzbühel, to relocate all these caches. Herr Dr. [Ludwig] Gesek, then the head of the Section Cinéma Française, as well as the Austrian Film Museum and editor of *Filmkunst*, saw the importance of preserving this archive, and spontaneously initiated a corresponding action; however, as a German—even though I did not belong to either the "Party" or the "Reichsfilmkammer"—I could not get permission to travel to the different zones of Germany, and had to turn back to Austria. When I arrived in Bielefeld in 1951, I immediately undertook several trips to Berlin and gathered all that I could still find in the different cellars, in the dust and rubble. I made the tragic discovery that a large part of [Murnau's] film legacy was missing, that the most interesting scenarios, for example *The Last Laugh, Faust, Sunrise, The Four Devils*, sometimes with original notes and caricatures of the actors, all the film trophies . . . the scrapbooks, even the memorial wreaths sent by his Hollywood friends, all had been stolen, not to mention the objects of art and value. Of all this, there was nothing left. . . . I had packed Murnau's library, which consisted of about 2,000 volumes, partly inherited from his friend the young Jewish poet [Hans] Ehrenbaum-Degele, and I had stored it in a cellar protected against bombs. The building was burned down in 1944. The cellar was completely flooded and buried under rubble. During my last stay in Berlin in 1952, the cellar was not yet cleared.[57]

To the problems enumerated by Plumpe-Murnau of safe and stable storage were added the advancing age and failing health of many interwar filmmakers. Sensitive to the mortality of both filmmakers and archivists, Eisner is quoted by Mannoni as having admonished Fritz Lang to "throw nothing into the trash! We welcome all for future generations: everything, for the future Langlois, Eisner and Mary, when we have all bitten the dust."[58] While she never explicitly connected her own wartime experience to her archival praxis in any of her postwar acquisitions correspondence, the losses she sustained—her mother and *Hedda*, not least among them—reverberate throughout her archival and scholarly work and inflect her entreaties to each of the interwar filmmakers with a palpable urgency.[59] Among Eisner's most often-repeated memories about the early postwar frenzy of acquisitions, the stories of how André Andrejew and Max Douy each came to deposit their early work with the CF illustrate the precarity of even the work and people who managed to survive the war. In Andrejew's case, he confessed to Eisner that many of his set designs and sketches had been fed by his valet to their fireplace during wartime fuel shortages in Paris; Douy, on the other hand, fatefully lent Eisner his personal collection of set designs and sketches for an exhibition the night before a catastrophic fire engulfed his apartment.

So struck by the good fortune of having sent the materials into safekeeping in the nick of time was Douy, Eisner said, that he formally placed the entire collection on permanent deposit with the CF.[60]

With respect to the politics and poetics of the archive, "salvage" offers more than an opportunity to consider how trauma shapes memory and cultural historiography; it opens the analysis of Eisner's work up to the generative discourse with affect theory that has recently been broached in archival theory proper with respect to social justice and appraisal, as well as queer historiography.[61] Eisner's archival praxis, when it is foregrounded on its own terms, has usually been described as highly skilled and highly personal.[62] Mannoni and Bergstrom have each emphasized the importance of her "lived history" to the work Eisner did in the postwar years; indeed, in her study of Eisner's archival correspondence with Robert Herlth, Rochus Gliese, and Emil Hasler, Bergstrom argues, "Beyond collecting for the museum, Eisner had a personal mission that could be felt more directly in [her acquisitions correspondence] than in her published writing. It is impossible not to feel how important it was to her to try to locate, protect and give a second life to the cinema she had known and loved in Berlin."[63] Sympathizing with Eisner's sense of conviction, attuning oneself to the love she felt for these films; this is the language of affect.[64] Indeed, it is my own feeling that Eisner's archival praxis is ripe for consideration with some of the tools and insights of affect theory; not as an intervention into that literature, but rather as a particular case that can be best illuminated and more fully appreciated through the lens of affect.

A second contemporary discourse informing my analysis of Eisner's archival praxis is that of queer historiography. As in the case of affect, I am suggesting that Eisner's work is meaningfully described by this body of literature, rather than that she contributed to it.[65] This discourse is particularly clarifying in the case of Eisner's archival praxis in that it offers modes for analysis oriented toward understanding the ways Eisner and her work did not conform to dominant contemporaneous models of archival work as either quasi-scientific and highly rational or embedded in the institutional and political projects of its state and private sponsors.[66] In attending explicitly to the ways norms are negotiated, and the ways that communities and individuals navigate systems of institutional privilege and power, queer historiography opens up a space for understanding and contextualizing the kind of work Eisner did at the CF, which has fallen through the cracks of film historiographical discourse on archives to date. Indeed, the resonances between Eisner's work and what Ann Cvetkovich describes as "queer archival method" are unmistakable; Cvetkovich argues that such archives "are collected out of an affective need, generate complex affective responses (both positive and negative), and enable affective approaches to history."[67] Eisner's efforts to archive and analyze the fast-disappearing remnants of a robust interwar corpus of art by and about people marked for annihilation by the Nazi regime—gay, queer, leftist, Jewish, dissenting—emerged in spite of a lack of validation within larger, more stable social structures of power that undergirded the work of peers such as Kracauer and Arnheim, or Barry and Lindgren, and continued under precarious and unpredictable institutional conditions through the early seventies. Indeed, her impulse to snap up that work teetering on the lip of the maw may have begun as the self-affirming retort to the dehumanizing treatment of Jews and of women she experienced and witnessed.[68] Traces of Eisner's affective engagements with her own history, with fellow refugees and exiles, and with collaborators and sympathizers are scattered thinly and unevenly across the CF's administrative archives, yet it's possible to discern several important themes throughout the correspondence, notes, and documentation available there.

One bright thread running throughout Eisner's postwar correspondence is her aversion to dealing with people she judges as having actively or passively benefited from Aryanization, and those who sympathized with the Nazi regime. Eisner dwells at length on her unreserved disgust for Leni Riefenstahl and Thea von Harbou in her memoirs and in the Horowitz and Shahid Saless documentaries, as well as her skepticism—allayed, she affirms, after tough questioning on her part—about G. W. Pabst's wartime behavior. Yet in private correspondence, she allows that her postwar acquisitions efforts depended, in many cases, on working with people she knew or suspected to have been Nazi sympathizers. In a 1959 shop-talk letter to fellow archivist Gerhardt Lamprecht, Eisner replies to a query of Lamprecht's about *Sehnsucht* (*Desire*, F. W. Murnau, 1921) and thanks him for shouldering the odious task of corresponding with Gussy Holl.[69] Pivoting—as if to say, *speaking of Nazis*—Eisner inquires whether Lamprecht might have current contact information for Werner Krauss, who was similarly disgraced by his affiliation with the regime.[70] Interestingly, Eisner uses the past perfect tense to describe Holl's Nazism, indicating actions begun or performed in the past that carry forward, or whose effects continue:

> Thank you for writing to Gussy Holl; for my part, I would be reluctant to do so, because Holl has been a terrible Nazi. You should try to save the

Jannings archive. By the way, do you know where Krauss is at the moment? I would like to ask him a few things about *Tartüff*. All I have is his address in Mondsee [Austria], which he gave me when we met in Hamburg. We talked about a lot then, but not about Murnau. If Holl could tell you something about the content of *Sehnsucht*, that would be nice.

Notwithstanding her distaste for dealing with Holl in 1959, Eisner would end up interviewing her about her work with Murnau. In the 1964 edition of her monograph, Eisner relies on Holl's description of *Sehnsucht* to complement the censor's report on the film, indicating that Holl has informed her of another Murnau picture called *Wahnsinn* ("Madness") predating *Sehnsucht*, in which Holl also acted.[71] The ambivalence here—loath to deal with them, yet even less inclined to let a good lead or source go—is characteristic of Eisner's dealings with filmmakers whose wartime behavior ran in a direction opposite to her own.[72] Seeing Ernst Busch again for the first time after the war, Eisner says, she was struck by his chilly mien; he demanded to know when exactly she had come to Paris—a coded question, designed to get at why she had come to Paris—and, in her telling: "I laughed and said, 'Oh, since thirty-three!' Then he became very nice to me, and said, 'You see, I ask that [of] everybody, because I don't want to give my hand to a Nazi. I want to know whom I give a hand to. So, you have been here since thirty-three? So, I can accept you.'" Explaining that she thought this was a good idea, she says she adopted the phrase and whenever she has been asked why she didn't return to live in Germany after the war, she replies, "I would never go back, because I don't know to whom I could give my hand."[73] Her memoirs make plain that while she did travel to Germany regularly for acquisitions, exhibitions, and film festivals beginning in 1954, she found the notion of a return or homecoming impossible, even as she acknowledged the difficulties of dealing with French former collaborators, sympathizers, and run-of-the-mill anti-Semites. In spite of having taken French nationality in the fifties, she describes with bitter amusement the regular, petty humiliations she experienced in France as a result of her accent and her Jewishness; upon being honored in 1982 as a *Chevalier de l'ordre national de la Légion d'honneur*, she saved a thought for a neighbor who had made a pointed recent effort to impugn Eisner's foreignness: "For that reason, and that reason alone, I wanted to get the Cross of the Legion of Honor as fast as possible, so that I could display it on my lapel in defiance of my hostile neighbor, for I am a better Frenchwoman than she."[74]

A second vivid, contrasting strand of Eisner's correspondence with the interwar German filmmakers, and one that ultimately marks her archival praxis more strongly, can be roughly described as her warmth. Affectionate and empathetic, Eisner's approach to filmmakers and their partners, wives, widows, children, heirs, and executors was guided by her attention to their health, living situations, financial stability, and family news. In letter after letter, Eisner will follow up on mundanities of a daughter's exams, summer travel plans and upcoming opportunities for a visit, health issues and medical news (theirs or her own), or a correspondent's thoughts on a current film release. Moreover, the affection seems to have been reciprocal and based on sincere enjoyment of each other's company in person and via post, rather than on eliciting generous donations to the CF, as Langlois's somewhat cynical take on it in his instructions to Michelle assumed.[75] Often Eisner will begin letters with thanks for the tasty marzipan, good chocolates, or book, with a note addressed to the partner, wife, or child of her correspondent on some matter of prior conversation or interest. Close friendships with Fritz Lang and Louise Brooks were initiated in the postwar period, producing hundreds of intimate letters that have been engaged in the secondary literature on Lang and Brooks themselves.[76] The subset of Eisner's letters with Louise Brooks that are held at the CF—which form part of an animated exchange between Brooks on one side and Meerson, Langlois, and Eisner on the other, sometimes addressed individually, more often in combination—abound with pet names, in-jokes, and, particularly on Brooks's part, humorous, sometimes outrageous disclosures about her health, sex life, and her most private insecurities, envies, and indulgences.[77] By and large, the tone of this correspondence—and Brooks's insistence on cheerleading Eisner's work and reputation in it in somewhat grandiose terms—seems unique among Eisner's friendships. Her correspondence with lifelong friends such as Edouard Roditi, while affectionate, seems less inclined toward the effusive display of the Brooks letters, yet no less moving a testament to genuine concern, regard, and love.[78]

In those cases of correspondence with strangers for acquisitions purposes, Eisner's decision to engage affectively and to disclose any shared personal history or experiences (often mentioning her time at the *Film-Kurier*, and, when in the company of a fellow exile, her departure from Germany before the war) seems to have elicited strong emotional responses. A poignant letter from Grace Metzner, the widow of art director Ernő Metzner, reads, in part:

> Thank you very much for your letter to my husband. I am sorry to have to tell you that he died in September 1953. I have a number of set-stills, sketches and other materials that may be of interest for the exhibition. . . . I am very glad to hand the material over to you, as I am sure they will be of much better use in your hands than if it stays locked away in my closets. . . . I would like to express my appreciation to you for showing this interest in my husbands [sic] work. Please let me know when the material arrives and wether [sic] it is what you expected.[79]

Similarly, in an early letter from Rochus Gliese—before Henri Langlois's supervision of acquisitions funds began to corrode the relationship between Gliese and the CF—he gushes: "I need not tell you how I look forward to fulfilling one of your heart's desires, and to no longer being the poorest-represented one in your worthy collection, for I consider your admirable establishment one of the real and rare cultural achievements of our wretched era."[80] Gliese's enthusiasm is comprised of equal measures, it seems, of pride in having been recognized by an esteemed organization and gratification in the knowledge that some small part of the antediluvian ecosystem in which he had thrived would, by virtue of Eisner's work, manage to weather the storm.

In light of Eisner's own experience of that "wretched era," it's possible to see these same conflicts with Langlois as characteristic of a third important affective quality permeating Eisner's archival praxis: that of her desire for belonging and community, which was different, and in some ways at odds with Langlois's own conception of his mission and principles as the social center of the CF. Eisner's efforts to reinforce social bonds with the people she brought into the CF's sphere is nowhere better exemplified than the case of the New German Cinema Group. Eisner's celebration of their work and her personal embrace of the filmmakers and their families has been understood to reflect on her generosity as much as it is supposed to have derived from an essentially nurturing, secondary status vis-à-vis the creative genius of Langlois. What this view fails to address is that the second half of Eisner's life revolved—by her own account, as a direct result of the trauma she experienced during the war—around the CF as a social node and safe harbor. Notwithstanding the propensity toward self-promotion shared by Herzog, Langlois, and others, Eisner's achievements at the CF consisted of much more than merely supplying encouragement and administrative support to famous men. That her affective investments in this work and these relationships have usually been construed in such blinkered, gendered terms suggests the degree to which the early histories of the CF were written by people whose social experience of the CF was shaped by the jostling, macho antics of Langlois and his partisans.

Belonging, for Eisner, seems to have been a question of affinity and shared experience, whereas for Langlois, the definition and enforcement of out-groups was central to any definition of his own in-group. Anecdotes illustrating the importance of demonstrating one's bona fides, of passing tests, and of affirming allegiance to Langlois or his proxies abound, particularly in connection with the crises of the late sixties and early seventies. These later instances have often been read as a result of Langlois's paranoid unraveling under toxic stress, but early peace-time examples provide insight into Langlois's baseline conception of how the CF as a community was defined. In his account of the history of the CF, Richard Roud describes the postwar Cercle du Cinéma's storied initiation ritual (which he, arriving in the early fifties, did not personally experience); in order to thin the ranks, Langlois instituted a policy, to be exercised at his sole discretion, of administering an entrance exam: "Typically, Langlois selected those who could become members by giving them a questionnaire to see how much they knew—and therefore presumably cared—about the cinema."[81] Part and parcel of Langlois's personal definition and practice of cinephilia was a conviction that competing models lacked real credibility, as François Truffaut's assessment, reported by Roud, indicates:

> Langlois and [André] Bazin were not great friends, you know. Langlois didn't have too much respect for critics. You can tell that when you read his own texts. They're very much like conversation . . . although often very apt. But Bazin's intelligence was more Sartrean, acutely reasoned. Sometimes his arguments had little to do with the actual film he was writing about. I think Langlois didn't like the professorial side of Bazin. Bazin was a professor, he was a proselytiser, and he was didactic. And Henri must have been against all that. He wanted to show films and let it go at that. He believed in education by osmosis, and I felt that way, too. But Bazin liked the Cinémathèque and he liked Langlois. And Bazin went to the Cinémathèque all the time.[82]

Certainly one could quibble with Truffaut's rigid binary differentiation, but his sense that the rivalry existed mostly on Langlois's side and that Langlois's cinephilia was strongly flavored by anti-intellectual notions of appreciation and taste has been echoed in many other accounts of the CF and of Langlois's biography.[83] The import of Langlois's fixation on defining out-groups for Eisner's own work is discernible primarily in the contrast between her move on the archival praxis side to build social networks and community

FIGURE 5. Eisner at the Cinémathèque française. Still from *Lotte Eisner in Germany* (S. M. Horowitz, 1980).

and her consistent efforts to push Langlois to be more attentive, more considerate, more empathetic to the filmmakers around whom Eisner hoped to cultivate CF collections. Writing almost seventy years after Eisner began the second phase of her career, Marika Cifor could have been describing Eisner's archival praxis when she argued that an appraisal process informed by affect theory creates "collections that are of deep value and significance to their communities. These collections are aimed at doing emotional justice to the experiences they reflect and memorialize."[84] Eisner, in forging an archival and scholarly methodology out of the trauma and loss she experienced during the first years of her exile, moved to bend the film archive toward emotional justice for the community of filmmakers who shared directly and indirectly in that pain.

Reframing this work with affect theory allows not only for a more robust understanding of how, where, and why Eisner did it, but also to what ends, and in what broader constellation of intellectual history. With Sara Ahmed's work on pain and witnessing, in which she argues that it is "the apparent loneliness of pain that requires it to be disclosed to a witness," we can recognize Eisner's self-description as a "witness of our cultural history," and her affinities with exile filmmakers, such as Sohrab Shahid Saless, as part of a concrete, positive definition of her archival praxis.[85] Eisner's work at the CF comes into focus in this context via the insights of archivists and scholars working to queer the archive, less by reading it, in the Benjaminian mode, "against the grain," but by conceiving of archives as potential nucleation sites for affective disruption within larger structures of power and influence.[86]

Moreover, it is in the context of queer historiography that we find precedent for the careful engagement with one of the most serious historiographical consequences of the intertwining of Eisner's life and her work. Up to this point, I have dealt only glancingly with the issue of Eisner's reliability as a witness, citing her autobiographical narratives somewhat gingerly, using the degree to which a given anecdote, fact, or account relates to her first-hand knowledge as a rule of thumb. My hesitation to deal more directly with the fact that in Eisner's memoirs, interviews, and, to an extent, in her scholarly work, she reported certain stories or assessments of character that strain credulity or rely on private (i.e., not reported in other sources or, for whatever reason, impossible to fact-check) information derives from a normative model of straight history. Under this rubric, Eisner's affective investment in her work is a liability, leaving her objectivity (thus credibility) vulnerable to a good story told by an old friend, or, more troublingly, to upcycling calumnies where personal resentments paved the way.[87] Yet strewn among those juicy morsels and snarky digs on the cutting room floor are vivid snatches of Eisner's experience that speak to the improvisations and contingencies of a life lived on margins, sometimes very thin ones, between norms and outside certain privileges.

Gossip has been theorized within queer theory and historiography as a signal mode of communication that is, in part by virtue of the status occupied by the parties to it, forced out of the mainstream and conducted between the lines, as Eve Kosofsky Sedgwick's touchstone definition puts it: "It is probably people with the experience of oppression or subordination who have the most *need* to know it; and I take the precious, devalued arts of gossip, immemorially associated in European thought with servants, with effeminate and gay men, with all women, to have to do not even so much with the transmission of necessary news as with the refinement of necessary skills for making, testing, and using unrationalized and provisional hypotheses about what *kinds* of people there are to be found in one's world."[88] In most instances, the most gossipy passages of Eisner's memoirs and scholarly publications are evocative of their specific moment, overlaid with the reflective retrospection of decades elapsed. In her memoirs, she describes specific emotions and thoughts she remembers having, but also comments on things she saw only in hindsight, moments at which she was crucially unaware of some larger context that would become clearer in time. It is in this uncanny register that she recalls snatches of ambient anti-Semitism in her childhood years as seeming both mundane and disturbing. From the other side of the war, the Chevalier's pin on her lapel, she is able to associate her early memories of racist nursery rhymes with the humiliation and affront she felt when her friend Anneliese von Rohrscheidt's father forbade their friendship, and to then connect these experiences not only to the ability she developed in exile, in hiding, to parse anti-Semitic remarks—determining which ones were lethal threats and which ones were intended to help their enunciator pass as a willing collaborator to the Occupation—but also to the persistent, oppressive reminders that such bigotry still flourished in postwar France.

So, too, Eisner's relationship to gender performance, feminism, and authority, in addition to being legible on the surface of her journalism, informed the ways she conceived of community and belonging in exile and at the CF, and the way she would describe her interwar social life from a postwar vantage point. Pamela VanHaitsma has argued that within feminist and queer historiography, "gossip may be reclaimed in positive terms, insofar as it serves as a productive form of imaginative and speculative work crucial to feminist historiography and consistent with traditional scholarly methodologies," suggesting further that by virtue of a frank and even enthusiastic address of "its associations with the illicit," gossip can work to "queer normative conceptions of historical materials and methods [making it] a particularly powerful resource for studying non-normative genders and sexualities."[89] Reading Eisner's memoirs with Sedgwick and VanHaitsma, we might linger on the following passage about her university days rooming with her cousin, Ina, with special interest:

> [Ina] was an odd duck, not exactly pretty, rather mannish. Paula once visited Freiburg and told me under her breath that I was much prettier than Ina. She still today recalls me in a white summer frock with red dots, and me looking very attractive and feminine. I'm not so sure about that; it was no triumph to be better-looking than my cousin, I only know that I was proud of my shapely, long legs, that I had bright eyes and long blonde hair. I never developed any great coquettishness, but I relished any opportunity to show off my legs. . . . People who saw me in the twenties in Berlin caused Marlene

Dietrich great consternation by spreading word that Lotte Eisner had much prettier legs than she did.[90]

This passage is illustrated with a photo of Eisner hamming it up as Struwwelpeter in a costume jumpsuit—featuring a wide lace collar and cuffs, an oversize satin bow tie, and amply puffed satiny shorts, cropped mid-thigh—with her short, dark hair on end, lips pursed, eyes bugged out: hardly the image conjured by her own description.[91] Eisner's uneasy sense of difference—between her gender identity and social expectations, between how she remembered herself and how her future sister-in-law described her, and the poignant, complicated distance she felt between herself and the cousin who shared her somewhat difficult lot as a young woman at university—is equally as striking in this passage as is her emphasis on the world in which she felt she did belong, one defined by the circulation of gossip about her legs and Dietrich's. Eisner's sense of pride in finding belonging, this passage makes clear, derived in part from feeling that while her gender and sexuality had not been accommodated within the world of her upbringing or education, at a critical moment she was finally able to shape her work around her chosen social world. Moreover, the network Eisner built around herself at the CF in the postwar period, if we read her memoirs alongside the administrative archive, was one in which intimacies and alliances crystallized around shared experiences of the interwar years in Berlin as much as those of trauma, loss, and exclusion in a variety of additional contexts. In view of the CF's famously poorly disciplined bureaucracy, these relationships, and their affective valences, shaped an archival logic that was idiosyncratic, even unaccountable to what Philippa Levine has called the "monochromatic" enforcement of power, instead offering "a creative means to see past a dominant creed, not to uncover an impossible truth but to identify the very operations of power, both when it succeeds and, as interestingly, when it fails."[92]

One of the more idiosyncratic aspects of Eisner's postwar publications and public remarks, across reviews, film histories, commentary, and interviews, is the frequency with which she asserts that sexuality is a rubric for stylistic, social, and aesthetic analysis. In the methodological remarks she makes about this belief, she describes it as a historicizing impulse. And, indeed, these references are typically dropped in the context of describing the social and cultural context of a filmmaker's work through the lens of their sexuality, as in the case of Murnau, to which we will shortly be returning.

However, in a few important cases, Eisner discloses information about a given subject's sexuality while describing a shared social milieu in the first person. Valeska Gert, Eisner claims, was a regular fixture of the sex parties that were frequently held in large private homes in Berlin during the twenties. Klaus Mann was terrified to recognize Eisner, she says, at a gay bar she frequented in the thirties, because he knew she was a journalist and he feared (rightly, it turns out, if posthumously) that she'd out him. And it was due to a deep, unusual affinity—one Eisner sidles up to the very edge of naming outright—that Greta Garbo kept Murnau's death mask because, euphemistically, "he had been as solitary as she."[93] As disturbing as it is that Eisner blithely outs all three of these people, without any indication of having asked or gotten consent on their part, it's clear that she thinks of these disclosures not just as tributes, but as ways of signaling her own positionality, in addition to her own status.[94] She casts herself, that is to say, as part of these worlds, privy to these relations.

The problems of reception Eisner's scholarly work has faced among the subsequent generations of Weimar cinema scholars—including claims that it was marred by her personal investments, too preoccupied with style, too focused on national identity, and, by implication, lacking intellectual heft and rigor—may derive from the fact that her writing and the archival praxis from which it arose were marked so strongly by qualities and methodologies that have only recently been taken up on their own terms by affect theory and queer historiography.[95] So too, Eisner's repudiations of feminism and consistent avowal of her own misogyny make her a somewhat troubling figure for feminist historiography and for feminists doing film historiography.[96] Finally, without the context of Eisner's interwar journalism, or her archival praxis, her postwar publications (of all her work, certainly this is the most readily and widely accessed) have often been read only selectively, in isolation from the experiences that shaped and informed her work.

Mannoni's description of Eisner in his history of the CF as "la seule historienne du cinéma" among the group of four can be read two ways; in the first, local sense, Mannoni's point is that Eisner was uniquely prepared to deal with the historiographical concerns of archival praxis.[97] However, "seule" can also be translated "lone," suggesting the solitary, forlorn, or unattached, and for Mannoni's effort to recuperate Eisner's reputation, these associations function as a kind of admonishment: Eisner is a film historian and an archivist who has been left out in the cold by subsequent generations of scholars and practitioners, he argues, at a cost to her reputation. I would add that to the extent that Eisner has been excluded from or marginalized within intellectual histories of the field of film studies, the potentialities of her work—and its apparent affinities with contemporary developments—have been occluded at a cost to the disciplinary imagination.

FOUR

"Lacunae Everywhere"

ITERATIVE HISTORIOGRAPHY AND
THE MIDCENTURY PALIMPSESTS

CONCURRENTLY WITH HER ARCHIVAL and administrative work at the Cinémathèque, Eisner researched, wrote, and published over seventy articles, three scholarly books, and one edited volume in the years between her return to Paris and her death in 1983. Although she is best known for her first postwar book—*L'écran démoniaque* (1952, 1965, first published as *The Haunted Screen* in 1969)—and most highly praised for her second—*F. W. Murnau* (first French edition in 1964, German in 1967, English in 1973)—the renown of these two publications may have contributed to the speed with which their fellows faded from regular citation and reference.[1] Many of the film historical articles Eisner published in high-profile French journals such as the *Cahiers du cinéma* and *Cinéma* treat the influence of German Expressionism and Max Reinhardt, as well as the effects of the unique German production culture of the interwar period on the stylistics of its cinema, all themes in common with Eisner's books. Yet in addition to these, she published consistently and prolifically on a range of topics, in a handful of different languages, and in a variety of formats, including film reviews, festival reports, survey articles, tributes and obituaries, and news and commentary.

Given the degree to which subsequent historians of Weimar cinema have tended to introduce their own interventions by way of a critique of *L'écran démoniaque* (*The Haunted Screen*), usually in combination with Kracauer's *From Caligari to Hitler*, it is remarkable that there has been so little attention paid to the question of when and how Eisner developed the ideas represented in this seminal volume. Indeed, each one of Eisner's books develops subjects on which she had previously published, and each in turn was revised extensively for every translation and republication. As a result, the arguments Eisner made on any one issue tended to vary over time, expanding with new evidence and reconfiguring in response to counterarguments and criticism.

Rather than observing the way a single iteration of any of these arguments in isolation behaves when pressure is focused on a certain point—for instance, the consistent reference to a singular German ethos in *The Haunted Screen*—I suggest that we understand Eisner's work and influence more fully by stepping back to watch the larger interconnected web of articles, books, interviews, methodological remarks, reviews, and commentary sway, stretch, or snag on any given question, German identity being just one example. From this vantage, it is possible to see where Eisner's personal sense of identity, exile, and trauma were in tension with contentious postwar French politics on the left and with auteur theory and contemporaneous film historical and theoretical writing more generally, and how her scholarly work was informed by her training and convictions as a film journalist, as well as her experience as an art historian and archivist.

Eisner's postwar publications are abundant; to annotate each and every member of the corpus in isolation risks a synchronic myopia. Instead, I treat the most important general characteristics of this body of work diachronically: the features on which I focus include the tone and context in which her work was articulated, as well as the methodological remarks Eisner offered over the course of these decades and the interlocutors and audiences she addressed. In addition to contextualizing her writing, I show how the contemporaneous reception of Eisner's publications shaped the ways they have been used and characterized since. Eisner found the way that younger French film theorists and critics engaged her work exasperating and reductive, and, I argue, she was right to be concerned about the association of her work with theirs; in hindsight, it is clear that she was not only marginalized and dismissed by these (mostly) younger men in the moment, but that subsequent assessments of the development of formalized film studies have tended to reinscribe this incomplete, deeply flawed narrative.

Foregrounding Eisner's own commentary about the importance of her work and its stakes, we see how vital and complex it actually was in its own time and, by the same token, what was forfeited in this particular case during the midcentury push to formalize scholarly film study. It is my contention that, in addition to the misfortune of having written some of the first widely read postwar works of film historiography and stylistic analysis—and as a consequence serving as one of the few benchmark thinkers who needed to

FIGURE 6. Eisner at her typewriter, in her Neuilly-sur-Seine home. Still from *Lotte Eisner in Germany* (S. M. Horowitz, 1980).

be debated or reckoned with in the burgeoning discipline's struggle to claim institutional space and legitimacy for itself—Eisner put herself in the singular, contrarian position of being a senior woman in the field who rejected feminism, a person interested in stylistic analysis, authorship, and genre, yet uninterested in participating in film theoretical discourse, and a scholar who insisted on referring to herself, not as one of this brave new breed called film historians, but instead in terms of her doctoral training in art history and archaeology. By rejecting all three of these labels and their respective alliances and intellectual genealogies—for each one, as we now know, would go on to become an important branch of institutional film study, within the academy and outside it—Eisner set her work on a narrow path as it passed from her hands into those of her disciplinary inheritors.

DISPUTATION AND ITS DISCONTENTS

One of the salient, symptomatic features of this period of Eisner's work is the extent to which she was actively participating in the debates and disputations of a discipline in the early stages of defining its methodologies, stakes, and purview across the pages of journals that, increasingly over the course of the following decades, defined themselves in opposition to each other. The majority of Eisner's postwar articles were published in the fifties in the pages of the *Cahiers du cinéma*, during what Daniel Fairfax has described as the journal's "'golden age' of French cinephilia."[2] In 1953 and 1954, however, Eisner also published in the *Cahiers* rival *Positif,* founded a year after *Cahiers*, and often described as having oriented itself as that journal's Left Bank, left flank antagonist. Throughout the postwar period, she also contributed regularly to Jonas Mekas's *Film Culture, Sight and Sound, CINÉMAtographe* (later stylized sans majuscule), *Cinéma, L'Âge du cinéma, L'Avant-scène. Cinéma,* and, early on, to *La Revue du cinéma*. Most of these were scholarly essays on film historical topics, but interspersed among them were festival reports from Venice, Cannes, and Berlin, contemporary film criticism, and commentary on a range of topics. In spite of such breadth and variety, Eisner is typically remembered for her books and not usually numbered among the key postwar participants in the highly contentious critical debates waged in the French- and English-language journals.

The auteur theory debates and their legacy in subsequent field discourse serve, together, as an acutely representative example of the dynamics of citation and engagement with Eisner's work at large. French, British, and US film studies discourse has long been preoccupied with the auteurist debates that raged during the first three decades of the postwar period. Despite having taken an early position on the question of locating and describing authorship in the cinema and having carefully articulated qualifications to that position over the course of the next thirty years, Eisner is rarely mentioned in connection with the French critics at *Cahiers* who advocated for auteur theory, and she is not typically identified as a contemporary party to that discourse. Nor was she later directly engaged by the Anglophone debates in the United Kingdom or United States, despite what some participants acknowledged was an established body of relevant work and incisive arguments on her part about the nature of film stylistics and the significance of collaborative or hierarchical production work flows for stylistic analysis.[3] In 1947, ten years before André Bazin's "De la politique des auteurs" ("On the *politique des auteurs*") appeared in *Cahiers,* Eisner laid out the key tenets of a model of stylistic analysis centering on authorship in the influential, short-lived *Cahiers* progenitor, *La Revue du cinéma*. Her opening salvo, before commencing the article's stylistic analysis of Fritz Lang's career to date, sets out the terms of the debate that would continue for decades: "From the first hundred meters, a film of quality reveals the style of its *metteur en scène*. The signature of a Stroheim, of a Griffith is detectable in a random sample from a reel."[4] She continues by arguing that although the German Fritz Lang films are differentiated from his French and American films, it's possible to discern in all of them his "complex mentality, his style of conceiving and realizing his vision of things, the traces of his origins, his education and his culture," asserting, as a principle, "one cannot deny that an artist is influenced by the atmosphere of a country."[5]

Eisner and Bazin were good friends and frequent interlocutors, and Bazin's idiosyncratic, sparing approach to citation is well established. Still, the reverberations of Eisner's 1947 argument are hard to miss a decade later, when Bazin clarifies the fundamental stakes of what he calls the *Cahiers* "family quarrel" about the *politique des auteurs*: "there can be no definitive criticism of genius or talent which does not first take into consideration the social determinism, the historical combination of circumstances and the technical background which to a large extent determine it." The echo of Eisner's earlier work is even more pronounced in Bazin's conclusion: "the *politique des auteurs* consists, in short, of choosing the persona factor in artistic creation as a standard of reference, and then assuming that it continues and even progresses from one film to the next.... Certain important films of quality [escape] this test, but these will systematically be considered inferior to those in which the personal stamp of the *auteur*, however run-of-the-mill the scenario, can be perceived even minutely."[6] Besides her article on Lang, Bazin also failed to reference a second article of Eisner's in *La Revue du cinéma* about the nature and origins of the vaunted Lubitsch touch in 1948, in which Eisner argues anew that any serious discussion of directorial style must historicize authorship. Whether as a result of Bazin's silence, or of their own incomplete review of the literature, the many auteur theorists who clustered around him and remained at *Cahiers* after his death in 1958 continued to neglect any explicit reference to either of Eisner's articles; indeed, as the so-called Young Turks at *Cahiers* ran with their own notion, the distance between their Hollywood-centric, deliberately provocative interpretation and Eisner's own model grew to be vast.[7] Even when Eisner has been credited as a participant in the early stages of the French auteur theory discourse, she is typically included only in oblique or passing reference. Thomas Elsaesser, for example, argued that Eisner's 1947 article on Lang helped to jumpstart postwar French interest in Lang's work, which became an important pillar of the discourse on auteur theory: "This revaluation was, of course, part of the more general revaluation of the American cinema, thanks to André Bazin and the *Cahiers du cinéma* critics, but perhaps none benefitted more from this change in attitude than Lang and Hitchcock.... Thanks in part to a seminal article on his style by Lotte Eisner that appeared in Paris in 1947, [Lang's] reputation began to undergo a sea-change, and he became for all intents and purposes a French director."[8] Elsaesser's list of Lang's influential admirers includes Éric Rohmer, Alexandre Astruc, Jacques Rivette, Jean-Luc Godard, and François Truffaut, as well as Jean Douchet, Philippe Demonsablon, Michel Mourlet, and Gérard Legrand, but not Eisner, in spite of her early and sustained interest in Lang.

Elsaesser may have reasoned that it would go without saying that Eisner had continued to publish on Lang and to establish a crucial archive of materials related to his work at the Cinémathèque française (CF), but it is a curious omission nevertheless, and one in keeping with the ways others have written retrospectively about the dynamics and membership of the *Cahiers* in-group. The first issues of *Cahiers* consistently trumpeted an upcoming contribution (one that wouldn't actually arrive until March 1952) by Lotte Eisner in their front matter. These teasers suggest that her association with *Cahiers* was thought to be one of the journal's selling points in its early days, but later accounts would gradually efface Eisner's name from the roster of its formative contributors. Daniel Fairfax has recently argued, misleadingly if not incorrectly, that the first woman to "penetrate" the "hitherto purely masculine grouping" of the *Cahiers* was Sylvie Pierre, with a review published in February 1967.[9] Fairfax, reporting Pierre's assessment of the situation, states that she was accepted into their ranks on the basis of her good looks and her marriage at the time to Jacques Aumont: "I was a very pretty girl, and since they were very macho, very seductive, very dandyish, seeing a smart, pretty girl write for them was amusing. They forgave me for being an intellectual because I was cute."[10] Although most accounts of the boys club atmosphere of the *Cahiers* focus on the late sixties—a period during which even contemporary groups that existed in a similar cultural and social frame of reference, such as rival *Positif*, decried the journal's "misogynist" culture—*Cahiers* indulged in frankly chauvinist commentary even during Bazin's tenure in the fifties, when Eisner published semi-regularly in its pages.[11] The winter 1953 issue of *Cahiers*, billed as a special issue celebrating the women of cinema, features one particularly pungent example: an omnibus piece titled, "F comme Femme," which presents an alphabetical list by name of female actors, each entry accompanied by a short statement gleefully objectifying the woman in question.[12] Quantifying the sex appeal of each actor by turn, these judgments illustrated with publicity and film stills cropped to isolate their breasts, legs, mouths, or naked bodies, the article at large is a parade of blithely misogynist bloviation, interrupted at its midpoint by an encomium to Asta Nielsen. This entry, one of the list's longest, historicizes Nielsen's acting style, recalling to readers the rapturous reception of Nielsen's work in the 1910s and 1920s, in particular her portrayal of Hamlet, and discussing the degree to which Pabst attributed the aesthetic triumph of *The Joyless Street* to Nielsen's contributions.[13] The juxtaposition of this entry with its fellows is jarring, and the credits list at the bottom of the piece takes care to separate out Eisner's byline on the Nielsen entry, attributing the rest of the article collectively to a list of young men: François Truffaut, Jacques Rivette, Philippe Demonsablon, Jean-José Richer, Michel Dorsday, and Frédéric Laclos.

Whether she was unaware of the context in which her contribution was going to be run or was simply mortified to see her name associated with the article in its final form, separate byline notwithstanding, Eisner appears to have suffered no little consternation. In the following issue, the first of the new year, a special note in bold type was included at the base of the table of contents: "Miss Lotte H. Eisner, fearing there remained some confusion, requested that we clarify that she wrote nothing in the article 'F comme Femme' in Issue 30 except the passage about Asta Nielsen."[14] Miss or not, Eisner liked the Nielsen piece well enough to rework it for publication in several other venues, and in spite of the evidence suggesting that its appearance in *Cahiers* embarrassed her, she doesn't seem to have considered withdrawing from future work with the journal; it was only her sixth article in *Cahiers*, but she would publish twenty more reviews, festival reports, film historical articles, and short sketches before 1958.[15] *Cahiers* chronicler James Hillier has described the winter of 1953 as the period in which the editorial shift became clearer, congealing with the January 1954 publication of Truffaut's polemical "A Certain Tendency of the French Cinema." Indeed, the tone of the final 1953 issue of *Cahiers* at large, and "F comme Femme" in particular, as a snapshot of this moment in the journal's history, suggests that by that pivotal winter, the cohort of young men under Bazin's tutelage felt at some liberty to steer the journal toward their most fervent interests, with or without the participation and approval of their elders.

Not unlike her recollections of beginning work at the *Film-Kurier*, Eisner framed her most important postwar associations with film publications as relationships emerging naturally from her social network. In a 1981 interview, Eisner recalls that it was her friendship with Jean George Auriol that had led her to publish after the war in *La Revue du cinéma* and her friendship with Bazin that led to her association with *Cahiers*.[16] And, despite the distance of nearly a thousand kilometers and a quarter century, the parallels between Eisner's status as the odd woman out at the *Film-Kurier* and at *Cahiers* are hard to miss; only this time in addition to her doctorate, gender, and privileged upbringing, she was also different in that she was between twenty and forty years older than most of her fellow film reviewers and had been living in France just about as long as some of them had.[17] While Laurent Mannoni has argued that Langlois's esteem for Eisner dramatically shifted after the publication of *L'écran démoniaque*, it seems clear that some of his younger acolytes continued to perceive Eisner primarily as an adjunct to Langlois.[18]

Reading Eisner's postwar scholarship and correspondence together with her remarks on methodology, it's possible to see the flashes of testiness in her public writing in light of a cranky undertone in some of her private correspondence, and to wonder whether these outbursts were in part a result of frustration with the behavior of the young Frenchmen—including the "Cahiers snobs"—she worked alongside, in combination with the resentment she felt about the incomplete and occasionally incorrect reception of her work.[19] In the latter category Eisner placed the persistence of a blatant misunderstanding of her thesis that German Expressionism and Max Reinhardt constituted two different influences on the stylistics of interwar German cinema; in spite of the clarity with which she distinguishes the two in *L'écran démoniaque*, Eisner took every opportunity to emphasize that she had never equated them. Over time these admonishments became progressively more strident; in a 1973 iteration of the same basic argument she has made since the mid-fifties, Eisner begins with an aggrieved, weary tone:

> Even at the risk of being considered a rigorous purist, I would like to offer, at long last, my own definition of the Expressionist film, for in most countries, especially in France, there seems to be an increasing tendency toward regarding all the "classic" German films of the twenties as Expressionistic. I suspect that, in spite of all my attempts at explanation in the book *L'écran démoniaque* . . . the latter's subtitle "The influence of Max Reinhardt and of Expressionism" has caused this misunderstanding because one sought to substitute *or* for *and*. In the first issue of *Cinéma 55* I published an article entitled "Mise en garde et mise au point" (Warning and Redefinition) which deals with the Expressionist school, or rather movement, and in which I tried to clarify my position, apparently without success. For in the 69th

and 70th issues of *Cinéma 62* (i.e., quite a few years later) a certain gentleman declared, in an article called "Actualité de l'expressionnisme," that Max Reinhardt was an undaunted Expressionist. (The gentleman in question, by the way, plagiarized my book rather unscrupulously by borrowing entire phrases and whole passages, from which he drew the wrong conclusions.)[20]

The fact that Eisner takes her first full page of this invited contribution to gripe about the mistakes others have made in their reception of *L'écran démoniaque* is striking. Moreover, given that the "certain gentleman" to whom she refers—one Paul Leutrat, whom she calls out by name in the *Édition définitive*—made a less lasting impression than she on the way interwar German cinema has been understood, her repeated detour for the sake of derogation suggests a resentment out of proportion to the situation at hand.[21] So, too, the letter to the editors of *Cinéma* following their 1964 publication of a promotional extract of her forthcoming *F. W. Murnau*.[22] Eisner's book has maintained its regard as a formidable contribution since it first appeared, garnering positive reviews upon release and withstanding the usual jostling of a crowded field, yet she accused *Cinéma* of "more than an indiscretion, an abuse of confidence" in running alongside the excerpt a filmography she had compiled and provided to them, she says, only for reference. They never asked her or her publisher's permission, Eisner writes, and they might instead have used Theodore Huff's already-published filmography.[23] Eisner protests that the effect of running her filmography alongside the excerpt was to have caused "grave harm to the publication of my work"; in their reply printed underneath, the editors apologize and affirm that they hope the success of the book proves such fear unwarranted. While in neither of these cases is Eisner in the wrong—failing to ask permission to publish her work and plagiarizing it are each serious trespasses—nor does she sit entirely in the right; senior scholars can usually refrain from such exaggerated public shaming of their juniors, precisely because of their disparity in status. The fact that Eisner didn't—in light of what we know about the precarity of Eisner's existence in France from 1933 on, as well as the aftershocks of wartime trauma, the nature of the CF's dynamics during this period, and her position there—suggests that she may not have been able to see any such disparity. A few remarks from Eisner's correspondence may offer some context as to why such territorial posturing might have seemed necessary to her at the time.

In 1946, Eisner initiated an exchange with Siegfried Kracauer in which she offered to submit to *La Revue du cinéma* a version of his recent article "Hollywood's Terror Film," and broached the possible translation of *From*

Caligari to Hitler for publication in France by the CF. Less than a month later, Kracauer replied from MoMA with enthusiasm, adding that he and Lili were delighted to hear that Eisner had "managed to survive the war and [continued] to work as before, and, we hope, with more resonance than ever" at the CF. He confirms his interest in publishing the article and can't seem to resist preening a bit: "I will add that this article created a little sensation here. Editorials in *PM*, *New York Post*, and other newspapers commented upon my article—not to mention two radio talks about it." He continues, "I will ask Princeton to send me the proofs of my chapter on Caligari and the introduction to my book, which is of general interest."[24] The next letter in the exchange held in the CF's administrative archives marks an abrupt about-face; read next to Kracauer's follow-up, one wonders whether in the intervening period, a holiday letter inquiring about the status of these projects, perhaps in impatient tones, might have been received. If so, it was not retained in the file, for dated over three months later, and unsigned, the next letter in the series begins with a curious disclaimer:

Dear Mr. Kracauer,

Browsing the Cinémathèque's mail, I came across your letter to Mademoiselle Escoffier. So, you've come to France and want to see us goose-stepping? Here, the whole world is late, nobody responds to letters, we forget our appointments, we wake up when we feel like it, and we nap when we feel like it. It's nothing to get upset about, and it would be better for you not to think of or write to people, to help them when they need it, and not send them your best wishes for Christmas. I'm surprised that you've so soon forgotten the pleasant disorder of Paris. I know that at the Museum of Modern Art, you're perfectly respected by everyone and very famous, meanwhile I'm happy here and hard-pressed.[25]

Two months later, Kracauer ventured the following reply:

Dear Mademoiselle Eisner:

I'm very upset at the false impression my letter produced. Alas, it's partly my fault. In my impatience—which was down to my own difficult situation—I didn't realize that which I know now, of that you can be certain: that your situation in France is still much more difficult. And I feel horrible about it, and *I am terribly sorry* [in English]. Being, myself, a little to blame for your violent reaction, I don't protest. I am convinced that you well know, in the depths of your heart, how unjust your reproaches are: how could I, *I*, misunderstand the France I love forever, or mistake it for Germany, etc.? I, who hated the German mentality even in my youth? Really, it's ridiculous, but again, I know you know it. As for my articles: forget it! I already feel guilty enough to have, in a moment of forgetfulness, aggravated your difficulties. Regards from my wife, and our best wishes. *And let us forget about it* [in English].[26]

Henri Langlois made no effort to conceal his dislike for Kracauer, and he is sometimes credited with the often-repeated crack about *From Caligari to Hitler* suffering from too little actual knowledge of the films, because during the writing its author couldn't be bothered to look up at the screen from behind his midden of books. While Kracauer addressed himself to Eisner alone in his reply, the unkind letter of February 1947 is written in a different style than most of Eisner's correspondence at the CF, very much in the vein of Langlois's own.[27] Whether Eisner had indeed written the letter, or merely neglected to correct Kracauer's assumption that she had, in her regular correspondence with friend and fellow *Film Culture* contributor Herman G. Weinberg in the fifties, Eisner makes it clear that she resents what she sees as Kracauer's better-supported, more highly respected, and stable situation in the United States, remarking in one 1958 letter, referring to *Theory of Film*, "I hope to finish my book by [the] end of this year, if everything is okay with my work. It is so much easier in the States where you get a fellowship like Kracauer does. When is his book coming out?" and, a month later, "It is difficult with books. The Kracauer book [*From Caligari to Hitler*] is in my way in the States, as my book for him in France for translation. I am little interested in that book now, as I am writing my Murnau book."[28] Later, Eisner would make even less effort to conceal her resentment; in a 1981 interview with *Cinématographe* on her career at large, Eisner claims that it was Kracauer who was annoyed by the publication of her own work. At the prompting of her interviewers, who invited Eisner to share her opinion of Kracauer's book no doubt aware of the tenor of her remarks on it over the years, she asserts, "He believed the German cinema was his turf. I find that he is completely wrong about some things."[29] The difficulties Kracauer faced in the United States and the precarity of his situation have been discussed in the secondary literature at some length, but it is important to point out that during the war and into the postwar period, unlike Eisner, he was able to make his living by working as a researcher, writer, and public intellectual.[30] Even in those quarters where he was disparaged as insufficiently sophisticated, he was not begrudged the dignity of consideration by his peers as a substantial intellect.[31] Whether her colleagues perceived and treated Eisner as Langlois's secretary or as one of the day's preeminent historians, she behaved, to a certain extent, as though it needed to be constantly reasserted that she was to be taken seriously.

In published remarks she made referring to Kracauer's *From Caligari to Hitler*, Eisner often introduced the book's thesis—that the rise of Hitler and Nazism was prefigured in the films of the interwar period—as a straw man. In a 1953 article published in *Positif*, following the first edition of *L'écran démoniaque*, Eisner describes her working methods, the stakes of film historiography, and the craft of writing. In this piece, we see the rhetoric she adopts in the introductory remarks to *L'écran démoniaque*, *The Haunted Screen*, and *F. W. Murnau*, as well as a few pointed remarks about the flaws in what she identified as competing methodologies: remarks that she would go on to reiterate in many interviews and several publications to follow, as time went on, with greater candor and less charity. She begins by describing the state of historical understanding and scholarship on film as underdeveloped: "This is a curious fact: today we know the prehistory of humanity better than we know the first quarter century, or even the first thirty to thirty-five years, of the period that has elapsed since the invention of the cinematograph. There are lacunae everywhere to fill, errors to rectify, doubts, disputes that should be cleared up, new discoveries of facts or people that have been neglected, previously forgotten, [that have] yet to be intercalated."[32] For the "true historiographer of cinema," she writes, "the first task is to do deep excavation worthy of an archaeologist . . . which is to say, to read and re-read meticulously the cinema catalogues, old reviews and journals, to examine them page by page." Once steeped in the materials of the period, one must work to establish the facts by rigorous cross-reference: "This means tracking down the exact dates of production, the dates of release, the names of the filmmakers, technicians, actors, knowing how to read between the lines sometimes, how to weigh and evaluate old studio gossip for what it might signify or reveal." Beyond culling the facts from period accounts and records, she considers talking to people who lived through it an essential component of any solid historiographical method: "And above all, one must refer to the testimony of those still living, seeming to emerge from the mists of a bygone era; one must question the old actors, the old art directors, screenwriters, cameramen and set designers of yesteryear. They are always happy to enlighten us, to correct our errors, to give us confirmation or denials; for them it is an occasion to recall the 'good old days,' to draw on their often-unerring memory." Clearly, this describes Eisner's own methodology, particularly the approach she would go on to employ in *F. W. Murnau* when she began writing the monograph four years later. Yet she differentiates it carefully from that taken in the previous year's *L'écran démoniaque*: "There is another path, open to those who would write a history of a single national cinema (my *L'écran démoniaque* is a first attempt at this). Here, one must use the methods of art history, thereby endeavoring to write a history of tendencies and artistic evolutions, which is to say a history of different styles, schools, or technical developments—inasmuch as they explain style. It's important to try to analyze the key films," she argues, by actually watching them and seeking out any opportunity to see them again. Only then, Eisner says, in a Riegelian inflection reminiscent of her doctoral work, can the historian draw out the elements that allow one to "crystallize the style, the technique of this or that specific *metteur en scène*, and then to outline the different cinematic traditions" of the nation in question, with rigorous thoroughness and a certain critical distance serving as the primary protections against bias.

Turning, next, to this very question of bias, Eisner begins by tracing a boundary between interested narration and skewed:

> And here is the thorniest point: to each author his own political opinion. Can one remain impartial, or, better yet, should one? I think that there is a way of thinking, an independence to preserve; a clarity of judgment to safeguard. But a history of cinema written from a sectarian point of view, that of a zealot—the extrapolation from a set of facts narrowly conforming to a party line—can never detach itself from unproductive prejudices, arbitrary judgments and preconceptions.... A fanatical blindness can be just as dangerous as total indifference, or facile indulgence, a kind of weakness that doesn't dare defend its judgments. Retrospection always encourages, to some extent, taking on the seductive role of the prophet, and, too often, the attribution to events a greater significance than they really had in their time. On the other hand, certain conclusions are not inconsequential, they become the necessary explanation of myriad facts. One cannot, as it were, write the history of German cinema before 1933 without thinking that it preceded, at least in a certain regard, the advent of Hitler.[33]

Moving from a more direct register into an elevated, supercilious passive voice riddled with double negatives as she circles closer to her intended target, Eisner concludes her musings on good and bad historiographical praxis with a thinly veiled reference to Kracauer's book, allowing that there is at least a temporal similarity between anticipation and simple antecedence: the films did indeed come first. Concluding the article, Eisner observes that the task—"attempting to retrace an artistic evolution *sine ira et studio*"—is by no means an easy one, yet the degree of difficulty should not be taken as an excuse for the kind of dry, colorless writing that can result from uninspired historical research. And then, in a move familiar to readers of her *Film-Kurier* coverage, as well as her postwar interviews, Eisner compares the historiographer to the critic: They "must know how to nurse a sacred wrath against the mediocrity of a purely commercial production," eschewing both credulous acceptance of "the substitutes for art, bad films" made by producers who have no respect for their audiences, and snobbishness, or what she dismissively refers to as "l'art pour l'art." "In addition," Eisner declares, "there will always be a vital touchstone: the question of discerning the quality of a film, of probing the sincerity with which it has been realized. Moreover, we can classify readers, just as we can spectators, into two distinct groups: those who are moved by the uncompromising and desperate humanity of a *Monsieur Verdoux*, and those who prefer the so-called problems of the type encountered in young adult or Vicky [*sic*] Baum novels, of a *Mrs. Minniver* [*sic*]. Ultimately, one must know how to choose for whom one wants to write." This ideal critic-historian is immediately recognizable in the reader-conscious diction and analytical approach of Eisner's dissertation, as much as in her *Film-Kurier* coverage of the *Kulturfilm* and the avant-garde.[34]

If there are hallmarks of Eisner's thinking and writing throughout her career, constitutive principles from which the work she did across multiple disciplines and idioms radiates, certainly foremost among them would be this notion of respect for one's audience. Framed in the negative, it is perhaps the single constant across her criticism of literature, theater, film, art, music, and scholarship; in its paradigmatic formulation, her complaint is that through a bad work, its producer talks down to the audience, betraying in that underestimation nothing so much as their own inadequacy and smallness of spirit. As praise, it unifies her appreciation for minor works of favorite artists, for experimental and conventional aesthetic approaches alike, and, perhaps most importantly, the unabashed appreciation for expression across the high/low culture divide that bedeviled many of her fellow cinephiles, especially those eager to legitimize the medium as an object of serious contemplation.[35]

Tellingly, a comprehensive summary of Eisner's critical stance is presented in a 1969 piece called "Kitsch in the Cinema."[36] As we've seen, Eisner believed that her own discernment—"[my] nose for originality and the gift for putting my discoveries into words"—was her greatest strength; she believed that her life's work had been, in essence, exercising that discernment in various domains, and communicating it clearly and persuasively.[37] Thus, the inherent subjectivity of identifying and defining kitsch makes it an ideal object of contemplation, the candid mirror reflecting back the attitudes and assumptions of the critic, along with their shortcomings.

Stipulating at the outset—with the support of a quote from fellow interwar Berlin critic Herbert Ihering—that kitsch in the cinema is more difficult to define than in any other figurative art, and that in any medium it will be both a subjective and historically contingent judgment, Eisner centers her discussion around her personal experience as an archivist, critic, and art historian. After giving a handful of examples of shifts in her own personal opinion of certain films with the passing of time and the dawning recognition of an alternative context—rendering what was once understood as affectation, in this new light, as "a remarkable expression of the sentiments of the age"—Eisner defines kitsch as the quality of having an artificial *Stimmung*, connoted with falseness and "a reactionary attitude." Cycling through examples, many of them big budget and prestige pictures, each exemplifying a variety of more general shortcomings and missteps, Eisner arrives at the heart of her argument: "In what are known as anticipation films, horror films or erotic films, it is far easier to define the tendency toward kitsch. . . . When a director does not have the power of persuasion and the genius to impose the absurdity of another world on us as if it were real, kitsch is inevitable." She continues,

> What leads to deviations of taste, in both horror films and pseudo-erotic films, is the exploitation of the voyeurism and base instincts of the general public. When Erich von Stroheim shows us a repellent cripple avidly gazing at the beautiful Mae Murray in *Merry Widow* (1925) or a similar scene in the rediscovered sequences of *Queen Kelly* (1928) with another cripple and the beautiful Gloria Swanson, what translates such scenes into great art is the corrosive shock effect of genius. . . . In Stroheim's films, in which perversions are often raised to grandiose dimensions, disgust can become the measure of eroticism.[38]

Fundamentally, she argues, the difference between art and kitsch can be summed up by the difference between Stroheim's treatment of the bathing scene in *Queen Kelly*, which Eisner describes as "highly erotic," and cheesecake publicity stills that "have the same vulgar attraction as certain visiting cards handed out by expensive brothels. Eroticism is as far removed from kitsch as the genuine terror one feels at the great (and very rare) horror films," such as *Nosferatu*. She concludes, "One can say, quite definitely, that kitsch in the cinema, as in all other forms, is unpardonable mediocrity." While she sometimes argues that such mediocrity results from a mistaken notion of what will give the film commercial appeal, Eisner more often faults either the producer's failures of imagination and intelligence, or their underestimation of their audience. In her criticism of documentary and avant-garde film, she places greater emphasis on this final failing—that of respect for audiences—given the nature of distribution and exhibition channels for such films.

Along these same lines, and in a striking counterpoint to Rudolf Arnheim's contemporaneous assessments, Eisner consistently registered her impatience with Maya Deren, arguing in a 1954 review of *Meshes of the Afternoon* that Deren's references both to psychoanalytic theory and to European painting exemplify a larger trend resulting from the diversion of young filmmakers from wartime documentary to the postwar avant-garde and art film. In general, Eisner argues, this group had descended into an aestheticized haze, asking whether "the hasty return to the oneiric and to psychoanalysis is really a safety valve, the only possible escape for young beings who suffer from narcissistic or homosexual erotic complexes and repression, for these rootless [people] attempting ineptly to adapt themselves to old European cultures."[39] A harsh, dubious critique, no doubt, but one informed by Eisner's suspicion that the economic boom and repressive social norms in the postwar period might have the same corrosive effect on US filmmakers that similar conditions post–Dawes Plan had on German filmmakers and artists.[40] Indeed, in the same article, Eisner celebrates what she sees as the "very pure, affirmed homosexual character" of *Fireworks* (Kenneth Anger, 1949), likening it to *Un chant d'amour* (Jean Genet, 1950). Eisner reiterates the theme of much of her *Film-Kurier* work on the cross-pollination between avant-garde and commercial cinema stylistics, quoting Henry Miller in support of her long-held view on the topic, moving from a discussion of the US avant-garde's stylistic borrowing from Méliès, Richter, Ruttmann, and Fischinger into a merciless panning of Deren's *Meshes of the Afternoon*. Invoking Lewis Jacobs's 1949 assessment of the influences of interwar German stylistics—particularly the traces of *Caligari*, *The Golem* (*Der Golem, wie er in die Welt kam*, Boese and Wegener, 1920), *Der letzte Mann*, and *Variété* in the work of Sybil Watson and Melville Weber, and the "first wave of the American avant-garde" more generally—Eisner argues that Maya Deren has merely pilfered elements of Dadaism and French surrealism, "mixing [them] rather peculiarly with her recollections of German chiaroscuro."[41] Eisner states that the film owes its "obvious visual beauty" to Alexander Hammid's photography: "But Maya Deren, ever so 'high-brow,' has the ambition to create what she calls an 'especially filmic time and space' by rather puerile means. . . . The heroines, portrayed by Maya Deren herself, [are] beautiful, mysterious creatures who look like committed vegetarians and recall the anemic virgins of Rosetti, [sic] sleepwalking through this so-called 'twentieth-century mythological journey,'" amid allusions to the films of Luis Buñuel, Germain Dulac, and Murnau. Eisner claims Deren stole the second sequence of the film—in which the shadow of the young woman is cast over a cut flower on the pavement, and an extended hand, disembodied from the figure, picks it up—from what she judges to be one of the most beautiful passages of Murnau's *Tabu*, and she charges that the film at large is dusted with what she derides as facile "flirtation" with the ideas of Einstein, Freud, and André Breton. In 1967, Guido Aristarco would lodge a strikingly similar critique of the New American Cinema group's work and their claims to novelty—in which he, too, traces precedent to the work of Méliès, Dulac, and Richter in the twenties—arguing, further, that the avant-garde of the twenties, "at least the most committed among them intended to contribute to changing the world; their 'search for new languages' went beyond the 'stylistic surface.' The New American Cinema, on the contrary, affirms that the world is what it is, and cannot, must not be changed." Like Eisner, Aristarco describes the self-fashioning and aesthetics of the postwar US avant-garde, and particularly the New American Cinema group, as troublingly uninterested in a self-reflexive historical-stylistic consciousness, instead preferring to don the mantle of novelty despite its poor fit, an impulse Aristarco denounces as "anarcho-nihilistic in essence." The filmmakers, Aristarco charges, are fundamentally unconcerned with revolutionary change, leading, he claims, to a situation in which "a film like *Chelsea Girls* [dir. Morrissey and Warhol, 1966] proceeds directly from the underground, with perhaps some Dostoyevskian pretension, to the red carpets of a Central Park cinema."[42] Aristarco's stance, as Irene Rozsa and Masha Salazkina have argued, drew from "the old humanist tradition of Marxist critique," on the one hand, and what they call "the more generally textual orientation of European film theory of the 1960s and 1970s," on the other, describing the latter as "particularly powerful in the French film critical tradition, best known through its elaboration in the works of André Bazin, but widely shared by the widest range of critics and filmmakers associated with New Cinemas around the world, particularly in

Europe." Rozsa and Salazkina find, more generally, that "Aristarco's ... vocal rejection of what [he] saw as incipient signs of [a] reactionary aesthetics ... is hardly surprising, and can be seen as symptomatic of the European critical reaction at large."[43]

Yet the hostility of such critiques on Eisner's part is best understood in the context of her remarks on methodology and what she identified as the key differences between her own modes of film analysis and those of other contemporary critics and scholars. Apart from the *Positif* article discussed above, most of Eisner's comments on methodology were articulated in the context of interviews, often with more junior film critics or historians, or reviews of their work. A dismissive 1961 review of Bob Bergut's *Erich von Stroheim*, manages to include a swipe at *Cahiers* by way of faint praise; she finds the book lacking in many regards, suggests that it would have been done better by a different group of authors and that its author "allowed Stroheim to bamboozle him," but grants that at least "Bergut does not go in much for the brand of philosophical or sophistical theorising which a certain ultra-highbrow clan of critics has applied to Hitchcock, nor for film jargon only comprehensible to the initiated. (This kind of writing, incidentally, has recently infuriated Fritz Lang, who is shocked by their claims that his work reaches its height in *Le Tigre d'Echnapour* [sic] and that, by comparison, a film like *M* is of negligible importance.)"[44] Leaving aside, for the moment, the posture of alliance and privileged communication with Lang that Eisner adopts here, the key point is her identification contra such "ultra-highbrow" theory and criticism. In the 1981 *Cinématographe* interview, Eisner also identifies her work by way of a series of contrasts: "I was neither a semiologist, nor a structuralist. I watched films from a visual point of view, that is to say, as an art historian. That's why, I believe, my books are a little different from others, from those that are much more theoretical."[45] Remaining aloof from these currents, Eisner also expressed reservations about the variety of auteur theory some at *Cahiers* advocated, arguing in a 1974 interview with Edmund Luft, "I believe it is very important to not, as is so often done today, take a given director and say that he is a genius, without ever explaining why." Instead, she argues, one has to show the internal logic of the work, to elucidate the characterization from within.[46] Turning, for a vocabulary and intellectual framework, to her academic training, Eisner would describe *L'écran démoniaque* as an "art historical" work, *F. W. Murnau* as an "archaeological" or "philological" effort, and *Fritz Lang* as a quasi-biographical study, deeply influenced by her conversations and friendship with her subject. Yet for all this apparent variation, there are important continuities among these three projects. Eisner took each new edition or translation as an opportunity to update and refine her arguments and evidence, and it's possible, reading the books in their multiple editions alongside the articles she was publishing in conversation with the books, to see the development of several important lines of inquiry and argument.

THROUGHLINES

In broad strokes, Eisner's postwar work goes in three directions, each corresponding to—if not entirely contained by—one of her books. With *L'écran démoniaque*, she refined a model of stylistic analysis that borrowed from art historical vocabulary and methods yet was centered about the moving image and had been adapted to its medium-specific properties. This model invokes terminology proper to the analysis and description of painting and graphic arts, and, not unlike the comparative stylistic analysis of her dissertation, it trades in attribution (i.e., authorship) as a fundamental stylistic property, albeit by nuancing the basic premise of auteur theory by way of a decisive turn toward historicization.

As she explains in the foreword to the 1969 English-language edition, she has confined her analysis to "some of the intellectual, artistic, and technical developments which the German cinema underwent [during] the last decade of the silent period," which she says she will describe with reference to some specialized terminology, including "demoniac," *Weltanschauung, Kammerspielfilm, Stimmung, Umwelt,* and, "As an historian of art I have also allowed myself the licence [*sic*] of a few technical terms": *chiaroscuro, grisaille,* and *sfumato*.[47] An important frame of reference Eisner doesn't mention, although it has remained one of the book's most distinctive features for her readers, increasingly so over time, is Germany and the Germans. Whether put off by the book's opening assertion that "the German mind had difficulty in adjusting itself to the collapse of the imperial dream," and that as a result of the interwar social, economic, and political upheaval, the "inner disquiet of the nation took on truly gigantic proportions," or by later claims—including that the tragedy of *The Last Laugh* "can only be understood in a country where uniform is King, not to say God [, and that a] non-German mind will have difficulty in comprehending all its tragic implications"—some readers have argued that Eisner, like Kracauer, assumes the validity of a unitary, reified national character.[48] However, as I've argued, apart from these references, the 1952, 1965, and 1969 editions of the book all confine discussion of Germany and the Germans almost entirely to these two passages. The bulk of her references to national character or identity are best understood in the context of a slightly different argument, one she made more or less continuously throughout her postwar scholarship, most pointedly in opposition to Nazi film historian Oskar Kalbus, about the need to historicize authorship.

In the first two major articles Eisner published after returning to Paris, she began to develop arguments about the nature of authorship under a film industrial, collaborative creative system that would form the bedrock of *L'écran démoniaque*, and to structure her approaches to both *F. W. Murnau* and her monograph on Lang. The first article, on Fritz Lang, is a twenty-three-page case for comparative stylistic analysis centered on the film director, taking the diversity of production contexts for his German, French, and American films as an opportunity to test the notion that from their commonalities it could be possible to derive the picture of the director's influence, his "complex mentality, his style of conceiving and realizing his vision of things, the traces of his origins, his education and his culture."[49] Eisner devotes most of the article to tracing the visual tropes repeated and reiterated across Lang's films—candles (*Der müde Tod*, *Metropolis*), wet foliage, and portentous reflections in a store window (*M*, *Woman in the Window*)—alongside the ways his films departed from stylistic antecedents. In the latter category, Eisner places figures that she argues can be seen to have changed in his hands: Röhrig and Warm made the staircases in *Caligari* and *Der müde Tod*, but "in the differences of conception between the two realizations, one can divine that [Röhrig and Warm] imposed their ideas on Wiene, and that they were submitted to the will of Lang."[50] Crucially, however, Eisner does not stop here, with Lang as sole originator; although it isn't often isolated as a significant thread of her argument, the more important point she works to make, amid the highly subjective assertions of Lang's genius, is that comprehensive stylistic analysis requires historicizing the author and production context. In spite of any assertions to the contrary on the part of authors, she says, their work is fundamentally imbricated in the material circumstances of its production: "German intellectuals, determined to break with the customs and conventions of the old regime, saw the path of salvation in [the contemporary Russian theater of Stanislavski and Meyerhold], which itself had made a tabula rasa of all the preceding artistic principles. But they could not liberate themselves entirely from their ideology, nor from [their] *Weltanschauung*."[51] Reading this early article alongside her monograph, it's clear that certain interpretations were not to change in conversation or dispute with Lang over the long years of writing and revision, and that, contrary to what Lang biographer Patrick McGilligan has argued, Eisner's impressions or arguments about Lang's work seem to have shifted the ways Lang talked and thought about his own work, particularly in terms of the stylistic influence of Constructivism, elements of Expressionism, and futurist theater on Lang's *Nibelungen*.[52]

Yet this argument for historicizing style would not reach its fullest expression until 1948, with Eisner's next article on "The origins of the Lubitsch style," in which, without disclosing her own positionality, Eisner offers a vivid description of a world on the edge of her upbringing. Invoking attempts by Gilbert Seldes, Herman Weinberg, and Oskar Kalbus to describe the nature of and differences between Lubitsch's German and American films, she defines her research inquiry thusly: "Is it possible to recognize the continuity of personal style in Lubitsch, who was shaped by so many influences? Is there really a difference between the German Lubitsch and the American Lubitsch, who has proven so refined and *sophisticated*? [English] What, in short, are the origins of the 'Lubitsch touch'?" In answer, Eisner declares, "To understand the character of an artistic style, one must return to the source: the birth, the upbringing have an indelible influence."[53] She then relates a page-long description of the precise standing of Lubitsch's family within class and cultural hierarchies of early twentieth-century Berlin, a description she would condense and modify slightly in *L'écran démoniaque* and *The Haunted Screen* and would reference indirectly in the opening pages of her memoirs.[54] The "Konfektionaire," purveyor of ready-to-wear, was regarded by "the major fabric manufacturers and traders" such as Eisner's father "with a contemptuous indulgence," denoted by the name *Mantelmen*: a condescending rhyme with the word "gentlemen" (*Mantel* meaning "coat"), emphasizing their status as tradespeople, not properly peers to the upper middle class. She continues:

> It should, moreover, be emphasized that the flavor of this milieu, mostly Jews and many of them later cineastes, was not typically Jewish, but essentially of Berlin. . . . Before the Hitler-hypnosis provoked a collective madness and flattened all regional differences among Germans, Berliners had a reputation for being spirited, bullish, and alive to the ridiculous. In two centuries, this spirit became known as Berliner *Schusterjungenwitz* [roughly, urchin's wit],

associated with the apprentice cobblers, celebrated for their trenchant repartee.... In this spirit, the weaknesses and tribulations of others furnished a mean-spirited amusement, tempered with the fatalism of Jews who carried the recent memory of persecution, soon to be refreshed; a fatalism colored by nonchalant humor, and the somewhat cynical attitude of a people habituated to accepting the inevitable.[55]

In tracing this lineage back several hundred years and placing it firmly within a deep local history—contrasted emphatically to the ahistorical "flattening" of difference under Nazi historiography—Eisner repudiates Oskar Kalbus's assertion that the "effrontery" of Lubitsch's comedies was "foreign to the German race."[56]

Indeed, if we reorient the way Eisner tropes German identity around the axis of Kalbus, whom Eisner explicitly identifies as a target of her own critique here, the argument made in this article, in *L'écran démoniaque*, and elsewhere looks less like a regressive reification of the nation and national identity than a response in kind to what she saw as the co-optation of interwar history by a morally bankrupt historian. Eisner argues, in the opening stylistic genealogy of *L'écran démoniaque*, that "Mysticism and magic [are] the dark forces to which Germans have always been more than willing to commit themselves" citing Wilhelm Worringer's declaration that, "Inwardly discordant, always striving for the unattainable, [Nordic man] needs the spiritual unrest which is an incentive to the 'animation of the inorganic.' Mediterranean man, so perfectly harmonious, can never know this ecstasy of 'expressive abstraction.'" As a rebuttal to Kalbus, tit for tat, Eisner invokes the essentializing language of Worringer, which trades in notions of national cultural predisposition to make an argument for Expressionism, precisely that school of artistic production which art historians of Kalbus's ilk worked to pathologize and exclude from the Nazi canon. Indeed, in the volume Eisner cites in her 1948 article on Lubitsch, Kalbus argues, according to Joel Westerdale's summary, that any "unserious elements" in the German silent film were the result of foreign influence, and that, in general, German taste was aligned with "Nordic reserve, as opposed to the southern European penchant for grand gestures."[57]

Here it is useful to recall the epigraph of *The Haunted Screen*, in which Eisner quotes arch-conservative Leopold Ziegler: "German man is the supreme example of demoniac man. Demoniac indeed seems the abyss which cannot be filled, the yearning which cannot be assuaged, the thirst which cannot be slaked."[58] Ziegler (1881–1958) was a German philosopher associated with the conservative thinkers of the Weimar-era Conservative Revolution, a group encompassing figures as varied as Gottfried Benn, Hugo von Hofmannsthal, Ernst Jünger, Carl Schmitt, and Oswald Spengler. In contrast to Thomas Mann and others who were advocating for the fledgling republic, Ziegler argued that the republic was doomed and that a return to empire was desirable and imminent. Indeed, according to James F. Ward, Ziegler "presented the Reich as a permanent historical mission for Germany."[59] Victor Farías identifies a speech titled, "The Myth of the Reich," and the two-volume treatise *Das Heilige Reich der Deutschen* (*The Holy German Empire*, 1925) that Eisner cites in her epigraph as Ziegler's most important contributions to this interwar discourse. In the latter, according to Farías, "[Ziegler] made the Reich a transcendental entity that 'beyond any historical change will always remain the destiny and particular mission of Germans.'"[60] From this angle, it's possible to see Eisner's invocation of both Ziegler and Kalbus as parries: as if to say, even on its own terms, the revisionist historiography practiced by Conservative Revolution thinkers and Nazi historians was insupportable.

Reading the discourse on German identity peddled by thinkers like Ziegler and Kalbus against its grain, Eisner demonstrates that a narrative of interwar film culture that foregrounds the roles of leftists, Jews, and gay and queer artists is equally if not more plausible. Another version of this argument, suggestive yet less crisply articulated, pivots on the color brown. In discussing Reinhardt's influence on interwar film, Eisner quickly sketches the discreditable lineage of Julius Langbehn's *Rembrandt als Erzieher* (1890)—which argued that the painter could be claimed by racist advocates for Aryan purity, his signature palette conscripted in the conservative cause—through to Oswald Spengler, who argued that Rembrandt's "atelier brown" was a "protestant color," belonging properly to the gloomy "Faustian soul" of the revanchist German straining to produce his fascist destiny. Eisner uses "brown" and "brown shirt" metonymically in a number of postwar publications to signify Nazis and Nazism; in this passage from *The Haunted Screen* about Spengler and Langbehn, she appears to figure two visions of chiaroscuro: one is "Faustian," allied with the murky, noxious rhetoric of the reactionaries; the other is Reinhardt's. According to Eisner, "Nordic man's Faustian soul is committed to gloom, whereas Reinhardt—we should remember that he was Jewish—created his magical world with light, darkness serving only as the foil to the light. This was the twofold heritage of the German film."[61]

Eisner's allergy to overdetermined historiography, from either the left or the right, also undergirds her reading of Lubitsch's genre films. In what will become a signature move of Eisner's stylistic analysis of interwar films, she suggests that the production context and contemporary mediascape in which Lubitsch as an artist and person had marinated are the strongest influences on the films and provide the most effective inroads to analysis, rather than ideological critiques of plot. Remarking that Iris Barry "seems to be the only one to have deduced the part that had already been played in the development of the 'Lubitsch touch' by the old comedies of Mack Sennett and the Keystone films of Chaplin," Eisner argues that neither Riciotto Canudo's critique of *Madame du Barry*—that the film betrays its reactionary bent by trivializing the French Revolution—nor an assertion she attributes to Henry Roussell about the nasty spirit of *Anne Boleyn* indicating an appeal on Lubitsch's part to American puritanical revolt against "merry old England" stand up to scrutiny: "Siegfried Kracauer, not suspected of any partiality toward the Germany on its way to Nazism, has demonstrated that the large industrial powers, concerned to bring in foreign investment, had every interest in making films that pleased the Allies."[62] The French critics, she points out, claim that the foibles of Lubitsch's revolutionaries derive from the director's own hostility to the French. Yet, she continues,

> On the other hand, do we not find a Danton, a Robespierre, and a Marat (the latter portrayed by the unforgettable Antonin Artaud) grimacing painfully in Abel Gance's silent *Napoleon*, the grandiose French glorification of the Revolution? What, then, too, of the frenzied ogres that the great Dreyer himself showed in *Pages from Satan's Book* about the French Revolution? And this last in 1919, the year of *Madame du Barry*. In France they forget that Germany, in 1914–1918 no less, was obsessed by two plays about Danton that many people, under the despotic reign of Wilhelm II, considered allegories of freedom.[63]

Here, Eisner highlights two Max Reinhardt productions, mounted in 1916 and 1919, that evinced an irrepressibly liberal spirit: Georg Büchner's *La Mort de Danton* and *Danton*, by Romain Rolland. "Lubitsch," Eisner argues, "could have been as influenced by the revolutionary spirit of these two plays as by their topicality," but for him they were never more than a colorful backdrop for a love story. Kracauer, like Canudo, derides Lubitsch's triviality in reducing the storming of the Bastille to the dimensions of a lover's spat, which, in Eisner's view, takes up the wrong end of the question: "For Lubitsch, moreover, history is never more than a pretext for period costume dramas; silks and velvet lure the former fabric shop attendant and delight his connoisseur's eye." To readers familiar with *L'écran démoniaque* and *The*

Haunted Screen, the argument is a familiar one, only slightly modified for later publication in the chapter on Lubitsch and his costume films. In the latter, Eisner offers some finer detail as to the cross-pollination between Reinhardt and Lubitsch, and instead of bickering with Kalbus and Kracauer, or Canudo and Roussell, she interpolates Georges Sadoul in a footnote and attributes to him the remarks she says are Roussell's in the 1948 article.

Granting that Lubitsch is "superficial," Eisner argues that his orientation toward surfaces might be interesting on its own terms. Having come up in the world of ready-to-wear, inculcated in the Reinhardt school, Eisner argues, should we not look to the stylization of the costumes, sets, and mise en scène for the substance of Lubitsch's particularity? While holding that ideological critique is a limited approach to understanding the Lubitsch touch, Eisner is wary of apologia; hence, perhaps, her frequent mention of Lubitsch's "vulgarity" and dubious taste. Focusing on visual style and the interplay of influence and reference, she notes that "Lubitsch's psychology is hardly less superficial than that of a novelist like Vicki Baum; and when he returns to a Central Europe familiar to him, as in *To Be or Not to Be*, he makes such flagrant mistakes of taste that one suddenly finds, behind the director who became famous for his lightness of touch, the Berlin prankster from his beginnings."[64] Emphasizing the porousness of the boundaries between theater and film in twenties Berlin—in terms of personnel, property, stylistics, and source texts—Eisner builds a case for stylistic analysis as the critical approach best suited to a collaborative, industrial art.

In her next article in *La Revue du cinéma*, Eisner effectively sketches the primary arguments of *L'écran démoniaque*, tracing in the key films of the period the influence of Max Reinhardt, of Expressionism, and the unique production culture of the interwar German industry. Focusing primarily on the interplay of costume with set design and lighting, Eisner reprises her take on Lubitsch and his costume dramas before detailing the personnel, props, and aesthetics imported from Reinhardt's theatrical work, related to yet differentiated from the influence of a handful of important, largely forgotten set designers. The middle third of this article is given over to an analysis of the work of set designers in collaboration with directors and cameramen, threaded through with a lament:

> [To understand] the composition of costumes in most German films, it is necessary to consider that the director often had a background in painting, or, like Murnau, in art history. What's more, in certain cases, it can be difficult to discern the draughtsman behind the work, even if his name is cited

in the credits. Although the names of set designers [Otto] Hunte and [Erich] Kettelhut, and that of cameraman Carl Hoffmann are remembered, how many today know that the stylized costumes of *Nibelungen* are the work of Paul Gerd Guderian? It was Walter Reimann who created the costumes of *Cabinet of Dr. Caligari*, even though their perfect harmony of form with the set was the result of a close collaboration between the painter and the set designers Herman[n] Warm and Walter Röhrig.[65]

The prevalence of certain costumes—the ill-fitting overcoat and bowler, or the Biedermeier frock coat and top hat—she construes as a gesture on the part of the costume and set designers to what would have been a familiar frame of reference—Expressionism in the former case and Romanticism in the latter. And the failures of certain productions, such as *Genuine* (Robert Wiene, 1920), can be understood most clearly as the imperfect, glib, or confused implementation of those generic conventions; Eisner lays blame at the feet of both director Wiene and the painter César Klein, who overloaded the sets with what she judges as a half-baked mix of Jugendstil and Caligarism. Eisner will go on to develop this argument in greater depth with *L'écran démoniaque*—and in several articles in which she attempts to clarify what she sees as prevalent misreadings of the case made in *L'écran démoniaque*—but for the moment she leaves this subtle point to one side.

In some ways, while Eisner takes a more thorough approach to defining a critical film stylistics rubric than some other contemporary studies of interwar German film, the precision and the clarity of the case made in *L'écran démoniaque* remain just beyond this 1949 article, suggesting that in the intervening three years Eisner worked to shape a body of perceptive, well-supported observations into a comprehensive argument.[66] Kracauer's remarks on *Genuine* circa 1947 offer an interesting counterpoint; in *From Caligari to Hitler*, he spares a short paragraph for the film, offering the following assessment:

> Immediately after *Caligari*, Robert Wiene, meaning to strike while the iron was hot, engaged Carl Mayer and the painter Césare [sic] Klein for the production of another expressionist film: *Genuine* (1920). This fantasy, in which an exuberant décor competes with a far-fetched, bizarre story, is of importance only in that it marks a turning-point thematically.... The narrative shows Mayer's interest shifting from the tyrant to the instinct theme. All instinct films Mayer made after *Genuine* have one feature in common: they are laid in a lower middle-class world which is the meaningless remnant of a disintegrated society.[67]

The differences between Eisner's take on the film and Kracauer's are suggestive of the larger conflict between their approaches. For Kracauer, the stylistic elements of the film merit only passing, vague reference, in favor of a symptomatic, quasi-sociological analysis of the film's plot, its place in the larger trajectory of Mayer's filmography on a narrative level, and its relation to Kracauer's overarching thesis. By contrast, for Eisner, the film is interesting precisely in terms of the way its visual stylistic elements suggest the collaborative effort between Klein, Wiene, and Mayer, the generic context in which each of them had previously worked, and the larger, longer history of cross-pollination among the literary, theatrical, and artistic influences on the interwar German film industry. In short, Kracauer's analysis is focused on what *Genuine* prefigures in Mayer's work, which is in turn symptomatic of the "mute chaos" of the pre-Hitler period, whereas Eisner's analysis—even in truncated form circa 1949—works to historicize the visual style of the period.

MURNAU AND LANG, ALONG A CONTINUUM OF CONTROL

For Eisner, the variegated, sometimes contradictory juxtaposition of stylistic influences suggested by the costume and set design, acting styles, camera work, lighting, scenario, screenplay, and editing suggests that discussing the unitary intention of a film, let alone the unitary import, is a dubious proposition in all but a few, exalted cases. Moreover, without recourse to comparative stylistic analysis, such as other films made by the same filmmaking team minus one or two members, any assessments of the relative genius of directors should be avoided, as Eisner argues in her comments on methodology circa 1953 and 1974.[68]

The second major line of thinking developed in Eisner's postwar scholarship emerged from her archival praxis, and, unlike *L'écran démoniaque*—which expanded on previously published articles—it was only explored in a single article, published six years in advance of the book.[69] Articulated in sustained fashion in the evolving text of *F. W. Murnau*, it represents an inquiry into the nature and origins of film style that remains unparalleled. The presentation of Eisner's research and analysis is highly unusual, in that she foregrounds her source material and appears in narrative or explanatory passages as a humble, indefatigably curious figure in the first person. In the forewords to the 1967 German edition and the 1973 English edition, Eisner describes her approach.[70] Explaining that the structuring logic of the book was her response to the fragmented and elliptical nature of the source materials, she states in the German foreword that, while Murnau was well known in France, in part because of an active secondary literature, she felt she could not take the same "philological" approach for German readers, because his work remained relatively little known in the postwar period. Additionally, she says, she felt the need to adjust her language: "To a more 'objective' contemporary German audience, I needed to make a different case for [Murnau] and for the appreciation of his films. Moreover, in today's Germany, purple prose rings false, and there is a heightened sensitivity to phrases echoing the pompous blathering of *Blut und Boden* [the 'Blood and Soil' rhetoric of the Nazi party]."[71] Quoting a passage describing Murnau's death from the first French edition—in which she says that Salka Viertel closed those "eyes that so loved to see"—Eisner observes that to transpose the passage directly into German would have been in poor taste, and that such mawkish, "*Gartenlaube*" language might detract from what she identified as the key purpose of the book: "to give young people a sense of the twenties in Germany, and to acquaint them with their most sensitive filmmaker. For people who lived through that time, this book is an inducement to reminisce."[72] Curiously, Eisner felt no such compunction about the passage in the English edition, which translated the French original nearly word for word. She did, however, offer a different foreword for the English edition; this is both more technical—it discusses the difficulties of researching among prints of varying quality and provenance—and more personal:

> I know Lang and knew Pabst; but I never met Murnau. . . . I do not believe in books written in haste, and during the seven years I worked on this book I saw—thanks to Henri Langlois and the Cinémathèque française—Murnau's films again and again, in as many different copies and versions as I could find. Even so, the fragmented nature of the material is such that I am aware that others may yet find more aspects of Murnau's style than I have been able to discover in my "archaeological" pursuit. . . . In my previous book [*L'écran démoniaque*, both French editions and the English translation] I made a first attempt at an evaluation of Murnau, devoting separate chapters to *The Last Laugh*, *Tartuffe*, and *Faust*. Consequently, although in this book the reader will find constant reference to these films, I have felt it more important to put the most emphasis on his other works. I hope this will explain the disproportionately little space devoted specifically to these major films. Murnau died prematurely; he stays eternally young. My aim has been to trace the development of his style through that brief life, and

to demonstrate the often intransigent continuity of his artistic will, a will expressed in films made in Germany, in the United States, and on his island in the Pacific.[73]

This foreword suggests that the English edition presents essentially the same arguments as the two previous editions, but as the text itself will admit on numerous occasions, Eisner added fresh evidence and testimony to each as she conducted new interviews, accessed different prints of the films, and reviewed further documentation as it became available. Such additions included expansions of the first chapter with the reflections of Ottile Plumpe and Wolfgang Schramm, of the fifth chapter with a rediscovered film, and of the tenth chapter—on special effects and the three final German films—with the recollections of Fritz Arno Wagner. Eisner also moved materials from the French edition's appendixes into the main body of the text and revised her chapter on the discrepancies between three archival copies of *Nosferatu* with novel findings as she gathered evidence in archival research and interviews.

Aside from these expansions, as Janet Bergstrom has pointed out, one of the key shifts Eisner makes over time in the three editions was to contend with increasing force against the argument Karl Freund first made in 1947, and continued to flog in spite of Eisner's claims to the contrary, that it was in fact Carl Mayer who should have been credited with the innovations and successes of the Mayer-Murnau collaborations.[74] Bergstrom suggests that rather than diminishing Mayer's contributions, Eisner seeks instead to demonstrate that Murnau's involvement in workshopping and executing certain effects, and his conception of visual style more generally, were far greater than Freund had granted. In the English edition, Eisner argues that through comparative analysis of Mayer's screenplays and Murnau's shooting scripts it is possible to attribute to Murnau achievements Freund argues were Mayer's, yet "it is impossible to define the part played by each individual in the shooting of a film. Where does improvisation begin in the studio, or on location, and which member of the team originates it? Was it chance that produced the exquisite tracery on the walls in *Tartuffe*, when the footmen carrying candlesticks pause on the landing and the flames cast shadows of the wrought-iron staircase? And what about the similar image in *Sunrise*, shot by another cameraman? . . . We must suppose a single intention behind all these varying images."[75] Arguing that the development of Murnau's signature "mobile yet limpid luminosity" stretches beyond the films he made in collaboration with Mayer, and that contemporaries have disputed Freund's characterizations of the team's working methods, she offers the following statement, which can be taken as characteristic of the tone of the work as a whole:

> It is not my intention to belittle in any way the poetic greatness and essentially visual gifts of a man like Mayer. . . . Nevertheless, I think it is more natural to suppose that the extraordinary and close collaboration between on the one hand people like Mayer, Herlth, Röhrig, Gliese, together with such talented cameramen as Wagner, Freund, Hoffmann, [Charles] Rosher, and others, and on the other hand a director as perceptive and intuitive as Murnau was a rare and fruitful opportunity for the art of the cinema at that time, and one of the reasons for the almost ideal fulfillment it achieved.[76]

Although she returns repeatedly to the notion of Murnau's genius, what has made Eisner's book enduringly useful and esteemed is that in addition to being an assessment saturated with primary and secondary source material, as well as original and perceptive observations of her own about the films, it is one suffused with remarks of this kind: steeped in the material, humble about the ends to which analysis should be carried, and rigorous about explaining the rationale by which she makes assertions of taste or perception.

Notwithstanding these admirable qualities, this book, like a number of Eisner's postwar film reviews and the commentary she offered in her memoirs and interviews, is bespattered with remarks about homosexuality, race, and class as they relate to cinematic style that are suggestive and murky. In her commentary on *Fireworks* (Kenneth Anger, 1947) and, indirectly, on *Un chant d'amour* (Jean Genet, 1950), as well as in her remarks on Murnau's *Die Finanzen des Großherzogs* (1924) and *Tabu* (1931), Eisner makes reference to, in the first instance, a "very pure, affirmed homosexual character" and in Murnau's case, a "homosexual sensuality" legible on the surface of these films.[77] In the former case, Eisner appears to be grasping at a description of the film's content: both Anger and Genet depict men having sex with men on-screen. Yet in the latter, despite having left her language uncharacteristically imprecise, Eisner appears to be arguing that the way Murnau frames, lights, and tracks male characters in certain sequences is more plausibly sexualized than his treatment of female characters.[78] Describing Murnau's death in the English edition, Eisner offers the following statement: "The ancient Greeks represented death as a handsome young man, with the sombre and enigmatic beauty which the young Filipino who drove Murnau to his death no doubt possessed. Everyone's private life is sacred, and if we touch here in passing on the homosexual tendencies in Murnau which his brother Robert always tried to refute, it is merely because they may explain certain elements latent in his style, and for example certain vagaries of sensibility in *Faust*. Murnau's natural predispositions were as decisive a factor in the subtlety of his art as in his premature death."[79] Essentializing Murnau's homosexuality as a fatal gift and a "natural predisposition," Eisner slips into a register unfamiliar to the book at large: conjectural, falsely decorous, yet obviously intended to render tribute to Murnau. The posture of this passage at large is typified in a gesture that leaves a wary reader bemused: Eisner continues, darkly "Venomous tongues did not fail to set to work in the great Babel of Hollywood," a statement she footnotes as follows, "See the insinuations mentioned by Kenneth Anger in *Cahiers du cinéma* and in his book, *Hollywood Babylon*."[80] Ostensibly wagging a finger at Anger, Eisner all but points her reader to his allegations about the causes of Murnau's fatal distraction. Performatively contrasting her own interest in Murnau's sexuality with Anger's, she outlines a distinction without difference between those who stoop to insinuate and those who only refer their readers to several places in which those insinuations have been published. Eisner's narration in this passage is tangled and contradictory, seeming to signal a privileged knowledge she cannot rightly disclose in one moment, yet casting ludicrous aspersions in another. Continually referring to the young man traveling with Murnau as "the Filipino"—even though at one point she appears to know and call him by the name Stevenson—this passage also exemplifies what Nicholas Baer has argued is an "essentialist, Orientalist" discourse in some of Eisner's early film criticism.[81] In *The Haunted Screen*, Eisner offers the following, slightly shifted argument about a homosexual cinematic style, attributing Murnau's nuance, again, to a tragic fate:

> Murnau had homosexual tendencies. In his attempt to escape from himself, he did not express himself with the artistic continuity which makes it so easy to analyse the style of, say, Lang. But all of his films bear the impress of his inner complexity, of the struggle he waged within himself against a world in which he remained despairingly alien. Only in his last film, *Tabu*, did he seem to have found peace and a little happiness in surroundings which abolish the guilt-feelings inherent in European morality.... Murnau, born in 1888, lived under the ominous shadow which the inhuman Paragraph 175 of the pre-1918 German Penal Code, lending itself to all the horrors of blackmail, cast over him and those like him.[82]

As we've seen, Eisner was staunchly opposed to the infamous Paragraph 175 as far back as the twenties, calling the law "extortionate" in a 1929 film review. Here, as in Eisner's other arguments for historicizing authorship—and for understanding the ways that intergenerational trauma inflects cultural production—the connection is made directly and unequivocally, but with little specificity. In common with Eisner's discussions of Lubitsch, the historical context of the artist's upbringing and milieu is assumed to have influenced the ways he worked, to be at the root of the artist's style, in spite of variation across the span of his career.

In contrast to her introduction to the English edition of *Murnau*, in which Eisner describes the "often intransigent continuity in his artistic style," in this passage from *L'écran démoniaque* above, it is Lang whom Eisner holds up as the exemplar of "artistic continuity," a quality attributed indirectly to the solidity of his personhood, his self-knowledge, and his (relatively) frictionless passage through the corridors of power. From her earliest articles about Lang through the monograph that was ultimately published after Lang's death, the dominant personal characteristic Eisner reads in his filmmaking style is his desire for control. Indeed, control as a function of power and artistic mastery is one of the operative principles within Eisner's larger critical rubric.[83] Although she argues throughout *Murnau* that the director was the originator of key innovations in his films, she emphasizes that his collaborative spirit led to even greater achievements for the filmmaking team as a whole; in spite of celebrating some of Lang's primary collaborators, such as Fritz Arno Wagner, in all of her postwar writing on Lang, she argued that the defining characteristic of his work was his insistence on bending the profilmic world, as well as cast and crew, to his vision.

Fritz Lang was the third marquee work Eisner published in the postwar period, and by at least two definitions, it was the most difficult of all three. It took the longest to write, in part because of Lang's insistence on reviewing and suggesting numerous revisions to the manuscript, and it remained unpublished during his lifetime. Structured, basically, as a heavily annotated filmography, the 1976 English-language edition of the book is stylistically uneven, pocked with strange errors and repetitions, and overbearing in its insistence, sometimes against the testimony of its own evidence, on the singular genius of Lang. The posthumously published, French-language edition (1984) was edited by Eisner with the help of Bernard Eisenschitz, who helped Eisner correct a number of the problems in the original edition without fundamentally altering the arguments made by Eisner and Lang. Drawing on extensive interviews and correspondence with Lang and some of his collaborators, in addition to original materials and documents of Lang's, Eisner supplements plot summary and production details with her own observations about visual style, contemporaneous reviews and trade press coverage of the films, and biographical information provided by Lang. In the final analysis, however, the volume fails to offer either the depth or the originality of research on display in *F. W. Murnau* and *L'écran démoniaque*. "It is much more difficult," Eisner admits in her preface, "for me to write about Fritz Lang than about F. W. Murnau" because of their long friendship. Many of her readers have come to the conclusion that it was also the result of Lang's collaboration in the volume; as Eisner put it: "Each chapter as finished has been submitted to him for approval and for verification of dates and facts. While never attempting to influence my critical point of view, Lang commented extensively on those facts which had on occasion been misrepresented."[84] In spite of her protestations to the contrary, and the several disagreements between them that Eisner flags in the text of her monograph, she frequently took on the role of Lang's ally, weighing in on matters of critical opinion or theory in Lang's stead, or expressing on his behalf his displeasure.

In a certain light, these statements suggest the territorial posturing discussed earlier. In the preface to *Fritz Lang*, Eisner takes the opportunity of mentioning her work on Murnau as a point of contrast to the present volume to note that she, unlike others, confined herself "to a description of [Murnau's] style and working method, in order not to fall into the trap indicated by Goethe: 'If you cannot interpret, read into it.' I never attempted, then, subjective interpretation of the 'eternal emotional themes' in the work of this long-dead artist, which was the aim of an author of a monograph on Murnau that succeeded my own." This paralipsis would appear to be little more than a gratuitous insult to Charles Jameux's 1965 book on Murnau, but I emphasize it here in order to differentiate it strongly from a similar remark further into the preface to the Lang monograph that suggests another aspect of her allegiance with Lang.[85] Just a few sentences on, Eisner declares, "Much has been written about Lang. It is not my concern to criticise the monographs that have been published on him, all of which Lang himself considers inadequate. For my own part I do not claim to have produced a definitive study. . . . This book is, I believe however, the first attempt to do justice" to Lang's work.[86] Again, an apophasis awkwardly cloaked in false (if conventional) humility: the peculiar, maybe intentionally risible effect of Eisner's rhetoric aside, this remark implies that Eisner speaks for Lang with his permission and blessing. Emphasizing her privileged connection and communication with Lang was one of the ways Eisner signaled her relevance to a younger cohort, and in some important ways, she appears to have cultivated the alliance not merely for its professional expedience, but for protection.

One of the more prominent features of Eisner's postwar work, and perhaps the defining quality of the interviews she gave as she shifted from publishing relatively frequently to her later role as a mentor and symbolic figure, is precisely this rhetorical pattern by which she aligns herself with famous people, emphasizing her personal connections with them. Articles on Peter Lorre, G. W. Pabst, Erich von Stroheim, Fritz Lang, and finally Werner Herzog all trade in an image of Eisner as insider. This gradual, decades-long change is encapsulated in a set of three pieces Eisner published about Lang's *Das Testament des Dr. Mabuse*, the first in the *Film-Kurier* in 1932, the second immediately after arriving in Paris, in 1933, and the third, a call-back to these earlier pieces she published in *Cahiers* toward the end of her time regularly contributing to the journal.

The first article, titled "A Forest Is Dismantled: Fritz Lang Begins Shooting," like many of Eisner's on-set pieces at the *Film-Kurier*, sketches a vivid description of a trip she made out to a night shoot for *Das Testament des Dr. Mabuse*. On her way out to the set by car, she passes a suburban jumble of bourgeois homes and apartment blocks and arrives at a surreal scene: Karl Vollbrecht and Emil Hasler have been a month in working on the set—rigging a manufactured forest with scaffolding for lighting and cameras—for the night-time car chase scene. Describing the cables as snaking like jungle vines through the set, she says Lang ordered his crew to chop down all the trees, so that they might erect the forest of his mind's eye, telling her that to his way of thinking it is a "shame that there is always an incongruity between man and camera. We need a camera's eye" to achieve a truly filmic effect.[87] However, in keeping with much of her on-set coverage, Eisner devotes most of the article to her observations about Lang's collaborators and closes the piece with a celebration of the partnership between Lang and his cameraman, Fritz Arno Wagner, who "squats on his perch, fanatically devoted to his work, the exquisite cameraman that a director like Lang must have. And in his collaboration with Lang's vision, the unity of conception that the work must have is forged."[88]

The second version of this article, drastically pared down for publication in *L'Intransigeant*, performs a different model of appreciation and advocacy.

The film had been banned in Germany and was soon to be released in France. Eliminating any mention of Lang's collaborators and the collective labor being poured into creating the scene's effect, Eisner focuses in on Lang as the singular visionary.[89] Whether it was edited down in this way to appeal to a French readership not acquainted with the points of reference—the particularities of this suburban landscape, the collaborators whose names would have been well known to her specialist German readership—or simply for reasons of space, the second version does accord with the squabbles and uneasy accommodations Eisner would go on to make with her postwar French colleagues: the focus on singular over and against collective authorship, the strident tenor of her praise for Lang, and the evacuation of a certain charm and wit on the narrator's part. In both *L'écran démoniaque* and *Murnau*, of course, Eisner argues her case for a model of film scholarship much more in the vein of her interwar work—although she always described it in terms of her doctoral training, rather than her journalism—but the fact of her needing to argue the point is essential to understanding the directions in which her postwar scholarship ran.

The third piece, published in 1957 near the end of her regular *Cahiers* years, is a brief comment on taxi rides in Germany, titled "Taxi Chauffeurs." She begins, "I really enjoy, when I find myself in foreign lands, the chance to chat with taxi drivers," and offers two illustrations of the point. One time, she says, she happened to get a ride from a former studio driver for Nero Film, who, upon learning of Eisner's professional background, told her that he once drove out to a night shoot for a Lang picture and ended up on film in the car chase. "Weren't you there that night to pick up a journalist?" she says she asked him, "That was me." Another time, she says, she got a ride on a trip in the GDR from Erich Pommer's former driver: "We chatted, then, as I got ready to get out of the cab, he said: 'Now, dear Madam, would you be so good as to satisfy my curiosity on one point' (he asked me in a very ceremonious manner), 'Why is it that you deem Murnau the superior *metteur en scène* to Fritz Lang?'"[90] The tone and the topic do recall the perceptive sketches Eisner published in the interwar years, but they take place in a different diegetic universe, one common to many of Eisner's postwar recollections: pinging endlessly with improbable coincidence, populated, apparently exclusively, with luminaries of the interwar period, and narrated by a quick-witted, almost swaggering persona. This is the Lotte Eisner of most of the interviews she gave as she entered her seventies and eighties, and of her memoirs. While certain peculiar rhymes across some of these stories suggest that they were crafted with intention, I would argue that, on balance, they make the most sense in the context of the persistent precarity of her existence.[91] If she waged a peace with the uncertainties of her work at the CF with Langlois, and the still-chaotic jostling of the field of scholarly film study just beginning to gel in the sixties—these developments raising the stakes of territorial competition for resources, credibility, and institutional backing—one of her lifelines was this font of stories she began to tap with increasing frequency in the postwar decades.

Conclusion

THE WOOLLY MAMMOTH
OF THE CINÉMATHÈQUE

IN 1979, TWO INDEPENDENT FILMMAKERS—Sohrab Shahid Saless, the celebrated Iranian director working in exile in Germany, and S. Mark Horowitz, an American neophyte—each made a short documentary film about Eisner. Shahid Saless's film, *Die langen Ferien der Lotte H. Eisner* (*The Long Vacation of Lotte H. Eisner*), filmed in June of that year, was a German production emerging out of a friendship between the director and Eisner, years in planning with a budget of 150,000 marks underwritten by West Deutsche Rundfunk.[1] Horowitz's film, *Lotte Eisner in Germany*, cost around $17,000 and was funded entirely out of pocket by the director after his graduation from the University of California, Berkeley.[2] Horowitz shot his interviews with Eisner in English over four days in the middle of December, and he was motivated by what he would later call "an emotional encounter between acolyte and hero," not with Eisner herself, but with Werner Herzog.

In virtually all of the interviews Eisner gave about her life and career—most of them dating from her last twenty years in exile—the narrative of her identity and her accomplishments remained remarkably consistent. Not only do these interviews recount the same handful of events and reflections, but they often do so in the same phrases, in the same intonations, even across languages. Between the two documentaries at hand, Eisner provides the usual anecdotes and musings, yet the films diverge in interesting ways, reflecting not only the differences in how they were conceived and how they were designed to function for each director, but two fundamentally different ideas of how and why Eisner herself mattered. Of these ideas, one—Horowitz and Herzog's—would come to define the conventional wisdom about Eisner and percolate gradually into the contemporary discourses on her work, ultimately, I argue, to its detriment. The second, on partial view in Shahid Saless's film, suggests ways of engaging Eisner that rhyme with those I've proposed here; I posit that in this film, we see the hint of an alternate, counterfactual trajectory in which, before her passing and in the years following, Eisner's life and career might have been understood more fully and the importance of her work appreciated sooner.

By 1979, Shahid Saless had been living and working in German exile for half a decade, and his standing as one of the most acclaimed directors associated with the New German Cinema was largely secure. According to Shahid Saless scholar Michelle Langford, his appearance at the 1974 Berlin International Film Festival marked a key juncture in his career; already a well-known filmmaker on the Iranian scene by this point, the two films he presented at the festival—*A Simple Event* (1973) and *Still Life* (1974)—"took the Berlinale by storm," the latter winning Shahid Saless the Silver Bear. However, when Shahid Saless returned to Iran to begin shooting his third feature film, *Quarantine*, production was interrupted several days in by the authorities, and the project was abruptly curtailed. Frustrated, and in hopes of riding the success of his debut at the Berlinale to greater heights in what he wagered would be a less repressive production environment, Shahid Saless went into self-imposed exile in Germany in 1975, where he would make thirteen films over the course of the next eighteen years.[3] While his return to Germany was met with a flush of press reports, as Langford has argued, Shahid Saless occupied a complicated, fraught position "between self-othering and exceptionalism": aspiring, not unreasonably, to be considered and treated as a peer among New German Cinema filmmakers like Werner Herzog and Wim Wenders, yet caught in bureaucratic limbo in terms of his immigration and residency status, constrained in his ability to take on independent projects and to travel. It is in this context that the relationship between Eisner and Shahid Saless first germinated.

In addition to her outspoken admiration of Shahid Saless's films, which she first encountered at the 1974 Berlinale, Eisner's status as the doyenne of the Cinémathèque française and, per Herzog, the godmother of New German Cinema would have been known to Shahid Saless from the first moments of their acquaintance. According to Eisner, their friendship grew out of her regard for his films and their shared experience as exiles; she would later say that she herself had little interest in being the subject of a documentary and that her participation in Shahid Saless's project was entirely a testament to this friendship.[4] Indeed, in Langford's description of Shahid Saless's ambivalence, shades of Eisner's own self-othering and exceptionalism are recognizable: Eisner was complexly different and undeniably marginalized, yet, as we have seen, she rejected feminist politics of solidarity and collective action in regressive, sometimes hypocritical terms. At the root of some of the most gnarled contradictions in her work and personal attitudes lay the fact that Eisner existed, for most of her life, in interstitial, temporary, contingent, and marginal spaces, both in times of material and economic privilege and in those of privation and insecurity. Her family had prospered at a fleeting moment of unprecedented freedom for German Jews, characterized by largely peaceful economic, political, and social assimilation. Institutional space for women in higher education opened at precisely the moment of her coming of age (and closed, resoundingly, shortly thereafter), and the profession of film journalism was new and dynamic enough for a person in Eisner's position—no fan, barely an initiate—to get a foothold and learn on the job as the industry itself flourished. Over time, each of these provisional, fortuitous privileges was yanked out from beneath Eisner's feet; in common with Shahid Saless, she could attribute her unfulfilled potential and dashed ambitions, in large part, to forces outside her control. Affinities, friendship, and mutual regard notwithstanding, the context of West German filmmaking and the *Vergangenheitsbewältigung* were definitive: Shahid Saless might not have been so well positioned—both personally and in terms of the support available for projects reckoning with recent German history—to make such a documentary had he been forced to rely on the postwar French state or private subvention. Likewise, he may not have been as interested in Eisner had he been embraced by the French Nouvelle Vague, given the oppositional tenor of Eisner's engagement with some of the movement's main protagonists.

Among the filmmakers Eisner mentored and celebrated, perhaps none is better known than Werner Herzog. Since the earliest years of their friendship, he has credited Eisner publicly as one of the first and most influential supporters of his career and the New German Cinema movement at large. While they often verge on the hyperbolic, his sincere tributes to Eisner hinge on her connection to interwar German film culture, her embrace of New German Cinema, and of Herzog's films in particular:

> She was the missing link, our collective conscience, a fugitive from Nazism, and for many years the single living person in the world who knew everyone in cinema from its first hour on, a veritable woolly mammoth. Lotte was one of the most important film historians the world has ever seen.... So she alone had the authority, insight and the personality to declare us legitimate, and it

was vitally important when she insisted that what my generation was doing in Germany was as legitimate as the film culture that Murnau, Lang and the other Weimar cinema filmmakers had created all those years previously.⁵

The autumn following Shahid Saless's fateful Berlinale, in an episode chronicled contemporaneously in a diary that would later be published as *Of Walking in Ice* (1979), Herzog trekked on foot from Munich to an ailing Eisner's bedside in a pilgrimage he believed would stave off her death. This story and other tributes of Herzog's are part and parcel of the complex set of exchanges on the marketplace of social and financial capital between Herzog and Eisner, both during and after the span of her life. On the one hand, Herzog led efforts to secure financial support for Eisner and recognition of her life's work from the West German government, the fruits of which included a stipend to pay for in-home health care and some of the medical bills that began to accrue as her health failed.⁶ On the other hand, the stories and tributes Herzog has recounted regularly in public about Eisner since the 1970s are often less about Eisner and her work than they are about the honors her acquaintance conferred upon Herzog himself. A recent French-German coproduction, *Lotte Eisner, aucun lieu, nulle part* (*Ein Leben für den Film*, Timon Koulmasis, 2021) arrays new interviews with Herzog, Volker Schlöndorff, Martje Grohmann, Laurent Mannoni, Bernard Eisenschitz, Wim Wenders, and others alongside numerous excerpts from previous recorded interviews as a documentary tribute to Eisner, but the film takes its structure, large portions of its voice-over narration and the bulk of what is not given over to talking-head footage to imagery reenacting Herzog's 1979 memoir.⁷ The first and last words of Koulmasis's film, notwithstanding its efforts to foreground and celebrate Eisner herself, belong to Herzog and center his experience and recollections at the expense of established facts, to occasionally comical effect; in his introductory remarks, Herzog blithely claims that F. W. Murnau, who never met Eisner, was "enamored of her," and in his closing, he attributes the Nazi death threat against her to the publication *Der Stürmer*. Fortunately, the gravitational pull Herzog exerts is as conspicuous as it is powerful, meaning that for the Koulmasis film and these kinds of accounts more broadly, the degree to which these factual errors undermine Herzog's credibility as a narrator of Eisner's biography and legacy depends on what that credibility is presumed to consist of.

In Herzog's telling, good intentions notwithstanding, the operative metaphor is extinction; Eisner was an anachronism belonging to a bygone period. In a recent conversation with celebrity interviewer David Marchese, Herzog went so far as to imply that he exercised a kind of power over Eisner's life and her death: "Lotte Eisner was out of hospital when I arrived [on his aforementioned pilgrimage], and she lived another eight years, until she summoned me. That time I came by train. She said: 'There's still a spell upon me that I must not die. Can you lift it?' And I said: 'Of course, Lotte. If you die now, it seems to be all right.' . . . She said, 'I am saturated with life.' And I said to her, 'Lotte, hereby the spell is lifted.' She died eight days later, and I had absolutely no problem with it. It was a good death."[8] This interview at large is marked by the polemical contrarianism and high-spirited provocation Herzog often adopts in conversation with interpreters of his work and words, and it may not be a literal recitation of the conversations between Eisner and Herzog. Nevertheless, while Herzog describes Eisner as his "mentor" and refutes Marchese's suggestion that his 1974 pilgrimage was "megalomaniacal," he doubles down on the notion that there was a mystical connection between them; she gave him legitimacy, and in turn, he sustained her in her last years. In Herzog's frame of reference, Eisner was exceptional not because of what she actually did back in her own time, but for the marks she bore of not belonging to the present.

Eisner's mentorship of filmmakers associated with the New German Cinema movement can be framed in terms of her role as cultural arbiter at the CF, but it should also be considered in terms of her conflicted relationship to Germany and German identity. Eisner's personal history and her archival and historiographical work to salvage and recuperate interwar film culture represented an alternative vision of Germany in the twentieth century. In the late 1970s context of strife and reckoning, the emphatically anti-Nazi cast of her scholarship provided a context for the movement: radically different from what these filmmakers derogated as *Papas Kino*, certain fragmented lineages of Weimar-era filmmaking curtailed by the ascendance of Nazism and the war offered artistic parentage that could be affirmed, endorsed, even celebrated. Indeed, the last sentence of the 1969 edition of *The Haunted Screen* is devoted to a somewhat wistful affirmation of the Oberhausen group's potential to take up this legacy: "All we can do is to hope that these films of quality spell a new departure for the German cinema."[9] It should be noted that there is debate about how dramatically different (and to what ends) the filmmaking movements of the sixties were from predecessors and what the dis/continuities among and between West and East German film industries were prior to reunification.[10] Nevertheless, Eisner's affirmation of the New German Cinema group must be placed in the context of the work she had done to wrest historiographical narration of the interwar period from historians like Oskar Kalbus, on one front, and Siegfried Kracauer, on the other. If Kalbus—in the service of a larger attempt to generate the normative cultural historiography of the Third Reich—used Nazi ideology to pathologize interwar cinema, Kracauer could be said to have animated the doppelgänger of Kalbus's ideological critique, operating within the context of a broader agenda on the part of the US government and private foundations to mobilize social psychology, first in the war effort and later in the postwar restructuring of West German institutions.[11] Eisner, as we've seen, rejected both of these narratives; in the more oppositional moments of her historiographical praxis, she situated her work in direct and open refutation of Kalbus and Kracauer alike.

Concurrently with his involvement with the CF and the European festival circuit in the mid-seventies, Herzog was a semi-regular presence in the vibrant cinema scene of Berkeley, California, associated with the Pacific Film Archive (PFA) and the University of California. A number of important US and European filmmakers, critics, and scholars attended the screenings and discussions held at the PFA. This group included the aspiring filmmaker Mark Horowitz; after his graduation from the University and a stint in New York City, Horowitz decided to move to Europe to pursue a career in film. Making Eisner's acquaintance through a friend who attended the Sunday afternoon teas Eisner hosted in her Neuilly-sur-Seine apartment, Horowitz recalls that she encouraged him to apply for an internship on Herzog's current film, *Nosferatu the Vampyre* (1979). After a bizarre afternoon in Munich—involving a dental appointment, lunch, and a minor car accident with Herzog and Klaus Kinski—Horowitz was tasked by Herzog not with an internship but with returning to Paris to make a film about Eisner. Horowitz, his collaborator and the film's narrator Lesley Topping, and a cameraman would shoot their interviews in English with Eisner over the course of three days in her apartment and one at the CF, but it would take a year of somewhat anguished editing and reediting to finish the film. Horowitz, who ultimately left filmmaking in the 1990s for a career in journalism, describes his editing process as exceedingly difficult, saying that it was, in a sense, "my first magazine article," and that there was "no cinema" to the project. With initial plans of creating a formally experimental film out of the interview footage, Horowitz says that he became frustrated and ultimately arrived at a "less ambitious" structure for the film. He entered his documentary, *Lotte Eisner in Germany*, in the marketplace at Cannes, which resulted in its booking by the London, Poland, San Francisco, Rotterdam, and Chicago film festivals. The film was acquired by New Yorker Films—the independent distributor known for bringing the work of Bertolucci, Godard, Lanzmann, Rivette, and Sembène to the United States—for the college circuit in 1980, and it was screened at Film Forum for two weeks, but it has since languished in relative obscurity.[12]

In spite of their similar origins—in Eisner's long friendships with Shahid Saless and with Herzog—and the commonalities among the anecdotes she related to each filmmaker, the two films take distinct approaches on the level of style and narration. *Die langen Ferien der Lotte H. Eisner* opens with a montage sequence juxtaposing the rubble of postwar Berlin, memorials near the Berlin Wall, and footage of Hitler addressing rapt, vast crowds. Shahid Saless interpolates himself indirectly into the film by way of a voice-over reading of an affectionate letter from Eisner to Shahid Saless about the arrangements for a program of his films to be screened in Paris at the CF and the Centre Pompidou. This letter performs a double introduction, placing Shahid Saless firmly in the cohort of celebrated transnational filmmakers appearing on the European festival circuit and at the CF, and jokingly referring to Berlin as the "foreign city in which [Eisner] happened to be born." Proceeding largely chronologically from this point forward, Shahid Saless's film is punctuated by title cards demarcating signal periods of Eisner's life by time, place, key relationships, and thematic meditations.[13] Almost exactly at the halfway point of the film, the chronological rhythm and narration by Eisner are broken by an extended passage—titled by day and date: Sunday, June 24, 1979—in which we observe a gathering of some of Eisner's friends and admirers, communing affectionately around a lunch table. The film closes with footage of Venetian canals, streets, and a piazza, all strangely deserted, and a voice-over that recounts a recurring dream, presumably Eisner's, in which she is young again and waltzes in Venice with Nijinsky.[14]

A tribute to Eisner, but also the fashioning of what Hamid Naficy has called a "narrative home" in her story of exile, trauma, nostalgia, and ultimately of belonging, Shahid Saless's film reads both as an extended, comfortable conversation between friends and a meditation on and mediation of the meanings of displacement on his part.[15] Grasping at a stylistic description of the profoundly compassionate, bittersweet tone of the film, I have found Naficy's concept of an "accented cinema" useful; in spite of its origins in observations about narrative film, it can be meaningfully extended to documentary in this instance. Within Naficy's taxonomy of the "accented structures of feeling," a handful of key markers of a cinema of exile resonate strongly with Shahid Saless's documentary: nostalgia, the trope of the outsider, a critically reflexive stance, epistolarity, autobiographical rumination, and attention to displacement on multiple registers.

Among these, the divergences between Shahid Saless's film and Horowitz's are most evident in terms of nostalgia and historiography, the thematic mediation of outsiders and outsider status, and what Naficy describes as the "privileged chronotopes" of a cinema of exile. According to Naficy, the quality of nostalgia evinced by exile cinema is both thematic and stylistic: "Sadness, loneliness, and alienation are frequent themes, and sad, lonely, and alienated people are favorite characters in accented films. Only when the return to the homeland is found to be impossible, illusory, or undesirable, does the postmodernist semiosis set in. Then the nostalgia for the referent and the pain of separation from it may be transformed into a nostalgia for its synecdoches, fetishes, and signifieds—the frozen sounds and images of the homeland."[16] While it would be a stretch to define Eisner primarily as a sad, lonely, or alienated person, there is a marked difference in the way the past figures in Shahid Saless's film versus Horowitz's. In particular, the ways Eisner's early career and the milieu of 1920s Berlin are represented and framed in each film speak to divergent conceptions of what exactly was lost and the affective qualities of that loss. In Shahid Saless's film, the twenties are narrated through Eisner's career during the period: she recounts her transition from academia to journalism and from theater to film criticism. As she describes reaching her stride as a journalist in the early thirties, Shahid Saless cuts to archival footage of Joseph Goebbels speaking and of the state-sponsored vandalism of Jewish-owned businesses. Eisner's experiences during the twenties are arrayed in a sequence emphasizing her frustrations and the fragility of the social and political fabric into which they were woven. An irretrievable, irredeemable past is thematized in terms of interruption, discontinuity, and loss.

Horowitz's film, by contrast, proceeds without strict chronological order, its associative narrative structure held together by Topping's voice-over, which provides contextual information and transitions. Eisner's narration is broken into roughly seven sections, each organized around a key anecdote. These anecdotes all relate to signal memories of her interactions with famous friends and acquaintances, offering irreverent, humorous sketches of their subjects. She recounts meeting Bertolt Brecht and reading the handwritten draft of *Baal* he had given to a friend of Eisner's he was wooing. She retells the story of seeing Louise Brooks reading Schopenhauer on Pabst's set, perhaps as a pretext for mentioning their close friendship in the postwar period, and spins a somewhat far-fetched yarn about being invited by Leni Riefenstahl to tea with Hitler, saying she declined but later wished she had gone, in order to slip poison into his drink. She declaims from memory a few verses of Paul Verlaine's "La Chanson de Gaspard Hauser," and says that a similar performance inspired Herzog's film. The usual stories about meeting Henri Langlois and his antics at the CF are also trotted out. Film stills and photographs are used to illustrate the people and activities Eisner invokes, and the documentary is punctuated by four sequences during which Topping provides a summary, transition, or explanatory aside over a long shot of Parisian city- and riverscapes, with the occasional intercession of the musical soundtrack.

One of the fundamental differences between the two films lies in how they hail the past: it's a difference in historiographical terms. Both films contain a key passage in which Eisner directly addresses the question of nostalgia and her relationship to Germany, yet the way each director deploys this passage indicates radically different interpretations of its significance. Hewing almost verbatim to the same expressions and sentiments in each version, Eisner remarks that having reached her eighties it strikes her as somewhat odd that she feels no connection to Germany per se, but rather to German culture and to certain young German filmmakers. Horowitz chose to place this remark close to the beginning of his film, and it serves as a springboard for the first passage about her experience of Berlin during the twenties. The effect of this placement is that Eisner's nostalgia takes on a regressive cast, fetishizing the period as halcyon and thereby isolating it. Shahid Saless, on the other hand, places these remarks in the final moments of the film, in a section titled, "Longing for the Past." Here, they reverberate in unresolved, even plaintive tones; her displacement is foregrounded and her (be)longing is contextualized as the product not of a fondness for the good old days but of being buffeted about by cataclysmic shocks to her political, social, and economic status.

On this last point, Naficy's observations about the outsider status of the exile describe Shahid Saless's approach well: "The authority of the exiles as filmmaking authors is derived from their position as subjects inhabiting interstitial spaces and sites of struggle. Indeed, all great authorship is predicated on distance—banishment and exile of sorts—from the larger society.

The resulting tensions and ambivalences produce the complexity and the intensity that are so characteristic of great works of art and literature."¹⁷ This characterization resonates with Shahid Saless's film on two levels: both in terms of the place of *Die langen Ferien der Lotte H. Eisner* within his oeuvre and in terms of Eisner's own narrative of identity, which is predominated in her telling by the trope of the outsider. As a child who struggled with social and familial expectations of her gender performance; as a woman, however ambivalently, in the male-dominated professions of academia and journalism during the twenties; as a historian of ancient Greek art on the editorial staff of a bracingly contemporary film industry trade paper; as an assimilated Jew; as a German naturalized only as of late middle age in France; and as a film scholar among cinephiles: Eisner's work throughout her life was characterized by nothing so much as being both attuned to and bedeviled by the difficulties of outsider status in her social and professional networks.

For Horowitz, by contrast, the selection, arrangement, and contextualization of Eisner's anecdotes work to produce an image of her status as perpetual insider from the twenties onward. *Lotte Eisner in Germany* is, in effect, an animated autograph book, in large part because of the ways the voice-over frames each anecdote, highlighting the illustrious subjects of her recollections rather than the thematic, historical, or personal resonances that the Shahid Saless film identifies. This view of Eisner's status and authority dovetails with Herzog's narrative of his own anointment, one in which Horowitz was likewise invested: that is, the importance of emphasizing Eisner's connections to interwar luminaries over her own story in all its particularities, and her body of work in all its subtleties, is that her endorsement of contemporary filmmakers can then take on a certain gravitas. Joan Scott has invoked the term "fantasy echo" to describe the elective affinities involved in narrating the self as part of an intellectual or political lineage.¹⁸ According to Scott, when an actor in the present calls upon foremothers and -fathers, it is both necessarily an aspirational move, and one that selectively ignores certain irreducible differences. Herzog, by virtue of existing in and responding to a distinct historical moment, cannot be considered except on an abstract level a peer of, say, Murnau's, and in this way his avowal of continuity can be understood, fundamentally, as an act of historical narration, of historiography.

This brings us to the final key feature of the stylistic rubric and an interesting reversal of roles. Within Naficy's formulation, the prevalence of "privileged chronotopes" in the cinema of exile reflects the "rupture of displacement." According to Naficy,

> Accented films encode, embody, and imagine the home, exile, and transitional sites in certain privileged chronotopes that link the inherited space-time of the homeland to the constructed space-time of the exile and diaspora. One typical media response to the rupture of displacement is to create a utopian prelapsarian chronotope of the homeland that is uncontaminated by contemporary facts.... The rendition of life in exile, too, initially tends to be just as cathected with dislocatory affect, but it is manifested in dystopian and dysphoric imagining of the contemporary times.[19]

A key to the difference between the ways these two films at hand approach Eisner, her displacement, and her status at the time of filming is suggested by their two titles: *Lotte Eisner in Germany* versus *Die langen Ferien der Lotte H. Eisner* (*The Long Vacation of Lotte H. Eisner*). The former indicates a privileged chronotope—a fixed, static, and storied past—whereas the latter gestures, somewhat ironically, toward an ongoing present. Both films reveal the origins of the phrase in a conversation Eisner had with her brother-in-law, Eugène, upon arriving in 1933 in Paris. Yet, importantly, the melancholy spirit of this quip permeates Shahid Saless's film, whereas it is a passing remark left to the voice-over in Horowitz's. And while Horowitz's film ultimately offers an unambiguously celebratory take on Eisner's experience of the interwar years, Shahid Saless's film holds both the light and the shade of her life in Berlin and in exile steadily within view, refusing to cast her past or her present as utopian or dystopian, choosing instead to emphasize the dissonance, the uncertainty, and the fundamentally surprising and discontinuous nature of experience on a granular level.

In Shahid Saless's film, unlike Horowitz's, we see Eisner interacting with a circle of admiring friends and quietly taking in a summer afternoon. Here, rather than submit to being regaled by her, we (with Shahid Saless) observe Eisner. We glimpse a small part of her world in motion, instead of that portion in amber. This sequence, in which Shahid Saless's film departs from Naficy's model, also functions powerfully as a statement on the nature of belonging; in it, Eisner is part of a chosen family of filmmakers and artists, perhaps a reflection of what Shahid Saless saw in and around her. In this sense, the film testifies to what was lost—a career, a home, a German Jewish narrative of assimilation and history—by Eisner when she was uprooted in 1933, and later, even more violently, in 1941, yet it also bears witness to the belonging, on an affective register, that she found late in life within the very circles in which Shahid Saless himself craved to be included. Horowitz, as Herzog's deputy, works to stabilize a distinct and fixed view of Eisner's status as a mythic figure belonging, in a proprietary sense, to a bygone era, whose relevance to the present is predicated on her power to endow those to whom the present belongs, in that same sense, with authority and cultural capital.

If Shahid Saless were in some important and deeply generative ways unmoored as he began working in Germany in the mid-seventies, one powerful opportunity for connection with his peers in Europe, particularly the New German Cinema group, would have been his friendship with Eisner. Membership in the cluster of young filmmakers orbiting Eisner may have promised the nebulous belonging that escaped Shahid Saless during this period. In this way, we might see both Shahid Saless's own experience and his aspirations reflected in the way Eisner is depicted, and the way her story is edited, framed, and interpreted by his documentary. Horowitz takes a more direct approach toward Eisner as CF elder, and he reinforces the narrative often recounted by Herzog, Langlois, and others in the introductory and explanatory voice-over sections: Eisner was less a cofounder than a steadfast assistant to Langlois as he built the CF.

Langlois, Herzog, Horowitz, and others share a certain amount of the credit for propagating and popularizing this version of history. Yet, if Eisner had taken a different tack or had rejected this narrative of the CF's and her own history, perhaps the story might not have sufficed for so long. In spite of the fact that certain of Eisner's peers were remarkably prolific self-promoters, and that her status as a single, "foreign" woman who worked to earn a living undoubtedly contributed to the way she talked about herself and her own accomplishments, the degree to which Eisner is a predictable, consistent supporting character in the histories she narrates is notable. And while many of her peers in the world of interwar German film journalism used publications based on or comprised of their newspaper work as their tickets out of Nazi Germany, Eisner started over in France, and this extensive body of work from the late twenties and early thirties has been largely overlooked since then, in no small part because of the dismissive remarks she herself offered on it.

Perhaps the most striking example of this disparagement lies in the last pages of her memoirs, in an exchange between Martje Grohmann and Eisner in which Grohmann asserts that she took the liberty of perusing all of the back issues containing Eisner's work at the *Film-Kurier*, and that she found it consisted almost exclusively of "insignificant, marginal crap" (*kleinen Scheißdreck am Rande*) compared to the juicier, more substantive assignments given to Eisner's male peers.[20] If Grohmann really did look through all of Eisner's work at the *Film-Kurier*, I struggle to understand how she could have made such a characterization; if, instead, she was repeating back her impression of Eisner's own take on it, it strikes me as a measure of the degree to which Eisner had internalized and rationalized the disparity in recognition between those male peers and herself. These remarks are offered in the book's forty-third chapter, titled, "Misogyny," which runs only a little over two pages. In it, Eisner tells Grohmann that she doesn't think there is a contradiction between her own misogyny and her anti-racism; she thinks that feminism ends up ghettoizing women and the work they do and that her resistance to such marginalization is consistent across religion, race, and gender. Moreover, she says, she had been poorly done by many women over the course of her career, especially in the early days, and didn't think the same could be said of men. Disavowing the work and leaning into the social details of her interwar life might have been easier than continuing to fight for recognition and equal treatment on the basis of her writing, and over time, perhaps it made more sense to stake a claim elsewhere and to invoke the interwar work as a foil.

So, too, the disintegration and brutalization of the institutions and networks she came up through in the twenties and thirties may help explain her willingness to narrate her later life so emphatically in terms of the CF and the New German Cinema movement. To a significant degree, the currency of both of these realms was a kind of performative cinephilia—articulated in explicit opposition to self-consciously intellectual film study—and Herzog and the disciples of Langlois were less interested in the kind of rigorous industrial and aesthetic analysis Eisner honed in the interwar period with her journalistic work than they were in the social networks and cultural capital of their own moment. The narratives about Eisner propagated by Eisner herself, as well as by Grohmann, Horowitz, Herzog, Roud, and others fixate on questions of influence and authority, defining her achievements in terms of her role as a tastemaker, mentor, and critic. As a result they elide the discontinuities in her narratives of identity; the unfulfilled potential of her early work; and the importance of trauma, recuperation, and salvage to Eisner's postwar work. Shahid Saless's film demonstrates how Eisner's postwar career was imbricated with these traumas by framing her early career in terms of the interruptions and disjunctures that shaped it. In this way, in spite of the fact that the second half of the film largely conforms to the received wisdom about her work at the CF, Shahid Saless suggests an approach to understanding the breadth and significance of Eisner's legacy.

TOWARD A GLEANER'S HISTORIOGRAPHY

In spite of conforming to a chronological, quasi biographical narrative structure in this study, I have attempted to shift the weight of inquiry, in order to avoid falling back on either the logics of hagiography or what Bishnupriya Ghosh has called the "additive model of historical recuperation where one more marginal community is 'found' through exemplary historiographical antics."[21] Eisner's work lies squarely within the wheelhouse of Weimar cinema studies, and it hasn't been neglected for reasons contemporary scholars are apt to own; simply moving to install Eisner in the disciplinary pantheon runs some risk of reinscribing those logics, be they endemic or inadvertent. Due to the relatively recent consolidation and institutionalization of film studies as an academic discipline—which is often dated in the US context to the 1970s—many contemporary scholars in the field either lived through the founding battles for resources, institutional support, and legitimacy, or they were trained and mentored by the people who did. The field experienced extraordinary latitude in its early years of growth, and in many of its institutional incarnations it has been the beneficiary of insights, methodologies, and solidarities with the diverse and vital peer disciplines that are its intellectual siblings and older cousins, including art history and literary studies; cultural history; ethnic and area studies; and feminist, sexuality, and gender studies.

Yet in addition to the privileges of youth, the field bears some of its burdens; it has taken some time for academic film study to not only grow into or tailor the awkward fit of borrowed and hand-me-down methodologies, epistemologies, and heuristics from its institutional relatives, but to fashion ideas and histories of its own. I submit that in addition to being different—in sometimes generative, sometimes risky ways—from most of her contemporaries throughout her life and her several careers, Eisner continues to cut a rather unusual figure in the present. Therefore, instead of performing the antics of "finding" Eisner, in the mode Ghosh cautions against, I have worked to tease apart some of the rationales by which her work had been siloed off. In reflecting on larger institutional, cultural, and historical forces that have acted on Eisner's legacy, as well as on the individuals who have described that legacy in influential ways, I've considered Shelley Stamp's call for "composite" approaches in feminist media historiography: "The close, careful archival histories produced by feminist historians . . . represent some of the very best scholarship on silent cinema and some of the strongest feminist research in the field. However, meticulous case studies of individual women and discrete historical moments have done little to disrupt conventional histories. They remain on a parallel track, interesting footnotes to the central story."[22] In this particular case, the challenge has been to demonstrate that, beyond filling a gap in the existing record, this study offers methods and findings that can do this work of disruption, of motivating intersection and interchange among previously parallel tracks.

The question of what relevance Eisner's work has for film studies today is an interesting and important one. Too important, in my view, to limit the scope of inquiry to a single category of her work, or a single contemporary branch of film study, not least because in fragmenting her work and selecting a concept, tool, or source of Eisner's in particular to be placed in conversation with today's discourse, there is some danger of losing sight of the historical specificity and interrelatedness of her contributions to a number of now-distinct domains of film study. Efforts such as Michael Wedel's to make the case for Eisner's relevance by positioning her work in the intellectual genealogy of cognitive film theory or film philosophies of world-building, while intriguing in certain ways, do Eisner's legacy a disservice by implying that minor recurrent terms deployed in her work, such as *Stimmung* and *Umwelt*—which had been theorized at length well before she invoked them and have continued to be debated in rarefied ways—constitute the work's most interesting or sophisticated aspects.[23] Not only did Eisner's usage of these particular terms change over the course of her lifetime, but she signaled different valences at each juncture by citing different sources and discourses nearly every time. The case for recollecting Eisner and her work, I fear, will leave readers cold if it is built on a wobbly line of citation and reference from a small handful of postwar publications and qualified with the assessment that, at any rate, she falls short of consideration as a "full-blown film theorist."[24] Defining in-groups in this way and limiting their membership in order to more highly concentrate the glamour that is accorded to initiates and entailed, in turn, upon their chroniclers, is a fundamentally conservative impulse, a gate-keeping ritual used to allocate institutional space and reinforce rigid intellectual genealogies.

In thinking about how Eisner related to her own time—especially when trying to understand the nimbus of associated meanings or affinities a particular citation might have suggested in the moment of their invocation—I have looked to Raymond Williams's guidance, in particular the argument he makes in *The Long Revolution* about the paradoxical nature of historiography: "We learn each element as a precipitate, but in the living experience of the time every element was in solution, an inseparable part of a complex whole."[25] For Williams, the historian's desk is a floodplain strewn with remains of the antediluvian, from which the manifold complexities of a liquid, teeming past must be extrapolated. In this model, the spectral and speculative alone perambulate, and while such an approach has been enormously generative, particularly in writing the histories of colonialism, slavery, and dispossession, a somewhat different approach is called for in the present case. Eisner was nourished by what she salvaged, and acknowledging the vitality, both extant and latent, of those remainders can extend and potentially enrich a model such as Williams's. Lyman Ward, the eminent fictional historian and protagonist of Wallace Stegner's *Angle of Repose*, offers a useful foil for the model I propose. Opining, as is his wont, on the noble, masculine craft—his/toriography, perhaps—Ward boasts of the historian's tenacity, his forbearance of the trivial and the womanly in his pursuit of useful facts:

> I have heard publishers, lamenting their hard life over Scotch and soda, complain that they must read a hundred bad manuscripts to find one good one. Having practiced the trade of history, I feel no stir of sympathy. A historian scans a thousand documents to find one fact that he can use. If he is working with correspondence, as I am, and with the correspondence of a woman to boot, he will wade toward his little islands of information through a dismal swamp of recipes, housekeeping details, children's diseases, insignificant visitors, inconclusive conversations with people unknown to the historian, and recitations of what the writer did yesterday.[26]

To the august, condescending Ward, such "islands" might be: industrial capitalism's predations; famous visitors to his grandmother's western salon; their conclusive conversations? Adult diseases? Ward's vision is, from this angle, what I described as "straight historiography" in my discussion of Eisner's reputation as a witness: Ward's his/toriography is a photo negative of the feminist and queer historiography that guided my own approach to Eisner. A history of the swamp, in contrast to that of the islands, is a history of collectives, networks, roots, and weeds; it requires a historiographical approach that takes as a given the interdependence of such ecosystems, the richness of women's work, and the temporal, performative dimensions of the maligned "recitation" of gendered, quotidian experience.

Historiography thus reframed becomes the work of gleaners, turning over the fragments left after the harvest and attempting to make of them something restorative in the present, taking inspiration from Agnès Varda's *The Gleaners and I* (*Les glaneurs et la glaneuse*, 2000), in its attention to collective labor, feminist praxis, and the redemptive possibilities of a cinécriture of marginalia. Unlike the detective or the doctor—protagonists of a positivist historiography pitted against the withholding, infirm, often feminized figure of history—I prefer the ambivalence and halting, meandering gait of the gleaner.[27] Pausing to turn the fruits and vegetables of their labor over in dirty palms, with nourishment rather than forensics as their guiding principle, they follow behind the reaper, like Benjamin's historical materialist, and are arrested in their movement by flashes of recognition in a field of loam. While the urgency of Benjamin's eschatology is missing in this model, the explicitly feminist cast of slow scholarship affords alternative epistemologies that neither rehearse the patriarchal tropes of coverture and heredity bound up in genealogical historiography nor foreclose the vivacity of a fissiparous past at hand.[28]

Saidiya Hartman has argued persuasively that archives-based historiography "entails interrogating the production of our knowledge about the past," and that "The task of writing the impossible . . . has as its prerequisites the embrace of likely failure and the readiness to accept the ongoing, unfinished and provisional character of this effort, particularly when the arrangements of power occlude the very object that we desire to rescue."[29] Eisner was privileged, lucky, and tenacious, and she accommodated herself to institutional and intellectual structures of power and influence, at the same time as she resisted them. Yet when we apply the scrutiny that has tended to be reserved for claims about her accomplishments to the areas in which she is presumed—in part based on her own assessments—not to have contributed much of significance, we find that the harvest has left behind a feast. If we are today beginning to see gains in the academy's acceptance of methodologies, archives, and scholars who have until recently been entirely excluded, the discourse of novelty can cut both ways. Historicizing inroads and attending to instances in which such gains were subsequently undermined or overturned—what Stamp calls "vengeful forgetting"—may help us maintain the readiness Hartman recommends, to nourish and sustain such a self-reflexive trajectory.

One of the unanswerable questions haunting this study is what a stable, salaried institutional berth in the United States would have changed about Eisner's work. Asking why Eisner didn't come to the United States for safe harbor in the 1930s like so many of her colleagues and compatriots runs some risk of erroneously implying that their trajectory was natural or inevitable; yet she had similar credentials, if not the necessary social connections, to several of the most famous exiled film scholars in the United States during the postwar period, including Siegfried Kracauer and Rudolf Arnheim.[30] In the absence of curatorial work, would Eisner have extended her writing and thinking in directions only hinted at in the work she did produce? Would she have developed her thesis about the relationship between the aesthetics of interwar German film and its production culture into that long-promised stand-alone volume focused on art directors? Without the pressure of daily administrative and organizational work at the CF, would she, like Arnheim, have written and thought more expansively, more "obstinately" about aesthetic theory, perhaps expounding on a theory of the kinetic, sequence-oriented visual analysis she favored, as opposed to the plot- or author-oriented stylistic analysis adopted from literary studies by some early practitioners of scholarly film studies? Would she have taken up the question of Nazi film historiography in more programmatic, perhaps more readily recognizable terms had she been working elbow-to-elbow with Kracauer, Thomas Mann, or Hannah Arendt?

Would she have returned to her *Film-Kurier* era work on production culture, exploring her interest in labor, effects, and style in the industrial or independent film milieux? We've seen Eisner's countering of Arnheim's praise for Maya Deren, but what kind of rebuttal might she have offered to Hortense Powdermaker's bleak take on the means and ends of control, manipulation, and agency in industrial film production? I am particularly intrigued by the dissonance between Eisner's lifelong interest in experimentation, persuasion, and creativity in the producer-audience relationship and Powdermaker's infamous assessment, not so unlike Kracauer's (or Adorno and Horkheimer's) in its pessimism, that "In Hollywood, the concept of man as a passive creature to be manipulated extends to those who work for the studios, to personal and social relationships, to the audiences in the theaters and to the characters in the movies. The basic freedom of being able to choose between alternatives is absent. The gifted people who have the capacity for choice cannot exercise it; the executives who technically have the freedom of choice do not actually have it, because they usually lack the knowledge and imagination necessary for making such a choice."[31] Eisner, as we have seen, often argued that a lack of imagination and little respect for audiences was the primary impediment to good filmmaking, yet she construed this observation in a critique almost diametrically opposed to

Powdermaker's: Eisner, by contrast with Powdermaker, was an insatiable consumer of films across virtually all stylistic registers and production regimes, and she expressed unreserved hope in the potential of film art for humanistic achievement.

One thing is relatively certain: research and writing time remaining equal, swapping her administrative and organizational work at the Cinémathèque française for more stable and better-remunerated administrative and pedagogical work at an academic institution in the United States could hardly have increased her publishing productivity in pure numbers, even if it is likely that such a scenario would have shifted the venues, languages, and registers of discourse in which she published. The subsequent reception of her work has been clouded by a number of factors, including the field's patterns and norms of citation, her work's accessibility to English-language readers, and its exposure to criticism. This exposure has had a measurably corrosive effect; indeed, I show that weathering—which follows gendered, linguistic, class-, race-, and citizenship-based channels—was largely a function of her work's emergence early in the development of the field. Film scholars working to establish a profile in Weimar cinema studies have often focused on demonstrating that her work is superannuated, rather than on trying to understand the ways it was bound up in the circumstances of her life.

If we read Eisner carefully and take her cues as to which discourses, which scholars she intended to address or debate with her work, we can see, for example, that *The Haunted Screen* is hardly an art historical helpmate to *From Caligari to Hitler*, unworthy of substantive critique on its own terms, as has been so often assumed. Upon attentive rereading, it becomes clear that *The Haunted Screen* is part and parcel of Eisner's archival salvage work, her anti-fascist and anti-war arts journalism, as well as her curatorial and critical advocacy for young filmmakers. I have also argued that Eisner's archival work and the scholarship that emerged out of it are clarified with reference to contemporary work in queer historiography and archive studies in terms not only of her commitments to foregrounding and celebrating marginalized artists and communities, but also in terms of her belonging in these social worlds and her traumatic experience of exile.

It is my further contention that the *Film-Kurier* work should be better known, given the prominent place her byline occupied in this influential publication; her contributions to the paper flesh out existing understanding of the vibrant early film and media discourse in the trade press and offer entry points to still-unexplored trajectories in the intellectual history of the field today. Indeed, although I reviewed the entirety of this corpus, there were a number of important and interesting threads I could not, for reasons of space and my own lack of the necessary expertise, take up. I did not, for instance, discuss Eisner's theater criticism, reportage, and commentary in relation to her film journalism, although this comprises a substantial portion of her work at the *Film-Kurier*. Her theater coverage is of historical interest in that she comments contemporaneously and in detail about important historical productions and producers, and the impact of political and economic change on state-funded theatrical art and artists. In addition, it was articulated, as I indicated with respect to her film criticism, from a vantage point that differed in crucial ways from that of the better-known Berlin theater critics, including Alfred Kerr and Herbert Ihering, as well as her colleagues who worked, as she did, across film and theater criticism, like Willy Haas, Hans Feld, and Ernst Jäger, all of whom have been the subject of much critical interest on the part of contemporary scholars of interwar German cinema. Moreover, it plainly informed her postwar writing on filmmakers such as Ernst Lubitsch and inspired her most perceptive and nuanced rebuttals to contemporaneous models of film stylistic analytics propounded by her French colleagues and US-based peers.

Eisner's interwar writing on film spectatorship, on exhibition, on educational films and filmmaking curriculum, as well as her travel writing all beg to be examined in greater detail and placed in conversation, not only with the usual suspects—Rudolf Arnheim, Béla Balázs, and Siegfried Kracauer—but with the work of other women who worked as film critics and journalists in the interwar period, such as Iris Barry, Winifred Bryher, Colette, C. A. Lejeune, and Louise Straus-Ernst. Indeed, Eisner cited both Barry and Lejeune's film criticism in positive terms, suggesting that a comparative study articulating such alternative constellations in the intellectual history of interwar film discourse draws strength not only from present-day contexts and calls for revision to the largely male-dominated histories of early film journalism, but also from real relationships of reading and citation among these women. Additionally, Eisner's interwar journalism reflected and participated in contemporary debates on the German left about antiracism, political and aesthetic praxis, and Jewish assimilation. Her interest in the anti-Black racism of Hollywood films, which she relates to German fascism via eugenics and anti-Semitism, was likely influenced by larger discourses on the German left of the interwar period that placed the Soviet and US approaches to race, class, and art in tension, refracting the domestic political and economic conflict of the Weimar Republic. In my discussion of her *Film-Kurier* film criticism and her postwar work on Murnau, I gesture at some of the ways Eisner's commentary about the relations between European and non-European people—in economic, affective, and political terms—suggest an ambivalent, likely class- and race-bound attitude toward decolonization, sexuality, and power. Particularly in light of her postwar work of salvage, I think the question of Eisner's emphatically positive, yet deeply prejudiced commentary about the work of certain non-European filmmakers is worth reading for its investments in race, class, and colonial relations.

Wary of recuperative reading for its own sake, I nevertheless maintain that the self-reflexive, considered approach outlined here as a gleaner's historiography is well suited to the tasks of discerning the mechanisms by which an intellectual history of film studies that downplayed Eisner's achievements and influence operated, demonstrating the inconsistencies in those logics and the oversights that have resulted from them. In offering a more holistic view of her career, in reading her work with the same care and interest that has long been lavished on the work of some of her peers, and with an eye toward what has been left behind in previous waves of scholarly Weimar film historiography, I have hoped to whet the appetites of feminist media historiographers, not just for Eisner's work, but for the kind of historiographical work that asks what more there is to be learned today from other sources, forebears, or lineages that have been discarded and selected against.

APPENDIX

Film-Kurier Bibliography, by the Numbers

All charts created by the author, based on the author's complete catalog of Lotte Eisner's *Film-Kurier* bibliography.

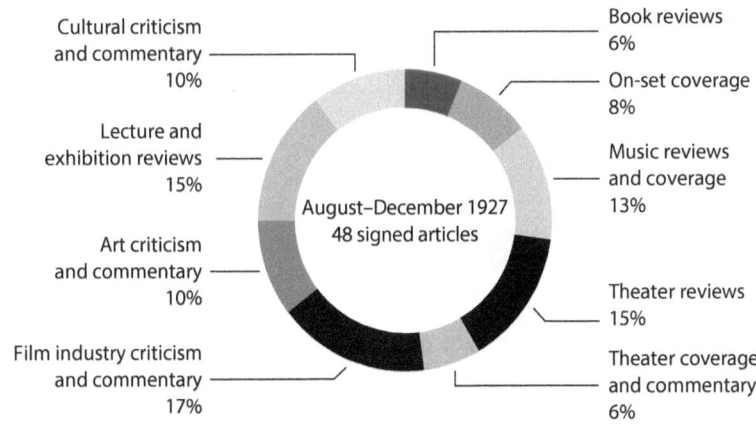

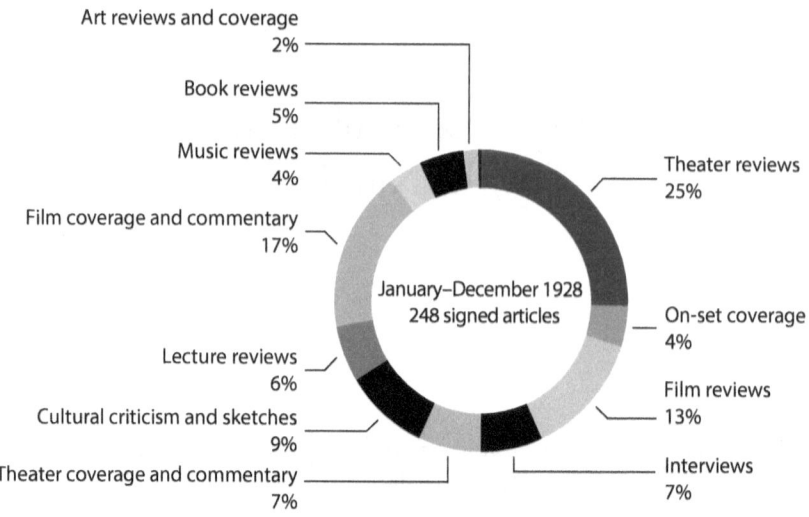

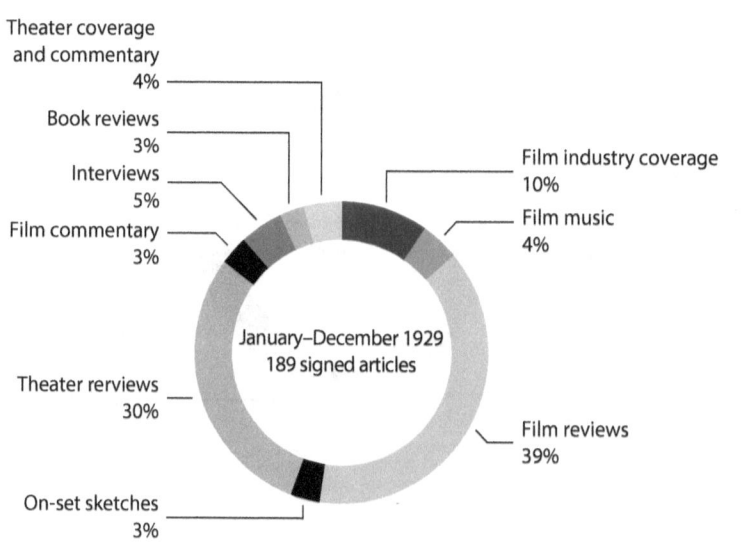

164 • APPENDIX

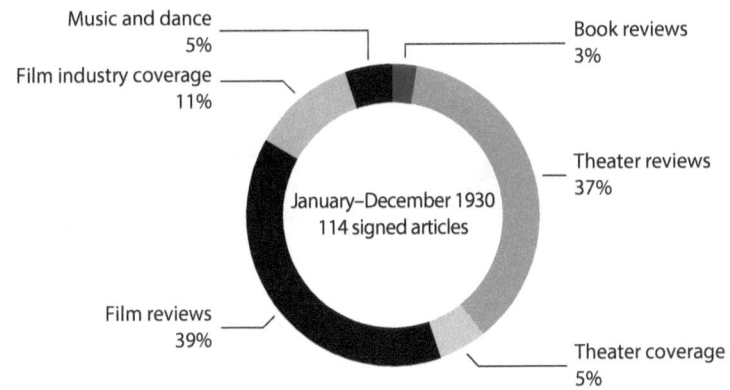

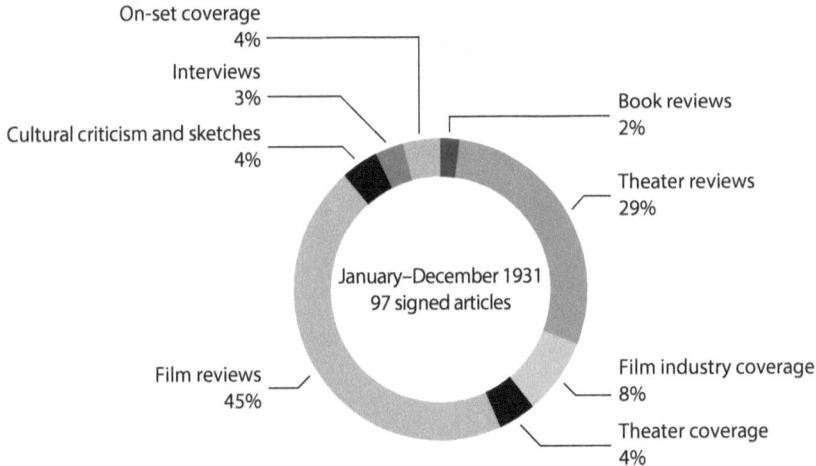

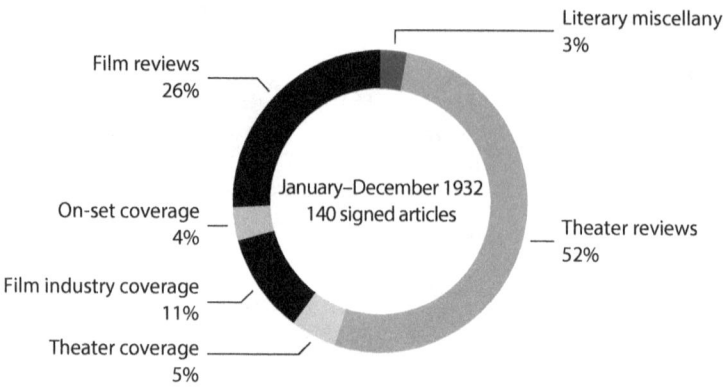

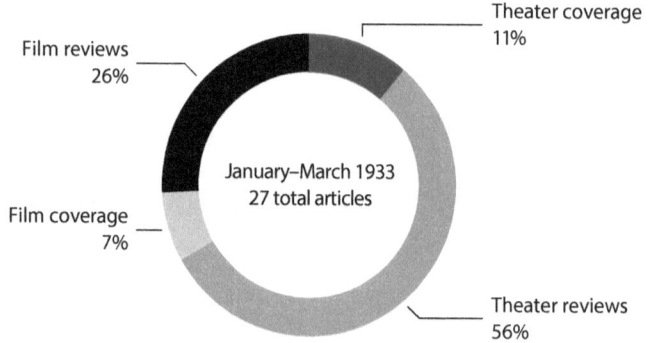

166 • APPENDIX

NOTES

INTRODUCTION

1. Lotte Eisner, *Ich hatte einst ein schönes Vaterland* (Heidelberg: Wunderhorn, 1984), 291. Grohmann was married to—and made the acquaintance of Eisner through—Werner Herzog. They were amicably separated during the time she cared for Eisner, and they later divorced.

2. Jeffrey Herf, *Reactionary Modernism: Technology, Culture, and Politics in Weimar and the Third Reich* (Cambridge: Cambridge University Press, 1984).

3. These include Thomas Elsaesser, *Weimar Cinema and After: Germany's Historical Imaginary* (London: Routledge, 2000), Tim Bergfelder, Erica Carter, and Deniz Göktürk, eds., *The German Cinema Book* (London: BFI, 2003), Dietrich Scheunemann, ed., *Expressionist Film: New Perspectives* (Rochester, NY: Camden House, 2003), Anton Kaes, *Shell Shock Cinema* (Princeton, NJ: Princeton University Press, 2009), Noah Isenberg, *Weimar Cinema: An Essential Guide to the Classic Films of the Era* (New York: Columbia University Press, 2009), and Stephen Brockmann, *A Critical History of German Film* (Rochester, NY: Camden House, 2010).

4. Sabine Hake, *German National Cinema* (New York: Routledge, 2002), viii.

5. Noah Isenberg, "Review," *Monatshefte* 98, no. 1 (2006): 153.

6. Indeed, Lenssen mistakenly reports that Eisner began writing again first in 1950, and she demonstrates only a little familiarity with the postwar publications aside from *L'écran démoniaque*, *Murnau*, and *Fritz Lang*. Claudia Lenssen, "'Die Klassiker': Die Rezeption von Lotte H. Eisner und Siegfried Kracauer," in *Recherche: Film. Quellen und Methoden der Filmforschung*, ed. Hans-Michael Bock and Wolfgang Jacobsen (Munich: edition text + kritik, 1997), 67–82.

7. Elsaesser, *Weimar Cinema and After*, 21; see footnotes 18 and 19 to his second chapter, "Expressionist Film or Weimar Cinema? With Siegfried Kracauer and Lotte Eisner (Once More) to the Movies."

8. Elsaesser, *Weimar Cinema and After*, 51, 25.

9. Elsaesser, *Weimar Cinema and After*, 37.

10. "One of the secrets of the success of the classical German film was the perfect technical harmony achieved by long *Regiensitzungen*, discussions on the mise-en-scène of the film to be made which sometimes lasted for two months or more before the actual filming began, and to which the director invited everybody due to work on the film, from the chief designer and chief cameraman to the workmen in charge of the lighting. . . . At these *Regiensitzungen* everyone was heard; like everybody else, the cameraman could ask for changes in the sets if he thought he saw a way of achieving a better result." Eisner, *The Haunted Screen*, 36–37.

11. Lotte Eisner, *F. W. Murnau* (London: Secker & Warburg, 1973), 7; Lotte Eisner, *Fritz Lang* (London: Secker & Warburg, 1976), 8.

12. Elsaesser, *Weimar Cinema and After*, 36. Elsaesser's dismissive, indirect reference to *Kunstwollen* undermines the claims he makes to originality at Eisner's expense. He works entirely within Alois Riegl's formulation of *Kunstwollen* when he states that, in contrast to Eisner's, his approach operates under "another paradigm altogether: that of style as design, and of design as at once a form of disguise and enhancement, suggesting that so-called 'Expressionism' in Weimar cinema has determinate modernising or constructivist functions, creating for the cinema a space not only among the arts but making it a vehicle also of the emergent lifestyle technologies and leisure industries, such as fashion, decor and display." As we'll see, not only is this actually a simple instantiation of *Kunstwollen*, Elsaesser protests too much: while she, too, was deeply influenced by Riegl's ideas, Eisner never actually invokes the term in *The Haunted Screen*. The confusion suggested by this muddling of *Kunstwollen* and auteur theory—independently of the fact that it isn't an accurate summary of Eisner's work—is indicative of larger problems with Elsaesser's preemptive stance vis-à-vis Eisner.

13. Hake, *German National Cinema*, 27.

14. Namely, Asta Nielsen, Greta Garbo, and Louise Brooks. Discussing the latter—in a passage that resonates strongly with her analysis of *The Joyless Street* (*cf.* 256–63)—Eisner remarks, "Pabst's remarkable evolution must . . . be seen as an encounter with an actress who needed no directing, but could move across the screen causing the work of art to be born by her mere presence." Eisner, *The Haunted Screen* (Berkeley: University of California Press, 2008), 296.

15. Eisner, *The Haunted Screen*, 298.

16. Siegfried Kracauer, *From Caligari to Hitler* (Princeton, NJ: Princeton University Press, 1947), 178–79.

17. Kracauer, *From Caligari to Hitler*, 99.

18. This passage is also representative in that Kracauer makes indirect reference, with the phrase, "instinctive reluctance to attempt emancipation," to Erich Fromm's *Escape from Freedom* (New York: Farrar & Rinehart, 1941), one of the key points of reference for *From Caligari to Hitler*. As throughout the book, Kracauer suggests that such an inclination in German men is less a matter of interpretation than of fact.

19. Eisner commented at length in private correspondence and occasionally in interviews about the vagaries of translation and the degree to which she ultimately found it necessary to supervise the translation of her work. Kracauer's difficulties

with English have been discussed at some length in the secondary literature; see in particular, Johannes von Moltke and Kristy Rawson, *Siegfried Kracauer's American Writings* (Berkeley: University of California Press, 2012) and Anton Kaes, "Siegfried Kracauer: Film Historian in Exile," in *Escape to Life: German Intellectuals in New York*, ed. Eckart Goebel and Sigrid Weigel (Berlin: de Gruyter, 2013).

20. Leonardo Quaresima, "Introduction to the 2004 Edition: Rereading Kracauer," in Siegfried Kracauer, *From Caligari to Hitler: A Psychological Study of the German Film* (Princeton, NJ: Princeton University Press, 2004). By supplements, I mean those written by editors, commentators, and the like. The materials appended to the main body of *The Haunted Screen*—the foreword to the English language edition, the summary of the *Dreigroschenoper* lawsuit, the film- and bibliographies, and all end matter—were all authored by Eisner herself.

21. Barry Salt, "From Caligari to Who?," *Sight and Sound* 48, no. 2 (1979): 119–23.

22. Eisner, *The Haunted Screen*, 47.

23. She had already covered these themes, respectively, in *The Haunted Screen*, 260–63, and 39–44; in "Les origines de style Lubitsch," *La Revue du Cinéma* 17 (September 1948): 3–15, and *The Haunted Screen*, 82 and 309–11; *The Haunted Screen*, 36–37, 207–22, and her monograph on the director, *F. W. Murnau*, which had been available for fifteen years in French (six years in English) prior to Salt's article. The unique German production system and its effects on style are discussed extensively in Eisner's interwar journalism, as well as virtually all of her postwar scholarship, including her 1947 "Notes sur le style de Fritz Lang," *La Revue du cinéma* 5 (February 1947): 3–26, *The Haunted Screen* (see especially 36–37 on the *Regiensitzungen*), and her monographs on Murnau and Fritz Lang (the latter first published in English three years in advance of Salt's article).

24. Salt, "From Caligari to Who?," 121.

25. Elsaesser, *Weimar Cinema and After*, 234–35.

26. Elsaesser, *Weimar Cinema and After*, 223.

27. A similar spirit informs the textual analysis offered throughout the book, which emphatically reinscribes male anxiety and subjectivity as the engine of stylistic and narrative signification for Weimar cinema at large, in spite of decades of feminist film theory and history that has persuasively argued against such parochial optics. Glaring examples of Elsaesser's insistent androcentrism include his curt dismissal of attempts to read *The Cabinet of Dr. Caligari* "from Jane's point of view," or his far-fetched take on *Pandora's Box* as properly centering about Alwa; "surely a contentious choice in terms of the plot," he admits, with the unmistakable tone of a goading provocation. According to Elsaesser, "A differently gendered reading [with Lulu at the center] is without pathos" because the film "prevents the (male and female?) viewer from constructing [Lulu] as victim, thus recovering one's emotional investment in her" (Elsaesser, *Weimar Cinema and After*, 272–73).

28. Elsaesser, comparing *The Haunted Screen* and *From Caligari to Hitler*: "On an even more personal level, both exiles also enjoyed patronage, and their books can be understood as addressing their benefactors—Eisner was working for Henri Langlois, and Kracauer wanted to express his gratitude to Iris Barry at MOMA

[*sic*] and the Institute of Social Research, as well as offering his services to the US government." Elsaesser, *Weimar Cinema and After*, 21.

29. See, for examples, Richard Roud, "The Moral Taste of Lotte Eisner," *Sight and Sound* 53, no. 2 (1984): 139–40, Marcel Martin, "De l'archéologie à l'histoire," *Image et son* 377 (November 1982): 127–30, Connie Greenbaum, "Entretien avec Lotte Eisner," *Image et son* 283 (April 1974): 67–69, and Herman Weinberg, "Review: *The Haunted Screen: Expressionism in the German Cinema and the Influence of Max Reinhardt*," *Film Comment* 6, no. 2 (1970): 60–62.

30. Richard Roud, "The Moral Taste of Lotte Eisner," 140.

31. Mannoni, "Kurtz et Eisner: Deux regards sur l'expressionnisme," in *Le cinéma expressionniste: De Caligari à Tim Burton*, ed. Jacques Aumont and Bernard Benoliel (Rennes, France: Presses Universitaires de Rennes, 2008), "Lotte Eisner, historienne des démons allemands," in *Le cinéma expressionniste allemand: Splendeurs d'une collection* (Paris: Éditions de La Martinière / La Cinémathèque française, 2006), and *Histoire de la Cinémathèque française* (Paris: Gallimard, 2006).

32. Indeed, while Eisner's later uses of *Stimmung* and *Umwelt* in *L'écran démoniaque* and *F. W. Murnau* draw explicitly on a lineage of usage through Novalis and Paul Wegener, respectively, Wedel interpolates reference to Heinrich Wölfflin, which, as I indicate in my study of Eisner's dissertation, is not entirely clear in the text itself.

33. Patrick Schollmeyer, "Lotte Eisner: Eine Archäologin als Filmkritikerin," *Thersites* 11 (2020): 324–42.

CHAPTER 1. FRÄULEIN DOKTOR EISNER

1. Lotte Eisner, *Ich hatte einst ein schönes Vaterland: Memoiren* (Heidelberg: Wunderhorn, 1984), 8–9.

2. In "*La seule historienne*," I discuss gossip as rhetorical mode in further detail.

3. Many of Eisner's stories about her family in her memoirs, particularly those about her sister, Steffi, are difficult to verify—for example, because they present accounts of private conversations that took place fifty years prior to the narration of her memoirs, or detail speculations on Eisner's part about a person's inner life—and are so blisteringly caustic that repeating or parsing them here without the benefit of any corroborating accounts or sources would be irresponsible. Other readers of Eisner's memoirs have discounted her credibility as a result of these episodes in which she flays family, colleagues, or acquaintances, arguing that along with the more outlandish tales she recited, they indicate a lack of impartiality and suggest an unreliable narrator. See Sudendorf, "'Nicht zur Öffentlichung': Zur Biographie des Filmjournalisten Ernst (Ejott) Jäger," *Filmexil* 5 (1994): 62. Grohmann's influence on the tone of the memoirs should not be disregarded, and certain flourishes strike me as likely to have been hers. My own rubric for inclusion is as follows: in cases where Eisner's stories deal mainly with her own experiences or illuminate something about how she saw herself or how she hoped she might move in the world, I have considered them.

4. Eisner, *Ich hatte*, 9.

5. Eisner expresses annoyance about her mother's propensity to tie up the telephone for hours talking with her sisters in Eisner, *Ich hatte*, 26; disparaging comments about her mother and sister and the ways Steffi was encouraged to behave, dress, eat, and approach her education are found in Eisner, *Ich hatte*, 12, 17, 18, 23, and 62.

6. Eisner, *Ich hatte*, 82.

7. I place emphasis on these articulations of difference because they correspond to important themes that will emerge over the course of her career and will play a role in the reception of her work during and after her life. I am not advocating here for the interpretation of Eisner's self-identification within contemporary paradigms of gender and sexuality, and it is important to note that, in general, her hostility to such norms did not come from a feminist perspective. On the contrary, Eisner's resentment of the ways gender norms were enforced was often expressed as bilious misogyny, lampooning what she considered typically feminine weaknesses and proclivities. This complicated, idiosyncratic attitude as set forth in her journalism is also discussed in the context of Eisner's work at the *Film-Kurier*.

8. Harriet Pass Freidenreich, *Female, Jewish, and Educated: The Lives of Central European University Women* (Bloomington: Indiana University Press, 2002), 30. Freidenreich's deeply researched study of these women and the educational environment in which they participated provides both the data on women's enrollment and a handful of case studies of university women, primarily women pursuing degrees in the sciences, medicine, and social sciences.

9. Freidenreich cites Schoenberger's memoirs—Margaret Mahler, *The Memoirs of Margaret S. Mahler* (New York: Free Press, 1988), 9—as the source for the quotation reproduced in *Female, Jewish, and Educated*, on page 32.

10. Eisner, *Ich hatte*, 83.

11. Eisner mentions at several junctures throughout her memoirs that while she was a passionate bather, she never learned how to swim; she attributes her love of the outdoors and mountaineering in particular to the influence of her father, Eisner, *Ich hatte*, 15.

12. Eisner, *Ich hatte*, 27.

13. Freidenreich, *Female, Jewish, and Educated*, 18–20 and passim.

14. In her memoirs, she declares: "I know that I have an Elektra complex and therefore I have never had a satisfactory love relationship because I have always compared my lover secretly with my father, and no one could measure up." Eisner, *Ich hatte*, 16. Eisner's brother would go on to pursue a career as a scholar specializing in the work of Heinrich Heine. For some contextual information about Fritz H. Eisner's career, see Jeffrey L. Sammons, "Phases of Heine Scholarship, 1957–1971," *The German Quarterly* 46, no. 1 (January 1973): 56–88.

15. Eisner, *Ich hatte*, 27.

16. Eisner, *Ich hatte*, 29.

17. Freidenreich, *Female, Jewish, and Educated*, 15.

18. Eisner, *Ich hatte*, 47.

19. Freidenreich, *Female, Jewish, and Educated*, 17. For a somewhat broader overview of this historical moment and the significance of Jewish assimilation into the German bourgeoisie at this particular juncture, see Paul Mendes-Flohr, "The Berlin Jew as Cosmopolitan," in *Berlin Metropolis: Jews and the New Culture, 1890–1918*, ed. Emily D. Bilski (Berkeley: University of California Press, 2000), 15–31.

20. Her remarks on the connection between education and assimilation are brief: Eisner, *Ich hatte*, 15.

21. Freidenreich, *Female, Jewish, and Educated*, 207. The figures are as follows: 570 of 22,229 students in 1908–09, 1,686 of 26,140 in 1911–12, and 3,184 of 27,641 in 1924–25.

22. Freidenreich, *Female, Jewish, and Educated*, 207.

23. Freidenreich, *Female, Jewish, and Educated*, 52. Fritz K. Ringer's *The Decline of the German Mandarins* (Cambridge, MA: Harvard University Press, 1969) offers a penetrating analysis of these gatekeeping tactics and reactionary conservatism within the professorate, in spite of Ringer's refusal to address women at German universities during this period, a position on which he doubled down in his uncharitable review of Patricia Mazón's first book.

24. Patricia M. Mazón, *Gender and the Modern Research University: The Admission of Women to German Higher Education, 1865–1914* (Stanford, CA: Stanford University Press, 2003), 86. Mazón has contributed significant work in this area, focusing on the cultural politics of turn-of-the-century German universities and the extended public debate beginning in the mid-nineteenth century about women in higher education with her dissertation, later book, and select articles focusing on literary representations participating in these debates, including "*Fräulein Doktor*": Literary Images of the First Female University Students in *Fin-de-Siècle* Germany," *Women in German Yearbook* 16 (2000): 129–50.

25. Eisner recounts the situation with some humor, although she says that she's certain she contracted measles from the family's children: Eisner, *Ich hatte*, 60.

26. The timeline of Eisner's university education is somewhat hazy. In the memoirs, Eisner says she passed her Abitur around the time she turned twenty, which would have been in March 1916. She implies that a three-month trip to Italy with family friend Charlotte Münchhausen occurred between the Abitur and her time enrolled in university in Berlin, but she also says 1920 was her only winter semester in Berlin, which leaves the period between 1916–20 unclear. Was she traveling the whole time? Did she misremember the dates? Was it actually closer to 1918 or 1919 when she enrolled at university? To add to the confusion, Münchhausen's diaries, excerpted in Kenneth D. McCrae, *Nuclear Dawn: F. E. Simon and the Race for Atomic Weapons in World War II* (Oxford: Oxford University Press, 2014), 7–10, date their Italian sojourn to 1921 quite specifically. Janet Bergstrom has inquired at Rostock about Eisner's enrollment dates, and they don't appear to match the timeline reported in Eisner's memoirs; see notes to "Out from the Shadows: Lotte Eisner's Significance as a Collector," *Cinema in the Eye of the Collector*, edited by André Habib, Louis Pelletier, and Jean-Pierre Sirois-Trahan (Amsterdam: Amsterdam University Press, 2022).

27. Martin Warnke, "On Heinrich Wölfflin," *Representations* 27 (Summer 1989): 172–87.

28. Warnke places the announcement in *Kunstchronik und Kunstmarkt* 58, nos. 47/48 (7–21 September 1923): 792.

29. Eisner, *Ich hatte*, 63–64.

30. Eisner, *Ich hatte*, 64.

31. There is a hale body of scholarship on the institutional history of the field; I have relied on Heinrich Dilly, *Kunstgeschichte als Institution: Studien zur Geschichte einer Disziplin* (Frankfurt: Suhrkamp, 1979), the literature review by Stefan Muthesius, "Towards an 'exakte Kunstwissenschaft'? A Report on Some Recent German Books on the Progress of mid-19th-Century Art History," *Journal of Art Historiography* 9 (December 2013): 1–37, as well as Eric Garberson, "Art History in the University: Toelken, Hotho, Kugler," *Journal of Art Historiography* 5 (December 2011): 1–89.

32. For contemporaneous assessment, see Stephen Bleecker Luce, "A Brief History of the Study of Greek Vase-Painting," *Proceedings of the American Philosophical Society* 57, no. 7 (1918): 649–68.

33. More recently, this model has been critiqued on the grounds that authorship and style can only be deduced from comparative analysis and inference, yet connoisseurship reifies an organic style inherent to a singular artist, much in the Romantic model; in effect, a pattern of style is understood to imply—and is then conflated with—an authorial presence. Whereas sorting, and the instantiation of subjective relations between and among the sorted objects, is inherent in the methodology, the epistemology of connoisseurship doesn't acknowledge that the connoisseur reifies the artistic personality, or, in a semiotic frame of reference suggested by Richard Neer, it collapses the signified and the referent: Richard Theodore Neer, *Pampoikilos: Representation, Style and Ideology in Attic Red-Figure* (Ann Arbor: UMI, 1998).

34. Andokides is among the individual artists whose development over a period of years is traced in order to demonstrate both individual and historical formal trajectories. In one of the more normative moments of the dissertation, Eisner attributes changes in Andokides's style to increasing confidence on the part of the artist: Lotte Eisner, "Die Entwicklung der Komposition auf griechischen Vasenbildern" (Rostock: University of Rostock, 1924), 20.

35. Eisner, "Entwicklung," 4.

36. Eisner, "Entwicklung," 3.

37. It is important to flag the use of "painterly" (*malerisch*)—although Eisner makes no effort in-text to cue her reader to one or another definition—because by her time it had been mobilized in pedagogical, aesthetic, and nationalist discourses over decades of German art historical scholarship, notably by Wölfflin, and because she would go on to implement it in her own later work on film. For a summary of the uses of *malerisch* in the German context, see Daniel Adler, "Painterly Politics: Wölfflin, Formalism, and German Academic Culture, 1885–1915," *Art History* 27, no. 3 (June 2004): 431–56.

38. Eisner, "Entwicklung," 20, 30–31.

39. Eisner, "Entwicklung," 85.

40. The dedication pages of both *Die Kunst der Griechen* and Eisner's dissertation read, simply: "Meinem Vater." Eisner's quotation of Salis is imperfect, but it conveys the spirit of his statement, cf. Arnold von Salis, *Die Kunst der Griechen* (Leipzig: S. Hirzel, 1919), 173.

41. Margarete Bieber, "Necrology," *American Journal of Archaeology* 62, no. 4 (October 1958): 429–30.

42. "The art historian will not be content to make such statements, for behind the dissipative variety are clearly distinguished two major styles which diverge in time, as in the history of modern art: Baroque and Rococo. The parallel can also be extended to the nature of the artistic achievement itself, and not merely an astonishing resemblance of the formal language, but very closely related traits throughout the intellectual and sensory disposition. It is not uncommon to hear of an 'antique baroque' and of an 'antique rococo.' If we delineate these terms here and apply them directly to two stages of the development of antiquity, it is done with explicit reservation. It is important not to equate periods of art that are so separated in terms of time; rather, these names have been chosen because a truly accurate and exhaustive conceptual definition of these stylistic groups has not yet been coined, including by the present author, nor does it seem that one is forthcoming." Salis, *Die Kunst der Griechen*, 252–53. Up until this juncture, the term *baroque* had been deployed in the context of Greek and Roman antiquity principally as a derogatory term, most notably by the influential German art historian Johann Joachim Winckelmann (1717–1768). For a summary of how the exhibition of the Pergamon Altar in Berlin the 1880s precipitated this shift in the context of the German and French academy, see Lionel Gossman, "Imperial Icon: The Pergamon Altar in Wilhelmine Germany," *Journal of Modern History* 78 (September 2006): 551–87.

43. Gottfried von Lücken, "Archaische griechische Vasenmalerei und Plastik," *Mitteilungen des deutschen archäologischen Instituts* 44 (1919): 47–174.

44. The article's full reference would be: Gottfried von Lücken, "Zur Entstehung des Bildes," *Zeitschrift für bildende Kunst* 57 (N.F. 33, 1922): 1–7.

45. The second dissertation, the *Habilitationsschrift*, submitted in order to obtain university teaching credentials, would be researched and written independently, demonstrating the potential of its author to contribute original scholarship.

46. Gottfried von Lücken, *Die Entwicklung der Parthenonskulpturen* (Augsburg: Dr. Benno Filser Verlag, 1930).

47. Gottfried von Lücken, Method of Photographically Reproducing Pictures Represented on Curved Surfaces, US Patent 1,456,954A, filed June 16, 1921, and issued 29 May 1923.

48. Riegl's work has rarely bobbed too far below the surface of contemporary debate in any number of academic disciplines concerned with aesthetic theory. Prominent contemporary Riegl scholar Margaret Olin remarks in her encyclopedia entry that he has "never [been] neglected by scholars," charting a brief history of the fervent and sustained twentieth-century reception of Riegl, in and out of translation, across ideological lines and disciplinary boundaries: Margaret Olin, "Riegl,

Alois," in *Encyclopedia of Aesthetics, Second Edition*, ed. Michael Kelly (Oxford: Oxford University Press, 2014),

49. Jas' Elsner, "From Empirical Evidence to the Big Picture: Some Reflections on Riegl's Concept of *Kunstwollen*," *Critical Inquiry* 32 (Summer 2006): 741–66.

50. Michael Gubser argues that Riegl's "oeuvre can be read as a sustained investigation of the concept of history itself, a steady effort to grasp history and time in artistic form—to treat art as time's visible surface." Gubser, "Time and History in Alois Riegl's Theory of Perception," *Journal of the History of Ideas* 66, no. 3 (July 2005): 451–74.

51. She also makes direct reference in this work to *Kunstwollen* from time to time; see, e.g., Lotte H. Eisner, "Die neue Jugend und der Film," *Film-Kurier*, January 1, 1928. The fact that she makes reference to neither *Kunstwollen* nor Riegl in her postwar work suggests that she, like many of Riegl's twentieth-century readers, had adapted these concepts to her own uses to the extent that reference back to Riegl's original formulation was no longer clarifying.

52. Olin, "Riegl, Alois," n.p.

53. For a selective but thorough history of *Stimmung* in the German aesthetic and philosophical context, see David Wellbery and Rebecca Pohl, "Stimmung," *new formations: a journal of culture/theory/politics* 93 (February 2017): 6–45. Riegl's definition of *Stimmung* changed over the course of his work, and it finds its most thorough explication in an essay devoted to defining it as the fundamental characteristic of modern (post-Renaissance) Western art; thus, only in the loosest sense could Eisner be invoking Riegl's definition: Alois Riegl, "Die Stimmung als Inhalt der modernen Kunst" [1899], in *Gesammelte Aufsätze*, ed. K. M. Swoboda (Augsburg: Filser, 1929).

54. Eisner, *Entwicklung*, 90.

55. Michael Wedel, "Through the Looking-Glass: Lotte H. Eisner and Éric Rohmer on Murnau," *Screen* 62, no. 3 (Autumn 2021): 391.

56. See Eisner, *The Haunted Screen*, 200, 203.

57. Eisner, *Ich hatte*, 64. Her dissertation is undoubtedly well written, but I quibble with Eisner's characterization of her own prose as properly Expressionist, granting that there is, nonetheless, a structural feature of the German language that can leave a reader declaiming even a work as grammatically and syntactically moderate as Eisner's dissertation rather breathless: in constructions using compound or separable verbs, the decisive, conjugated portion of the verb can take last position.

CHAPTER 2. A RELUCTANT BELLWETHER

1. Lotte Eisner, *Ich hatte einst ein schönes Vaterland: Memoiren* (Heidelberg: Wunderhorn, 1984), 77.

2. Feld also remembered meeting Eisner at a party and suggesting she write for the *Film-Kurier*, but in more muted tones, cf. Hans Feld, "Lotte Eisner: Beginn einer Karriere. Eine Federzeichnung mit dem Hintergrund von Weimar," *Filmexil* 22 (2005): 37–38.

3. After completing coursework in various branches of law, civil service, and administration in Berlin, Freiburg, and Würzburg, Feld wrote a dissertation combining aspects of these disciplines, titled "The Emergence of the Principle of Ministerial Responsibility in the European States." (Hans Feld, "Die Entstehung des Grundsatzes der Ministerverantwortlichkeit in den europäischen Staaten." Inaugural-Dissertation zur Erlangung der juristischen Doktorwürde der rechts- und staatswissenschaftlichen Fakultät der Julius Maximilians-Universität Würzburg, June 2, 1924.)

4. Rolf Aurich and Wolfgang Jacobsen, "Leidenschaftliche Vernunft: Der Journalist Hans Feld im Exil," *Filmexil* 22 (2005): 15.

5. These contributors included E. van Bloem, Ernst Chaparral, Philippe Fachon, Ruth Goetz, Henriette Grünberg, Willy Haas, L. Heider, Georg Herzberg, Edwin Hirrle, Walter Jerven, Walter Kirchheim, Max Kolpe, Margarete Lindau-Schulz, Kurt Lorenz, Paul Medina, Margot Meyer-Landers, Erwin Wolfgang Nack, Dr. Richard Otto, Paul Sorgenfrei, Walter Steinhauer, Georg Otto Stindt, Leo Weiß, and Curt Wesse. Additionally, many of the most prolific contributors used a handful of bylines—in some cases, quite cryptic—maybe in order to give the impression of a more diverse and dynamic set of editorial contributors.

6. Werner Sudendorf puts the 1925 circulation at twelve hundred, and by 1930, at around ten thousand in "'Nicht zur Öffentlichung': Zur Biographie des Filmjournalisten Ernst (Ejott) Jäger," *Filmexil* 5 (1994): 62.

7. Sudendorf frames Jäger's editorial accommodations to the regime and his close association with Leni Riefenstahl in terms of a larger cultural shift. Jäger was contracted by Riefenstahl to write a brochure on the making of *Triumph des Willens* (*Triumph of the Will*, Leni Riefenstahl, 1935), and he accompanied her as press agent for the US tour of *Olympia* in 1938. Cooper C. Graham has argued that Jäger was a peculiar, "ambiguous" character, and his role in the Riefenstahl publicity trip indicated mostly his need for work. Graham goes so far as to describe Jäger's parting of ways with Riefenstahl and Werner Klingeberg—the official leader of the trip, a Nazi Party and German Olympic Committee member—as a "defection." While Jäger did shortly thereafter publish a series of articles with the *Hollywood Tribune* titled "How Leni Riefenstahl Became Hitler's Girlfriend," Graham argues that Jäger's actions were the result of being caught between a rock and a hard place: "If his former Jewish wife and Social Democratic past made him untrustworthy to the Nazis, he had written too many Right-wing [sic] articles in Nazi Germany for the German émigré community in Los Angeles to trust him either." Cooper C. Graham, "'Olympia' in America, 1938: Leni Riefenstahl, Hollywood, and the Kristallnacht," *Historical Journal of Film, Radio and Television* 13, no. 4 (September 2006): 446. Rolf Aurich has attributed the vagaries of Jäger's alliances to economic precarity; struggling to find work as a press agent or writer in Hollywood during the forties and fifties, Jäger used Riefenstahl's name in whatever manner promised to be economically advantageous. Rolf Aurich, "Zwei Pressemenschen: Ewald André Dupont und Ernst Jäger," *Filmexil* 17 (2003): 33–34.

8. Thomas J. Saunders, *Hollywood in Berlin* (Berkeley: University of California Press, 1994), 37.

9. See the front page announcement, "Das offizielle Organ des Reichsverbandes," *Film-Kurier*, September 22, 1928.

10. According to Lucien Mandelik (via Werner Sudendorf and Anton Kaes), "Ernst Chaparral" was the pen name adopted by a Dr. Redlich.

11. Werner Sudendorf, "Täglich: Der *Film-Kurier*," in *Film . . . Stadt . . . Kino . . . Berlin . . .*, ed. Uta Berg-Ganschow and Wolfgang Jacobsen (Berlin: Argon Verlag, 1987), 131.

12. Werner Sudendorf, "Hans Feld. 15. Juli 1902–15. Juli 1992: Ein Gedenkblatt," *Filmexil* 1 (1992): 53.

13. Eisner, *Ich hatte*, 79.

14. "Margot Walter-Landa [*sic*]: Meine großen weichen Hüte," *Film-Kurier*, March 10, 1928.

15. Eisner, *Ich hatte*, 81–82.

16. In fairness to Feld—*pace* Aurich and Jacobsen—his tone and delivery varied considerably among his many bylines and different areas of coverage, and I am aware of important exceptions; cf. Hans Feld, "Film-Kritik: Der Singende Narr," *Film-Kurier*, June 4, 1929.

17. Feld left the *Film-Kurier* on March 31, 1931. His recollections of Eisner's work at the paper are reported in Hans Feld, "Jews in the Development of the German Film Industry: Notes from the Recollections of a Berlin Film Critic," *Leo Baeck Institute Year Book* 27 (1982): 361.

18. Heike Hurst, Dorothea Muenk, and Uscica Perabo. "Film . . . das ist so populo! Gespräch mit Lotte Eisner von Heike Hurst, Dorothea Muenk, and Uscica Perabo," *Frauen und Film* 11 (March 1977): 31.

19. Eisner, *Ich hatte*, 78. This apartment building—at Marbacher Str. 18—was recently marked with a memorial plaque noting Eisner's residence there.

20. In an interview conducted during the Venice Film Festival with Herbert Feinstein, Eisner emphasizes that she identified herself as a "film journalist," rather than a critic: Herbert Feinstein, "Lotte Eisner" (Los Angeles: Pacifica Radio Archives, 1968).

21. Hurst, et al., "Film . . . das ist so populo!," 31.

22. By my count, she used ten: Dr. Lotte H. Eisner, Dr. L. H. Eisner, L. H. Eisner, Lotte H. Eisner, L. H. E., Lo-Ha., -ner., Flapper, Lolott., and –lo–.

23. See the appendix: "*Film-Kurier* Bibliography, by the Numbers" for overview visualizations.

24. Lotte H. Eisner, "Zu einem Spießerfilm," *Film-Kurier*, September 14, 1927.

25. L. H. E., "Berufe," *Film-Kurier*, December 10, 1927.

26. Eisner uses the word "misogynist" to describe herself and her work in a number of places. Most examples I've come across she either indirectly attributes the remark to other people (as in, "people say I'm a misogynist"), in Hurst, et al., "Film . . . das ist so populo!," 35–36, and in the documentary *Lotte Eisner in*

Germany (S. M. Horowitz, 1981), or identifies it in her own work, as in Eisner, *Ich hatte*, 159.

27. Lynne Frame, "Gretchen, Girl, Garçonne? Weimar Science and Popular Culture in Search of the Ideal New Woman," in *Women in the Metropolis: Gender and Modernity in Weimar Culture*, ed. Katharina von Ankum (Berkeley: University of California Press, 1997): 13.

28. The above translation of the article's title is loose: "Wir haben Frühlingssorgen" more literally would be "We Have Springtime Concerns." "Frühlingssorgen" could also be rendered "Springtime Worries," or "Troubles." With "Struggles" I attempted to preserve the hyperbolic, ultimately snarky spirit of the title in the context of the piece.

29. Flapper, "Wir haben Frühlingssorgen," *Film-Kurier*, March 10, 1928.

30. Flapper, "Kurze Naturgeschichte der 'Dame von Welt,'" *Film-Kurier*, March 24, 1928.

31. Incidentally, this conceit—in which the initial phrase, often a statement or observation, is repeated at the end of the piece, having by that point acquired a new, usually ironic sheen—is one of the hallmarks of Eisner's writing style at the *Film-Kurier*.

32. Lolott., "Das Mädel von heute," *Film-Kurier*, March 24, 1928.

33. Eisner describes persistent sexual harassment and intimidation in the workplace by Jäger in her memoirs, arguing that because she rebuffed his sexual advances he plotted to besmirch her name with an offensive article published under her byline and thus trump up cause to fire her. Eisner implies that this behavior was part and parcel of a larger animus and that his eager accommodation of Nazi ideology and culture in his personal life and at the paper were related to his abusive treatment of the editorial staff members. I have found neither corroborating nor contradicting accounts in the scant secondary literature on Jäger, and the only source on Jäger to address these accusations by Eisner is dismissive without being specific: Sudendorf, "'Nicht zur Öffentlichung,'" 62.

34. Eisner, *Ich hatte*, 82–83.

35. She indicates the first sentence of her review of *Mädchen in Uniform*, "The impossible has come to pass: a film starring only women manages to be gripping, because it treats a human story on the level of social themes": Lotte H. Eisner, "Film-Kritik: Mädchen in Uniform," *Film-Kurier*, November 28, 1931.

36. An evocative example of this self-identification in her memoirs relates to another Flapper-signed piece from around this time: "Die Baker in Berlin: Josephine wird photovraphiert [sic]," *Film-Kurier*, September 10, 1928. She recalls that she scooped the other journalists on staff by snagging an interview on the hoof with the busy Baker and dictating the piece to a female secretary just before the issue went to print, a feat that gobsmacked her colleagues, none of whom had been able to schedule an interview with Baker. She casts herself as skillful, wily, and impressive, using the tools at her disposal to pull off a feat that earned the awe and respect of her male peers: Eisner, *Ich hatte*, 80–81.

37. Claims about having been sabotaged by women are made in her memoirs and in the interview with Hurst, et al. See also her passing remarks in the 1982 interview with Marcel Martin on feminist solidarity, in which she implies that prompting Eisner to affirm a female filmmaker is tantamount to "racism"; she appreciates Margarethe von Trotta's work, she emphasizes, but resents the implication that it is because either of them is a woman: "I think [Trotta's work is] excellent. But I don't like to always be talking, as people do nowadays, about 'women's films'; I find it racist. I never liked it when people called books, 'women's books': I am not at all a feminist in that sense." Marcel Martin, "De l'archéologie a l'histoire," *La Revue du cinéma: Image et son* 377 (November 1982): 130.

38. Lolott, "Sieben im Autobus," *Film-Kurier*, April 14, 1928. I published a translation of this piece in full as part of the article, "A Critic at Large: Lotte Eisner at the *Film-Kurier* (1927–1933)," *Journal of Cinema and Media Studies* 61, no. 3 (Spring 2022).

39. For example, Adorno's tin-eared pieces on jazz. These are summarized and contextualized (but not excused) in the interesting history by J. Bradford Robinson, "The Jazz Essays of Theodor Adorno: Some Thoughts on Jazz Reception in Weimar Germany," *Popular Music* 13, no. 1 (January 1994): 1–25.

40. Siegfried Kracauer, *The Mass Ornament*, translated by Thomas Y. Levin (Cambridge, MA: Harvard University Press, 1995), 76–77.

41. Patrice Petro, "Perceptions of Difference: Woman as Spectator and Spectacle" in *Women in the Metropolis*, edited by Katharina von Ankum (Berkeley: University of California Press, 1997), 41–62.

42. Kracauer, *The Mass Ornament*, 294.

43. Indeed, there is a strong family resemblance—an ugliness and crudity in common—among the female-coded tropes that figure in the Frankfurt School's imaginary. Kracauer's shopgirls of 1927 condense the traits of what Horkheimer and Adorno will later dub the "dupes" of the culture industry, as well as the horoscope-reading Angelenos of Adorno's screed against irrationalism, "The Stars Down to Earth," and they do so blithely: without hesitation, qualification, or a recognition of how gender figures with the nation and history in the films at hand, Kracauer deploys the shopgirl as both victim and perpetuator of the industry. See also, Theodor Adorno, *The Stars Down to Earth and Other Essays on the Irrational in Culture* (London: Routledge, 1994).

44. The correspondence between Eisner and Kracauer in later years as they published competing volumes on Weimar cinema history—from opposite sides of the Atlantic and with substantially different methodological and epistemological approaches—suggests that while they did know of each other during the time in the twenties and early thirties when they each covered film and culture in Berlin for their respective publications, they did not share a great deal in common, socially or otherwise. The chronology of publication suggests that it is possible that Eisner wrote this piece in response to Kracauer's original publication, but she may have heard or read similar sentiments elsewhere, too.

45. Heide Schlüpmann opens her influential essay on the patriarchal assumptions at the heart of Kracauer, Benjamin, and Adorno's criticisms of feminized, passive cinema spectatorship with an observation from Emilie Altenloh's dissertation, *Zur Soziologie des Kino* (Jena: Eugen Diederichs, 1914): "Für den begleitenden Herrn ist 'sie' dann aber angeblich mehr das Objekt der Beobachtung als die Vorgänge auf der weißen Wand." See Schlüpmann, "Kinosucht," *Frauen und Film* 33 (October 1982): 45–52.

46. Kracauer, *The Mass Ornament*, 295. I am sympathetic to Petro's and Schlüpmann's observations that Kracauer moderated the harshness of his critique with time and ultimately understood pleasure in cinemagoing as having some potential to be neither exclusively feminine nor deplorably inane. However, I maintain that the exercise of inverting this body of literature and seeing what falls out of its pockets is useful, because some of its constitutive assumptions and constructs still have currency; indeed, in certain conversations within contemporary cultural criticism, they are the coin of the realm.

47. L. H. E., "Schauspielerinnen," *Film-Kurier*, February 18, 1928.

48. Barbara Dju is possibly best known for her role in *Eine Nacht in Yoshiwara* (*One Night in Yoshiwara*, Emmerich Hanus, 1928; also featuring Alfred Abel and Rudolf Klein-Rogge), and as the model for several portraits and busts by her then husband Ernesto de Fiori, who ultimately fled to Brazil after his work was declared to be "degenerate." Lo-Ha.,"Neue Gesichter für den Film Barbara Dju," *Film-Kurier*, July 14, 1928.

49. Flapper, "Tausend Beinchen suchen . . .," *Film-Kurier*, August 28, 1928.

50. Lotte H. Eisner, "Spanischer Frühling. Jacobinermützen in Barcelona," *Film-Kurier*, May 2, 1931; Lo-Ha., "Carmen hat unrecht! Ich lad Euch allen ein, dort in Sevillas Mauern. . .," *Film-Kurier*, July 4, 1931; Lotte H. Eisner, "Kino-Sonntag in Amsterdam," *Film-Kurier*, October 20, 1928; —lo—, "Kleines Rivierakino," *Film-Kurier*, June 20, 1931. I published translations of the first and third in this short list as part of DeCelles, "A Critic at Large: Lotte Eisner at the *Film-Kurier* (1927–1933)," *Journal of Cinema and Media Studies* 62, no. 3 (Spring 2022).

51. L. H. E., "Begebenheit," *Film Kurier*, January 16, 1928.

52. Günter Jurczyk "Voll Mut—wenn's auch nicht stimmt: Gespräch mit der Filmhistorikerin Lotte Eisner," *Süddeutsche Zeitung* 204 (September 6, 1982): 15.

53. Lotte H. Eisner, "'Große Szene' in Staaken," *Film-Kurier*, November 24, 1927, and Lotte H. Eisner, "Theater im Film," *Film-Kurier*, December 15, 1927.

54. Lotte H. Eisner, "'Großkampftag' in Johannistal," *Film-Kurier,* December 7, 1927. Olaf Gulbransson (1873–1958) was a celebrated Norwegian caricaturist who lived and worked in Germany during the interwar period for the satirical weekly *Simplicissimus*.

55. Lo-Ha., "Glashaus. 'Haus Nr. 17' und ein Schornstein, der rauchen soll," *Film-Kurier*, February 15, 1928. The "perfidy of objects" is a quiet reference to Friedrich Vischer's *Auch Einer*, which Eisner will reprise with explicit citation in *L'écran démoniaque* (1952). See DeCelles, "A Critic at Large: Lotte Eisner at the *Film-Kurier* (1927–1933)."

56. Lo–Ha., "Glashaus. Mord in der Großstadt," *Film-Kurier*, February 22, 1928. See DeCelles, "A Critic at Large."

57. L. H. E., "Alfred Kerr über den Kritiker," *Film-Kurier*, March 23, 1928.

58. L. H. E., "Vom Tage: Die Probe aufs Exempel," *Film-Kurier*, March 13, 1928.

59. That ragged forbearance is on display in L. H. E., "Mitmenschen," *Film-Kurier*, February 1, 1928, and L. H. E., "Wie gefällt dir Dein Nachbar?," *Film-Kurier*, May 26, 1928; both are sketches of city life and moviegoing featuring chatty, backtalking Berliners at the theater out for human interaction, refreshments, and a movie, sometimes—much to the narrator's indignation—in that order. In the latter, Eisner begins: "When renting an apartment, you inquire about the neighbors. Even though, thank God, you will be separated from them by a few walls. When you buy a ticket at the theater, however, you recklessly leave all chance and mishap to blind fate." Caricaturing the bulkily garbed, conspicuously lunching, and excessively perfumed fellow audience members likely to be encountered, Eisner focuses her ire on the family that reliably sits just behind you and talks throughout the show. Whether Eisner would have known Resi Langer's work, I am not certain, yet these sketches by Eisner strike me as strongly reminiscent of Langer's commentary on theatergoers in *Kinotypen: Vor und hinter den Filmkulissen*, translated by Sara Hall in *The Promise of Cinema* (Berkeley: University of California Press, 2016), 161–64.

60. Paragraph 175, two down from the subject of the reviewed film, refers to a section of the German Criminal Code (originally adopted in 1871 and expanded under the Nazi regime) that outlawed a number of sexual acts, including sex between men. L. H. Eisner, "Film-Kritik: §173 Blutschande," *Film-Kurier*, October 18, 1929.

61. There is an odd error, possibly a result of garbled dictation or Eisner's untidy penmanship, in the article's lede: "150 years ago, when the young Hölderlin took his own life, Goethe wrote his Werther. It was the sensational topicality, the onset of tragic reality in the small town of Wetzlar, that inspired him to write his work." The person to whom Eisner is likely referring is Karl Wilhelm Jerusalem, a lawyer whose suicide in 1772 is said to have inspired that of Goethe's *Werther*, first published two years later in 1774, not the poet Friedrich Hölderlin, who wasn't even born until 1770, didn't die by his own hand, and whose work achieved its current renown well after his death, beginning in the early twentieth century.

62. L. H. E., "Vom Tage: Aktualität oder Sensation," *Film-Kurier*, February 18, 1928.

63. See, for example, Dr. L. H. Eisner, "Beiblatt zum Film-Kurier: Der Kulturfilm," *Film-Kurier*, March 21, 1928; -ner. "Hans Fischingers erster abstrakter Film," *Film-Kurier*, October 23, 1931; and her commentary on the paintings and films of Fernand Léger in "Der Maler der Objekte: Ausstellung Fernand Léger bei Flechtheim," *Film-Kurier*, February 17, 1928.

64. "Dilemma der Kulturfilmproduzenten," *Film-Kurier*, December 20, 1930.

65. L. H. E., "Weltkongreß sabotiert den Film!," *Film-Kurier*, August 14, 1929.

66. In his 2020 Domitor talk, Malcolm Cook flagged a strikingly similar, earlier assessment by George Warrington in an article titled "The Coming of

Cinema Advertising" (published in *Advertiser's Weekly*, September 16, 1916), in which he claims that advertising film's implementation of animation is proceeding too slowly, that it was "being held back because it is in the hands of men of little imagination."

67. I've used "Documentary" here, but the group's name is sometimes rendered "Union Educational and Cultural Filmmakers" in Anglophone secondary literature and translation. Eisner's position was articulated across a series of articles following a Kulturfilm international conference in The Hague: Dr. L. H. Eisner "Der deutsche Kulturfilm in Gefahr? Der italienische Krieg: Geheimpolitik im Bund," *Film-Kurier*, April 13, 1928; L. H. E., "Vor der Haager Konferenz," *Film-Kurier*, April 21, 1928; L. H. Eisner, "Film-Kritik: Pressevorführung des Lehrfilmbundes," *Film-Kurier*, April 27, 1928; Lotte H. Eisner, "Weitere Zuspitzung im Haag: Vierter Tag der Haager Lehrfilm-Konferenz," *Film-Kurier*, May 5, 1928; as well as in the overview, Dr. L. H. Eisner, "Der Kulturfilm: Forderungen für 1929," *Film-Kurier*, January 12, 1929.

68. Hans Cürlis, "Film Is Promotion," in *Promise of Cinema*, trans. Alex Bush (Oakland: University of California Press, 2016), 545–46. Originally published as "Film ist Werbung," *Film-Kurier*, August 11, 1929.

69. Including the following films, all produced by Cürlis at the Institute for Cultural Research: *Kohlennot und Friedensvertrag* (*Coal Shortage and Peace Treaty*, 1920/21), *Truppenfilm I* (*Troops I*, 1921), *Pariser Konferenz* (*The Paris Conference*, 1921), *Deutschland auf Abbruch* (*Germany Carved Up*, 1921), *Brotfilm* (*Bread*, 1921), *Entente-Paradies im Rheinland* (*An Entente Paradise in the Rhineland*, 1921), *Französische Wirtschaftsorganisation im Rheinland* (*French Economic Organization in the Rhineland*, 1921), *Die wirtschaftliche Bedeutung Oberschliesiens* (*The Economic Importance of Upper Silesia*, 1921), *Oberschliesiens* (*Upper Silesia*, 1921), *Truppenfilm II* (*Troops II*, 1921), *Unfruchtbare Milliarden und Wohnungselend* (*Fruitless Billions and Housing Misery*, 1921/22).

70. A contemporary review in the Social Democratic Party's circular, *Vorwärts*, derided the film as a piece of retrograde "nationalist-imperialist" propaganda: technically accomplished, but insensible to the cruelty of its own argument, "The fate of the natives under colonial rule is completely ignored; a few natives appear as little more than picturesque decoration on the landscape." Clearly unconvinced of the film's educational value, the reviewer notes that the viewing public at the screening "saw through [the film's] pseudoscientific propaganda" but warns, "The public will have to take care that the poison of capitalist and nationalist propaganda is not instilled into the minds of defenseless children." "Ein kolonialkapitalistischer Propagandafilm," *Vorwärts* 44, no. 45 (January 27, 1927): 2.

71. L. H. E., "Der Film in der Schule," *Film-Kurier*, April 12, 1928, L. H. E., "Für den Lehrer!," *Film-Kurier*, September 15, 1928, -ner., "Der Kulturfilm: Der Lehrfilm braucht die Schere," *Film-Kurier*, September 15, 1928, L. H. E., "Der Kulturfilm: Wo bleibt das gute Beiprogramm?" *Film-Kurier*, February 9, 1929, -ner., "Der Wissenschaftsfilm fordert: Mehr Einsicht bei Wissenschaftlern—Unterstützung beim Reich!," *Film-Kurier*, March 15, 1929, and L. H. E., "Staatliche Kulturfilmaufgaben,"

Film-Kurier, November 2, 1929. Eisner reported on film clubs for teachers, as well, and commented on the ways teachers were approaching the project of integrating film into the classroom in -ner., "Der Lehrer sieht es anders," and "Ufa-Filmschau vor Lehrern," *Film-Kurier*, October 13, 1930. In L. H. Eisner, "Zum Internationalen Lehrfilmkongreß: Was geschieht in Wien?," *Film-Kurier*, May 23, 1931, she argues for the integration of filmmaking curriculum in high schools and subsidies for equipment to be used by students in these programs.

72. Ian Aitken, "The Redemption of Physical Reality: Theories of Realism in Grierson, Kracauer, Bazin and Lukács," in *European Film Theory and Cinema: A Critical Introduction* (Bloomington: Indiana University Press, 2001) and John Grierson, *Grierson on Documentary*, ed. Forsyth Hardy (Berkeley: University of California Press, 1966).

73. L. H. E., "Das Kino braucht den Kulturfilm," *Film-Kurier*, September 27, 1930.

74. -ner., "Mehr Montage für den Kulturfilm!," *Film-Kurier*, December 13, 1930. Eisner's familiarity with Soviet montage emerged not only from her engagement with the films, but attendance at (and often coverage of) lectures given by Eisenstein, Pudovkin, and others in Berlin. Here, she singles out André Sauvage's 1928 *Études sur Paris* and Wilfried Basse's 1929 *Markt in Berlin*, lauding the formal and technical experimentation of each documentary.

75. Lotte H. Eisner, "Tabak-Kulturfilm der Ufa," *Film-Kurier*, September 22, 1928.

76. -ner. "Neuer Weg für den Landschaftsfilm," *Film-Kurier*, September 22, 1928. Lotte Reiniger was associated with the Institute for Cultural Research.

77. She considered the practice of having an actor read such accompanying lectures from scripts provided by the scientist whose work was at hand to be a necessary evil, because of the "didactic inhibition" and a clear disjoint between the performer and the material they were delivering; L. H. Eisner, "Gläserne Wundertiere," August 5, 1929.

78. Eisner makes this case in dozens of her reviews and commentaries, but a particularly crystalline example is that in Lotte H. Eisner, "Kultur-Film-Sondervorführung für die Berliner Presse (Universum Film A.-G.)," *Film-Kurier*, March 17, 1928.

79. Antje Ehmann's chapter, "Rede, Gerede und Gegenrede: Film und Kultur im Diskurs der Weimarer Jahre," in the second volume of *Geschichte des dokumentarischen Films in Deutschland* discusses the *Film-Kurier*'s Kulturfilm coverage and acknowledges Eisner's work on the topic—even quoting from a small handful of samples—but Ehmann's primary concern is the broader picture, not Eisner's work in particular, and all address of Eisner's work is subsumed by Ehmann under a discussion of larger trends. Ehmann concludes that the beginnings of a dedicated film theoretical approach to Kulturfilm were curtailed by the conditions of crisis attending the end of the Weimar Republic: "Almost all those who gave pithiness and vitality to the German discourse [on Kulturfilm] in the Weimar years were forced, sooner or later, to leave the country: Rudolf Arnheim, Béla Balázs, Lotte H.

Eisner, Willy Haas, Hans Feld, Alfred Kerr, Siegfried Kracauer, and Hans Richter." Ehmann, "Rede, Gerede, und Gegenrede," 282–83.

80. Lotte H. Eisner, "Die schöne deutsche Heimat," and Hans Feld, "Die dokumentarischen Aufgaben des Kulturfilms," *Film-Kurier*, April 7, 1928.

81. Rudolf Arnheim, *Film Essays and Criticism* (Madison: University of Wisconsin Press, 1997).

82. Collections that feature good examples of such writing include Lewis Jacobs, *The Compound Cinema: The Film Writings of Harry Alan Potamkin* (New York: Teachers College Press, 1977), and Iris Barry, *Let's Go to the Movies* (New York: Arno Press, 1972 [1926]). Feld's writing has recently been assessed in the edited bibliography by Eva Orbanz, *Hans Feld: Redakteur und Kulturjournalist. Bibliografie Film-Kurier 1926–1932* (Munich: edition text + kritik, 2019), and it has been discussed at some length in the pages of the journal *Filmexil*.

83. See, for example Arnheim's "Film and Its Stepmother," in *Film Essays and Criticism*, 89–92, in which he takes issue with many of the problems Eisner identified across years of coverage of the Lampe Committee, including the punctiliousness of the Committee's standards, and their resistance to formal and aesthetic experimentation.

84. Richard Lowell MacDonald, "Film Appreciation and Cultural Leadership: Rudolf Arnheim, Roger Manvell, and Two Books Called '*Film*,'" *Canadian Journal of Film Studies* 23, no. 1 (Spring 2014): 124.

85. Rudolf Arnheim, *Film as Art* (Berkeley: University of California Press, 1957), 3–4.

86. Arnheim's *Film* (later republished as *Film as Art*) helped land him work in Rome, where he lived for six years until the outbreak of war in 1939, publishing a number of essays on film, including "A New Laocoön," and *Radio* (published in English in 1936); Shawn Vancour, "Arnheim on Radio: *Materialtheorie* and Beyond," in *Arnheim for Film and Media Studies*, ed. Scott Higgins (New York: Routledge, 2010), 177–94, and Roy R. Behrens, "Rudolf Arnheim: The Little Owl on the Shoulder of Athene," *Leonardo* 31, no. 3 (1998): 231–33. Kracauer's struggle to find safe passage to the United States has been reported in detail in the secondary literature, see especially Anton Kaes, "Siegfried Kracauer: Film Historian in Exile," in *Escape to Life: German Exiles in New York*, ed. Sigrid Weigel and Eckhart Goebel (New York: De Gruyter Verlag, 2013) as well as Miriam Hansen, *Cinema and Experience* (Berkeley: University of California Press, 2012).

87. See, for example, L. H. E., "Zeitschriften," and Lotte H. Eisner, "Avantgarde—Achtung!," *Film-Kurier*, May 26, 1928.

88. L. H. Eisner, "Avantgarde der Massen," *Film-Kurier*, August 31, 1929.

89. Eisner initiated a series of articles that would grow to include contributions by other *Film-Kurier* editors, titled "Das Feuilleton des Autors," which expounded on the importance of actors, writers, cinematographers, and set designers in all stages of production, particularly emphasizing the importance of including these people in the writing process: e.g., L. H. E., "Ein Komödiant könnt einen Autor lehren. . . . Der produktive Schauspieler," *Film-Kurier*, November 12, 1931; L. H. E.,

"Der produktive Kameramann wird zum Mitschöpfer: Wege zur Manuskript-Verwirklichung," *Film-Kurier*, November 26, 1931; —lo—, "Formkünstler werden Autoren: Ein interessantes Film-Triumvirat," *Film-Kurier*, May 19, 1932; Lotte H. Eisner, "Arnolt Bronnen sagt: 'Funk und Film haben nichts Gemeinsames,'" *Film-Kurier*, June 9, 1932.

90. Lotte H. Eisner, "*Aloma, die Blume der Südsee*," *Film-Kurier*, March 29, 1928.

91. Lotte H. Eisner, "The Utica Jubilee Singers," *Film-Kurier*, August 16, 1927.

92. Kira Thurman, "Singing the Civilizing Mission in the Land of Bach, Beethoven, and Brahms: The Fisk Jubilee Singers in Nineteenth-Century Germany," *Journal of World History* 27, no. 3 (September 2016): 444–45.

93. Together with Goslar and Rundt, Nussbaum shortly thereafter became an authorized translator of Langston Hughes's work: "The intellectual and material exchange between Nussbaum and African American modernists that took place between 1927 and her untimely death in 1931 produced a flood of translations and publications out of the trickle that had come before." Jonathan O. Wipplinger, *The Jazz Republic: Music, Race, and American Culture in Weimar Germany* (Ann Arbor: University of Michigan Press, 2017), 177–83.

94. Eisner uses the terms *Negersklaven* in the previous sentence, and *Negersänger* here to describe Jolson's blackface minstrelsy. I have chosen to translate them both into today's parlance because in context it seems clear to me that Eisner was using contemporaneously normalized language without special animus and in the absence of a robust German-language period discourse or nuanced vocabulary on the topic. Despite debate about the harms of the term *Neger* in contemporary versus historical German usage (whereas in contemporary parlance it is unambiguously understood as a racist slur, ca. 1929 it was used conventionally and with essentially equivalent meaning to the period US English word "Negro") tellingly, there is still no German term for blackface minstrelsy. I flag this choice in the interest of transparency—wanting neither to reinscribe racist conventions, nor to minimize or sanitize their historical usage—and in the spirit of defamiliarizing the white supremacist underpinnings of these terms.

95. L. H. Eisner, "Film Review: *The Jazz Singer*," *Film-Kurier*, November 27, 1929.

96. Linda Williams, *Playing the Race Card* (Princeton, NJ: Princeton University Press, 2001), 151–52.

97. Lotte H. Eisner, "Bürger, schützt Eure Anlagen!," *Film-Kurier*, August 9, 1927.

98. Eisner, *Ich hatte*, 152, and Sudendorf, "Hans Feld," 54.

99. While Eisner describes his departure as a "sacking," after which Feld was sent looking for new employment, this characterization may speak more to the spirit of the parting than the mechanics of it, as articles continued to run in the paper under his bylines intermittently for another five months. On March 31, 1932, the paper ran a discreet note near the usual space reserved for the theater review column Feld had established and run for years, stating that after his years of valuable contributions to the *Film-Kurier*, he had decided to pledge his services to the

producer-distributor Aafa: "the decision of a journalist manifestly committed to the development of quality film to actively engage in film production merits the attention of the industry."

100. See in particular: Lotte H. Eisner, "Kunst in Metern," *Film-Kurier*, November 10, 1927; Lotte H. Eisner, "Otto Rombach: Der heilige Krieg," *Film-Kurier*, May 24, 1928; Lotte H. Eisner, "R. C. Sheriff: Die andere Seite," *Film-Kurier*, August 30, 1929; L. H. Eisner, "Sommertheater... René Schickele: Hans im Schnakenloch," *Film-Kurier*, September 5, 1929; and Lotte H. Eisner, "Berliner Bühnen: Karl Kraus, Die letzte Nacht," *Film-Kurier*, January 16, 1930.

101. According to Eisner's recollections in her memoirs, as well as the documentaries *Lotte Eisner in Germany* (S. M. Horowitz, 1980) and *Die langen Ferien der Lotte H Eisner* (Sohrab Shahid Saless, 1979), the *Völkischer Beobachter* published a screed against Eisner and the *Film-Kurier*, which included the ominous declaration, "When heads roll, hers will be one of them." For a brief history of the paper's ownership, editorial politics, and imbrication with the NSDAP around this time, see Roland V. Layton Jr., "The 'Völkischer Beobachter,' 1920–1933: The Nazi Party Newspaper in the Weimar Era," *Central European History* 3, no. 4 (December 1970): 353–82.

CHAPTER 3. *"LA SEULE HISTORIENNE"*

1. Eisner, *Ich hatte einst ein schönes Vaterland: Memoiren* (Heidelberg: Wunderhorn, 1984), 173–74.
2. Eisner, *Ich hatte*, 174.
3. Eisner, *Ich hatte*, 177.
4. Eisner, *Ich hatte*, 174.
5. The remarks on Ernst Lubitsch's family are discussed further in chapter 4, "Throughlines."
6. Günter Jurczyk, "Voll Mut—wenn's auch nicht stimmt: Gespräch mit der Filmhistorikerin Lotte Eisner," *Süddeutsche Zeitung* 204 (September 6, 1982): 15.
7. Eisner, *Ich hatte*, 176.
8. "It was in part because Americans like Meyer Schapiro were in contact with Kracauer when he was in Paris, assisting him not only with the bureaucratic aspects of emigration but also with the intellectual and cultural transition that a move to America would require, that he did not give up hope in the following desperate years. Walter Benjamin, whom Kracauer saw regularly in Paris in this period... did not share this hope." Mark M. Anderson, "Siegfried Kracauer and Meyer Schapiro: A Friendship," *New German Critique* 54 (Autumn 1991): 18–29.
9. Miriam Hansen, "'With Skin and Hair': Kracauer's Theory of Film, Marseille 1940," *Critical Inquiry* 19 (Spring 1993): 446.
10. "Slip" in two senses: Eisner describes the novels as an inconspicuous way of keeping her German in practice without speaking it, which she feared would draw dangerous attention to her. Throughout her exile, Eisner worried about her

Berliner's accent in French: "When we were [learning French as] children, teachers didn't care as much about correct pronunciation as they do today." Eisner, *Ich hatte*, 177. Eisner also claims in her memoirs that during her time in hiding, she camouflaged her accent and nationality as Czech, circa 1941 in Montpellier; later, while living in hiding as Louise Escoffier of Strasbourg, she passed (probably more plausibly) as Alsatian, Eisner, *Ich hatte*, 203, 208, 213.

11. Eisner, *Ich hatte*, 191.
12. Eisner, *Ich hatte*, 192.
13. Eisner, *Ich hatte*, 179.
14. Edmund Luft, "Wir sind eigentlich alle vergessen worden; Lotte H. Eisner im Gespräch mit Edmund Luft," *Filmgeschichte* 16/17 (1974): 91.
15. Dr. Lotte H. Eisner, "Von einem, der auszog das 'Filmwesen' zu lernen. Was die Preussische Staatsbibliothek vom Film weiß," *Film-Kurier*, May 26, 1928. The title recalls the Grimm tale, "The Story of the Boy Who Went Forth to Learn What Fear Was." I published a translation of this article in its entirety in *Screen* 62, no. 3 (Autumn 2021): 382–85.
16. Lucien Patry, "Entretien avec Lotte Eisner, le 2 février 1980," *Films & documents* 332 (Autumn 1980): 25.
17. Georges Langlois, "Oeuvre et biographie d'Henri Langlois," *Films & documents* 332 (Autumn 1980): 7.
18. "Vexed" in that, as a consequence of his singular focus on acquisition at the expense of safe storage and preservation, several of the CF's storage facilities became film crematoria.
19. Glenn Myrent and Georges P. Langlois, *Henri Langlois: First Citizen of Cinema* (New York: Twayne, 1995), 27.
20. Eisner, *Ich hatte*, 181.
21. Myrent and Langlois, *Henri Langlois*, 30.
22. See Laurent Mannoni, "Lotte H. Eisner, Historienne des Démons Allemands," in *Le Cinéma expressionniste allemand: Splendeurs d'une collection* (Paris: Éditions de La Martinière/La Cinémathèque française, 2006), Laurent Mannoni, *Histoire de la Cinémathèque française* (Paris: Gallimard, 2006), and Laurent Mannoni and Richard Crangle, "Henri Langlois and the Musée du Cinéma," *Film History* 18, no. 3 (2006): 274–87.
23. In the event, according to Eisner's memoirs, Eugène was not able to meet her upon her arrival in Montpellier, but would continue to provide key contacts, connections, and information to Eisner during these first years of her life in hiding.
24. Eisner, *Ich hatte*, 207.
25. Rolf Aurich has flatly asserted that Hensel was "a spy" on the international archives scene, but he argues that the evidence suggests Langlois worked with Hensel only insofar as was necessary, and in the final analysis Langlois seems to have been working privately to thwart Hensel's efforts to confiscate certain films: see "The German Reich Film Archive in an International Context," in *The Emergence of Film Culture: Knowledge Production, Institution Building and the Fate of the Avant-Garde in Europe, 1919–1945*, ed. Malte Hagener (New York: Berghahn, 2014).

26. Eisner, *Ich hatte*, 210.

27. She is unequivocal about the date of the raid—in her memoirs, for example, she says "It was May 2, 1944. I remember this distinctly, even though I cannot recall dates usually" (Eisner, *Ich hatte*, 215)—but I was not able to verify the date or the number of people who were captured. It has been reported elsewhere that a raid on Figeac resulting in the deportation of between seven and eight hundred men occurred on May 11 and 12, 1944. These people were sent to Montauban and detained there; some of them were murdered at this juncture, and some still further transported to Dachau. Bergen-Belsen's publicly available data on the transports of prisoners to and from the camp during the six months following the date of the raid do not mention a single group of this size, or any groups arriving directly from Figeac.

28. Eisner, *Ich hatte*, 220.

29. Theresienstadt (Terezín) was unique among Nazi concentration camps in that it operated partially under Jewish administration and served as a ghetto and transit point—rather than primarily as a labor or extermination camp—as well as an important instrument of propaganda, purportedly modeling the living standards and operations of all camps to international observers. Living conditions were, nevertheless, abysmal by design. According to the US Holocaust Memorial Museum, roughly thirty-three thousand prisoners died there; "[Lücken] made inquiries for me at Theresienstadt and found out that my mother died in 1942, at the age of 76, but it was a 'natural' death. She was spared the journey to the gas chambers." Eisner, *Ich hatte*, 196, 221.

30. Mannoni, "Lotte H. Eisner, historienne des démons allemands," 6.

31. Julia Eisner, "Lotte Eisner in Exile: Reinvention and Relocation," in *Ach, sie haben ihre Sprache verloren: Filmautoren im Exil* (Munich: Edition Text + Kritik, 2017), 8–9.

32. One ready example is the ostensibly neutral accounting of the CF's history by Pierre Barbin, whose manifest conflicts of interest mar "Contribution à une histoire de la Cinémathèque française," *Journal of Film Preservation* 67 (2004): 15–30. Among the stranger issues with the piece is his insistence on referring to the CF's cofounder and first president as "Pierre-Auguste" Harlé; far more significant is his accusation that Langlois was an eager collaborator with the Nazi regime during the war who covered up his tracks after the war, and that Barbin's own installation at the CF was the result of an investigation of criminal fraud Langlois had been accused of perpetrating in concert with the ultimately discredited René Tréfousse. Contemporaneously, MoMA's Film Library was beset by feuds, power squabbles, and toxic red-baiting; see Robert Sitton, *Lady in the Dark: Iris Barry and the Art of Film* (New York: Columbia University Press, 2014), as well as the excellent Haidee Wasson, *Museum Movies: The Museum of Modern Art and the Birth of Art Cinema* (Berkeley: University of California Press, 2005), and Peter Decherney, *Hollywood and the Culture Elite: How the Movies Became American* (New York: Columbia, 2005).

33. Janet Bergstrom, "Out from the Shadows: Lotte Eisner's Significance as a Collector," *Cinema in the Eye of the Collector*, ed. André Habib, Louis Pelletier, and Jean-Pierre Sirois-Trahan (Amsterdam: Amsterdam University Press, 2022), 2.

34. Eisner, *Ich hatte*, 177.
35. Mannoni and Crangle, "Henri Langlois and the Musée du Cinéma," 281.
36. Eisner, *Ich hatte*, 258.
37. Numerous accounts of the Langlois Affair have reported its timeline and effects in detail; briefly, the circumstances are these: Langlois was asked to resign his position as director of the Cinémathèque française in February 1968 on the grounds that he had mismanaged its funds, holdings, and the process by which it granted access to outside researchers. The film festival impresario Pierre Barbin was installed in Langlois's post, which led to protests, boycotts, letter campaigns, public demonstrations, and staff resignations all organized under the name "Committee for the Defense of the Cinémathèque française." Langlois was reinstated by April 1968, and retrospectively the campaign came to be associated rhetorically, politically, and socially with the events of May 1968 in Paris and elsewhere. See Sylvia Harvey, *May '68 and Film Culture* (London: BFI Publishing, 1978).
38. Notes to Langlois embedded within Eisner's translation of a letter dated December 15, 1953, from Peter Röhrig to Eisner.
39. Note from Eisner to Langlois appended to Eisner's translation of a letter dated June 20, 1961, from Josef von Sternberg to Henri Langlois.
40. Letter from Rochus Gliese to Lotte Eisner, June 6, 1956.
41. Letter from Ewald Junge to Lotte Eisner, March 10, 1971.
42. Letter from Lotte Eisner to Ewald Junge, March 18, 1971.
43. Eisner, *Ich hatte*, 232.
44. Traces of Marie Epstein's work at the CF are preserved in its archives, some of it related to her regular business as preservationist, some to the deposit of her brother's work there. The above quotation is from a three-page note recording an oral history of her memories of the CF held there, but the contents of that note (excepting this quotation) closely map onto the text of the more readily accessible interview by Patry, "Entretien avec Marie Epstein."
45. Independently, it would seem, of any familiarity with her *Film-Kurier* work on the importance of intertitles, Enno Patalas has argued that Langlois "was not very interested in preserving or restoring [German silent film intertitles]. This was in marked contrast to Lotte Eisner, who was aware of the importance of titles, at least in German films of the 1920s, and who inspired me, 20 years ago, to begin searching for the titles of *Der müde Tod* (*Destiny*, Decla-Bioscop, 1921) and also *Nosferatu*, which were thought lost" in "On the Way to '*Nosferatu*,'" *Film History* 14, no. 1 (2002): 25–31.
46. In a choice that Sabine Lenk and André Stufkens claim clabbered relations between the CF and FIAF and precipitated the 1958 schism, Langlois diverted Michelle from her duties as Executive Secretary of FIAF toward a labor-intensive research and acquisitions mission benefiting only the CF; see their fascinating, somewhat partisan account in "'Then Began the Battle Royal': Marion Michelle and the FIAF Crisis," *The Moving Image* 13, no. 1 (Spring 2013): 199–217). A twenty-page set of instructions from Langlois for Michelle's trip (in which he, to Lenk and Stufkens's point, directs Michelle to send thank-you notes to everyone she interacts

with on CF—not FIAF—letterhead) held in the CF's administrative archives reveals a great deal about Langlois's philosophy of persuasion, adapted to what he thought would get the best results for Michelle: flattery, obsequiousness, emphasis on the nobility of the CF's mission, and the strategic deployment of impressive letters of introduction.

47. Letter from Lotte Eisner to Fritz Lang, October 24, 1960.

48. Many have described Langlois's preoccupation with costumes, in particular, as fetishistic; it is my speculation that more than his ardent pursuits of the trappings of cinema, it was his hostility toward self-consciously intellectual film study (particularly film theory) that ruffled feathers and provoked such accusations; e.g., Mannoni and Crangle say that Langlois defended himself "a little unconvincingly … against suspicions of fetishism," in "Henri Langlois and the Musée du Cinéma," 280.

49. Mannoni, "Lotte H. Eisner, Historienne des Démons Allemands," 21. In his history of the CF, Mannoni declares, "Of the four, Langlois, Meerson, Epstein and Eisner, Eisner was the most psychologically stable, the most intellectual, the most thoroughly cultured. In [the CF's inner circle], she was also the only film historian": Mannoni, *Histoire de la Cinémathèque française* (Paris: Gallimard, 2006), 56.

50. Throughout her correspondence held in the CF administrative archives, as well as her postwar publications, Eisner consistently refers not to "Weimar" or "interwar cinema," but to the "classical German cinema," a distinction that signals the art historical frame of reference within which Eisner operates, as much as it periodizes Eisner's work: substantial film studies discourse around "Weimar cinema" would not emerge until the mid-eighties.

51. See, for example, her letter of December 4, 1954, to Robert Herlth: "I hope to publish a larger multilingual work on classical German set design with the Cinémathèque."

52. See discussion in chapter 2, "Documentary and Avant-Garde Film: Criticism, Advocacy, Aesthetics."

53. Letter to Curtis Harrington, November 21, 1961 (original written in English): "Don't bother about the Cahiers snobs; they must always put a famous name to everything, instead of seeing really what it is about or recognizing a style really. It is so easy what they write and it glides down some reader's [sic] throat like oil. Brr."

54. Letter from Lotte Eisner to Robert Herlth, January 3, 1958.

55. I emphasize my focus on the extant traces because there are good indications that important documents related to her work at the CF are no longer (or never were) held in its administrative archives.

56. I use the term advisedly and relate it to Anjali Arondekar's critique of "salvage" historiography in the context of colonial archives in the following way: while it's true that Eisner's project could be construed as essentially empiricist, or a model "where the lost histories of the past [are] recuperated and reinstated within more liberatory histories of the present"—in that Eisner hoped to instantiate and limn an archive in defiance of Nazi cultural, social, political, and economic policy—I hope to demonstrate that its affinities with contemporary archive theory (particularly that informed by affect theory and queer historiography) derive from Eisner's

self-reflexive, improvisational archival praxis, informed by her ambivalence along several registers of positionality and belonging, including gender, nationality, class, and cultural identity. These, qualities, as I read Arondekar, resonate with her own interest in "an archival poetics of ordinary surplus." Anjali Arondekar, et al. "Queering Archives: A Roundtable Discussion," *Radical History Review* 122 (May 2015): 215–16.

57. Letter from Robert Plumpe-Murnau to Lotte Eisner, July 7, 1957.

58. Quoted in Mannoni, *Histoire*, 193.

59. It is everywhere, implicitly: Eisner would continue to use her nom de guerre in CF correspondence until the mid-sixties, and for a time it was the rare correspondent—most often, those with whom Eisner had been acquainted since the interwar period—who referred to her by her given name and the correct honorifics.

60. Both of these stories made their way into almost every interview Eisner gave on the history of the CF, as well as the pages of her memoirs; see, for example, Renaud Bezombes, Michel Celemenski, and Carine Varène, "Die Eisnerin: Entretien avec Lotte H. Eisner," *Cinématographe* 73 (December 1981): 36; Luft, "Wir sind eigentlich alle vergessen worden," 92; Patry, "Entretien avec Lotte Eisner, le 2 février 1980," 28, and Eisner, *Ich hatte*, 233–34.

61. Within archive studies, Marika Cifor's work has explored applications of social justice principles and approaches to appraisal and has suggested that insights of affect theory and queer historiography should inform archival practice: Marika Cifor, "Affecting Relations: Introducing Affect Theory to Archival Discourse," *Archival Science* 16 (2016): 7–31. The seminal text for applications of affect theory to queer historiography remains Ann Cvetkovich's *An Archive of Feeling: Trauma, Sexuality, and Lesbian Public Cultures* (Durham, NC: Duke University Press, 2003).

62. Julia Eisner holds that the correspondence and "practice of network-building" constitute "[Lotte] Eisner's crucial role in a revival of post-war international film culture." Julia Eisner, "Lotte Eisner: Pioneer of the Art and Craft of Collecting," *Screen* 62, no. 3 (Autumn 2021): 419.

63. Bergstrom, "Out from the Shadows," 2.

64. Interestingly, in her contribution to the *Screen* dossier, Julia Eisner also invokes affect, albeit on a somewhat different register: "The affective network that she was instrumental in constructing is characterized by intimate connections grounded amongst other sources in the shared trauma of persecution and a mutual recognition of life in exile. One outstanding example is Eisner's correspondence with film theorist and cultural critic, Siegfried Kracauer.... Much of the correspondence exemplifies this different type of attachment and genial communication." Julia Eisner, "Lotte Eisner: Pioneer of the Art and Craft of Collecting," 419. My own interpretation of the Kracauer correspondence differs (cf. "Disputation and Its Discontents" in chapter 4), but it is heartening to read that Julia Eisner's recuperation of the postwar archival work—informed by the family's private holdings of Lotte Eisner's correspondence—will also take an interest in its affective qualities.

65. One way of putting it is this: rather than moving to interpolate Eisner within the intellectual history of affect theory or queer theory, I argue that the work

is interpellated by it—that is, that her archival praxis is given a meaning, and set of useful relations and heuristics within such larger critical apparatuses.

66. The former is exemplified by Ernest Lindgren's BFI, the latter by Iris Barry's MoMA Film Library, particularly in the Cold War era. The East and West German state efforts to collect and preserve interwar film heritage came into stride nearly twenty years into Eisner's archival career and made acquisitions somewhat trickier for Eisner.

67. Arondekar, et al., "Queering Archives: A Roundtable Discussion," 225.

68. Self-affirming, yet as complicated as ever. In her memoirs, she introduces the section on her harrowing experience of her brief internment at the Vel d'Hiv with the following harsh, self-aggrandizing testament: "My inveterate misogyny can be ascribed primarily to this one week with 250 hysterical women, who selected me as their leader because I was cold. In times of crisis, I was always cold." Eisner says she spent the week consoling and reassuring her fellow internees before they were transported to Gurs and implies that it was the weakness she saw in their fear and despondency that galled her most: Eisner, *Ich hatte*, 197–99.

69. *Sehnsucht* starred Gussy Holl and her soon-to-be-ex-husband, Conrad Veidt; Veidt and his third wife, Ilona Prager, were exiled, like Eisner, in 1933. Holl went on to marry Emil Jannings; they remained (and flourished) in Nazi Germany, Jannings starring in a number of propaganda films.

70. Eisner's letter to Lamprecht is dated July 22, 1959; Krauss died a mere three months later, in late October 1959, in Vienna.

71. Lotte H. Eisner, *F. W. Murnau* (Paris: Le Terrain Vague, 1964), 136. This information drops out of the German edition of 1967 and is placed in a footnote (fn. 6, p. 130) in the 1973 US edition.

72. In a 1967 article, Eisner reflects on the contingency, and the complexity, of assessing the work of those filmmakers: Lotte Eisner, "Meetings with Pabst," *Sight and Sound* 36, no. 4 (Fall 1967): 209–10. Pabst was a particularly heartrending case for Eisner; later, she would argue that had he found success in Hollywood with a project—which she discusses in a 1937 article for Langlois's *Cinématographe*—about a group of passengers on a transatlantic steamer tricked into enacting the world war in miniature, he might have come out on the right side of history: see Lotte H. Eisner, "Le sujet que voudrait tourner G.-W. Pabst," *Cinematographe* 1 (March 1937): 7. Using Lang as a foil in the 1967 memorial piece, she argues that she didn't want to think of Pabst as a sympathizer, and had he stayed in Los Angeles, things could have been different: "Years passed, years that somehow buried all the resentment we had felt. . . . I wondered if Pabst, had he been able to shoot his film about the packetboat, might have had the strength to resist the temptation to direct films in Hitler's Germany. And I try to think of him now as the great director of *Pandora's Box*, *Diary of a Lost Girl*, and the sound films belonging to the era before 1933" (Eisner, "Meetings with Pabst," 210).

73. This anecdote is relayed about eighteen minutes into the film *Lotte Eisner in Germany* (S. M. Horowitz, 1981), as well as in the interview she gave to Brigitte Hervo, "Geist und Tat," *filmfaust* 9/10 (October/November 1978): 9.

74. Eisner, *Ich hatte*, 177–78.

75. It should be noted that Mannoni has suggested Eisner could be as calculating as Langlois was in negotiations with potential donors, although I would argue that this claim is best understood as a symptom of Mannoni's broader allergy to the doxa that Eisner merely carried out Langlois's acquisitions directives. In my view, the correspondence Mannoni cites in making this point is not representative of the larger body of Eisner's work, and the emphasis on her purportedly manipulative behavior fails to account for the simple fact that she needn't have gone so far out of her way to maintain friendships with some filmmakers and their families long past the point of acquisitions if it were a question of collecting the goods alone. Mannoni, "Kurtz et Eisner: Deux regards sur l'expressionnisme," in *Le cinéma expressioniste: De Caligari à Tim Burton*, ed. Jacques Aumont and Bernard Benoliel (Rennes, France: Presses Universitaires de Rennes, 2008), 32–58.

76. Lang's letters are discussed by Mannoni in *Histoire de la Cinémathèque française*. The Brooks correspondence is reprinted in part in Günter Krenn and Karin Moser, ed. *Louise Brooks: Rebellin, Ikone, Legende* (Wien: Verlag Filmarchiv Austria, 2006), and a selection of letters addressed to Langlois, Mary Meerson, and Eisner, dating from the late fifties is held at the CF. More are held in the private papers; Julia Eisner presented on a selection of these in May 2019 at the Amsterdam Eye conference.

77. See, for example, the exchange of letters of September 1963 from Brooks to Meerson with embedded messages for Eisner and Langlois; it relays some gossip about James Card, exhortations to Meerson and Langlois to get married and visit her in upstate New York, and a series of updates on her manuscript in progress and a developing dermatological situation. Mentioning her doctor's concern about a blood blister on her nose, and his proposed treatment plan, Brooks instructs Meerson to inform Eisner about the progress of a diet she's been following ("Tell Lotti [*sic*] I am not wrinkling up like a prune yet from my diet.") In her next epistle, dated September 12, 1963, Brooks signs off: "You make me so mad. Get MARRIED and come over. I may have a new nose tomorrow. The Doctor might remove my smeller and leave the red thing. Love, Louise."

78. Some of the letters between Roditi and Eisner, mostly about writing and translation, are held at the UCLA Special Collections Archive in the Roditi papers. An exchange of letters (held at USC among the Fritz Lang papers) between Eisner, Lang, and Herman Weinberg—in which Eisner mediates a dispute arising from the unauthorized use of a conversation with Lang recorded by Weinberg's daughter, Gretchen Berg—offers yet another view into Eisner's friendship with Lang, and with Weinberg. The correspondence between Weinberg and Eisner was collegial and friendly.

79. Letter from Grace Metzner to Lotte Eisner, May 15, 1955. Metzner was a director in his own right but is perhaps best known for his art direction and long collaboration in the twenties and early thirties with G. W. Pabst. Metzner, like Eisner, was exiled in 1933.

80. Letter from Rochus Gliese to Lotte Eisner, June 19, 1954.

81. This quotation is from an excerpt of Roud's *A Passion for Films* that was published as "Children of the Cinémathèque," *Sight and Sound* 52, no. 4 (Fall 1983): 252–57.

82. Roud, "Children of the Cinémathèque," 255.

83. It should also be noted that Langlois spent several years commuting by airplane to Montreal to lecture as a visiting professor at Sir George Williams University; maybe he wasn't figuratively or stereotypically so, but he was literally professorial.

84. Cifor, "Affecting Relations," 16.

85. Eisner, *Ich hatte*, 291 (see the introduction for quotation in full). Sara Ahmed, *The Cultural Politics of Emotion* (Edinburgh: Edinburgh University Press, 2004), 29.

86. Clare Hemmings has identified certain overreaches on the part of affect theory but concludes that it offers a valuable set of critical tools that moderate the more totalizing, determinist impulses within poststructuralist discourse on cultural institutions and power structures, including archives, in "Invoking Affect," *Cultural Studies* 19, no. 5 (2005): 548–67. My take here is also influenced by Anjali Arondekar's pivotal critique articulated in Arondekar, et al., "Queering Archives," and more fully in *For the Record* (Durham, NC: Duke University Press, 2009) of "against the grain" reading.

87. In the first camp, I would count the retelling of Fritz Lang's (in)famous story of his own departure from Berlin in her monograph on Lang, although in her memoirs she flags his tendency to embellish the story (Eisner, *Ich hatte*, 127). Gösta Werner did the work to double-check Lang's story and concluded that it could not have happened as Lang described. See "Fritz Lang and Goebbels: Myth and Facts," *Film Quarterly* 43, no. 3 (Spring 1990): 24–27. In the second camp, I would count some of Eisner's stories reported in the memoirs about her sister, Steffi, and Mary Meerson.

88. Sedgwick, *Epistemology of the Closet* (Berkeley: University of California Press, 1990), 23.

89. Pamela VanHaitsma, "Gossip as Rhetorical Methodology for Queer and Feminist Historiography," *Rhetoric Review* 35, no. 2 (2016): 135–47.

90. Eisner, *Ich hatte*, 60–61.

91. Heinrich Hoffman's collection of sinister cautionary tales for children bears the title of its first story's protagonist, Struwwelpeter or "Shaggy Peter," a boy whose slovenly personal hygiene results in devastating social isolation.

92. Philippa Levine, "Response," *Victorian Studies* 46, no. 2 (Winter 2004): 324–25.

93. Eisner claims that her father forbade her from attending such parties (although his death in 1924 would have liberated her from any such prohibition before the decade had half passed) and that she helped her friends make their outfits, but that Valeska Gert "never missed a one," in "Retour à Berlin," *Cinématographe* (May 1983): 4. The anecdote about Klaus Mann appears in several interviews, including in Sohrab Shahid Saless's film, *Die langen Ferien der Lotte H. Eisner*, and the Garbo remark in *Murnau* (Berkeley: University of California Press, 1973), 222.

94. In the case of F. W. Murnau, Eisner acknowledges that she is aware his family objects to any discussion of Murnau's sexuality and strenuously denies that he was gay; she argues that, their wishes notwithstanding, it's obvious that he was, and that his sexuality is of fundamental importance to any attempt to understand his artistic style. Eisner seems to be acting in good faith—although whether that matters is an open question—when she implies that the family's wishes are invalid on the grounds that Murnau was effectively out in his lifetime and that she doesn't want to humor or validate their rejection of his sexuality by either endorsing their view or remaining silent on this point.

95. These are the claims made, in order, by the following historians of Weimar cinema: Karsten Witte, "Ein oft gemischtes Glück," *Der Zeit* (October 31, 1986) and Werner Sudendorf, "Nicht zur Öffentlichung": Zur Biographie des Filmjournalisten Ernst (Ejott) Jäger," *Filmexil* 5 (1994), Thomas Elsaesser, *Weimar Cinema and After: Germany's Historical Imaginary* (London: Routledge, 2000), Noah Isenberg, "Introduction" in *Weimar Cinema: An Essential Guide to the Classic Films of the Era* (New York: Columbia University Press, 2009).

96. Although Claudia Breger's theorization of "feminine masculinities" suggests one possible avenue; see Breger, "Feminine Masculinities: Scientific and Literary Representation of 'Female Inversion' at the Turn of the Twentieth Century," *Journal of the History of Sexuality* 14, nos. 1–2 (January–April 2005): 76–106.

97. Mannoni, *Histoire*, 56.

CHAPTER 4. "LACUNAE EVERYWHERE"

1. *L'écran démoniaque* (Paris: André Bonne, 1952), *L'écran démoniaque: Édition définitive* (Paris: Le Terrain Vague, 1965), *The Haunted Screen* (Berkeley: University of California Press, 1969), *F. W. Murnau* (Paris: Le Terrain Vague, 1964), *Murnau: Der Klassiker des deutschen Films* (Hannover: Friedrich, 1967), *F. W. Murnau* (London: Secker & Warburg, 1973), and *Murnau* (Berkeley: University of California Press, 1973).

2. Daniel Fairfax, *The Red Years of Cahiers du Cinéma (1968–1973), Volume I: Ideology and Politics* (Amsterdam: Amsterdam University Press, 2021), 14.

3. Eisner had published English-language work in *Film Culture*, *Sight and Sound*, and *Film Quarterly* by this point, although the first edition of *The Haunted Screen* wouldn't appear until 1969.

4. Lotte Eisner, "Notes sur le style de Fritz Lang," *La Revue du cinéma* 5 (February 1947): 3–26.

5. Eisner, "Notes sur le style de Fritz Lang," 3, 20.

6. Interestingly, James Hillier—who mentions Eisner only once in his introduction to the first volume of his edited collection of essays from *Cahiers*, and never in the second volume—attributes the first stirrings of the authorship argument to a November 1946 article in *La Revue du cinéma* by Irving Pichel, in which Pichel states, "Creation must be the work of one person." Hillier, ed., *Cahiers du Cinéma*,

the 1950s: Neo-Realism, Hollywood, New Wave (Cambridge, MA: Harvard University Press, 1985), 5. The above translation of Bazin's article is Peter Graham's, reproduced in Hillier's book on pages 251–55.

7. Eisner is in good company here. Paula Amad has made the case that Colette was a "forgotten inspiration" and intellectual forebear to the *Cahiers* crowd, while maintaining that, at any rate, this fact is among the least interesting aspects of Colette's film criticism of the prewar period in the persuasive "'These Spectacles Are Never Forgotten': Memory and Reception in Colette's Film Criticism," *Camera Obscura* 20, no. 2 (2005): 118–63.

8. Thomas Elsaesser, "Too Big and Too Close: Alfred Hitchcock and Fritz Lang," *Hitchcock Annual* 12 (2003–2004): 1–41.

9. Fairfax's primary focus is the journal's dynamics in the late sixties and early seventies, during which period Eisner did not contribute to *Cahiers*; perhaps intending to say that Pierre was the first to be listed in the masthead, his mistake was in extending the claim to assert that Pierre was the first woman to write for *Cahiers*. Fairfax, *The Red Years*, 215.

10. Interview quoted in Fairfax, *The Red Years*, 215.

11. Richard Neupert, *A History of the French New Wave Cinema* (Madison: University of Wisconsin Press, 2007), 34.

12. The title translates to "F for Female," or more idiomatically, "W for Woman" in English.

13. "F comme Femme," *Cahiers du cinéma* 30 (Winter 1953): 29–41. Eisner's section on Nielsen runs pages 36–38.

14. *Cahiers du cinéma* 31 (January 1954): 1.

15. Eisner adapted the *Cahiers* Nielsen piece from the manuscript of *L'écran démoniaque* (1952) and would include a version in the revised definitive edition published in 1965, as well as all English-language editions of *The Haunted Screen*. Eisner incorporated another adaptation in the section "Filmschauspieler" of *Film, Rundfunk, und Fernsehen*, which she edited with Heinz Friedrich and published in 1958. In 1960, she published a Danish-language version in *Kosmorama*, titled "In Praise of Asta Nielsen," Lotte Eisner, "Zu Ehren von Asta Nielsen" *Kosmorama* 50 (October 1960): 6–7.

16. Auriol's *La Revue du cinéma* published its final issue in the fall of 1949, and Auriol died in April of 1950; Bazin died in 1958, the final year of Eisner's regular association with *Cahiers*.

17. François Truffaut, one of the younger members of this group, was born a little over year before Eisner was exiled to France. Like Eisner, he died in Neuilly-sur-Seine, just under a year after she did.

18. In a short sketch written by Roman Polanski and preserved at the CF, he recalls what he says was a characteristic interaction at a lunch out with Henri Langlois, Mary Meerson, and Lotte Eisner, throughout which Langlois held forth, animatedly, oblivious to the fact that loose threads from his sleeve were being dragged through some sauce on a plate before him as he gesticulated. Polanski describes

Meerson and Eisner attending maternally to him, supplying the ends of his sentences, and cooing about needing to repair his shirtsleeve for him.

19. See chapter 3, n. 53 for quotation from Eisner's letter to Curtis Harrington, November 21, 1961.

20. Lotte H. Eisner, "A Contribution to the Definition of the Expressionist Film," in *Expressionism as an International Literary Phenomenon*, ed. Ulrich Weisstein (Paris: Librarie Marcel Didier, 1973), 161.

21. There were other, more substantial critiques of her work that she could have engaged. Leonardo Quaresima writes that Raymond Borde, Freddy Buache, Francis Courtade, and Marcel Tariol's *Le cinéma réaliste allemand* (Lyon: Serdoc, 1965) was "explicitly directed against *L'écran démoniaque*" and allied itself with Kracauer's approach in opposition to Eisner's, which they deemed "old fashioned." Eisner engages the critique in *F. W. Murnau*, with a short chapter, titled "The Other Murnau, A 'Realist' Murnau?" in in which she disputes their claim that Murnau was actually a realist. Quaresima, "De faux amis: Kracauer et la filmologie," *Cinémas* 19, nos. 2–3 (2009): 333–58.

22. Lotte H. Eisner, "Les Secrets de Murnau," *Cinéma* 86 (May 1964): 105–6.

23. Theodore Huff, "An Index to the Films of F. W. Murnau," *Sight and Sound* (August 1948): 1–14.

24. Letter to Lotte Eisner from Siegfried Kracauer, October 20, 1946. Interestingly, all of the letters mentioned here between Eisner and Kracauer were written in French, with the exception of a few phrases of Kracauer's in English in the original, as indicated. A 1959 letter on an unrelated matter from Kracauer to Eisner held in the CF's administrative archives is the only correspondence I have seen there between the two conducted in their native German.

25. Letter to Siegfried Kracauer, February 4, 1947.

26. Letter to Lotte Eisner from Siegfried Kracauer, March 23, 1947.

27. *Pace* Mannoni, who attributed the letter of February 4 to Langlois and the Kracauer crack to Eisner in "Kurtz et Eisner: Deux regards sur l'expressionnisme," in *Le cinéma expressioniste: De Caligari à Tim Burton*, ed. Jacques Aumont and Bernard Benoliel (Rennes, France: Presses Universitaires de Rennes, 2008), 32–58. Julia Eisner has offered her own view of this correspondence and an alternate translation of some excerpts from it, in "Lotte Eisner: Pioneer of the Art and Craft of Collecting," *Screen* 62, no. 3 (Autumn 2021): 418–23.

28. Letters to Herman G. Weinberg from Lotte Eisner, April 28, 1958, and July 6, 1958, held at the New York Public Library, all written in English.

29. Renaud Bezombes, Michel Celemenski, and Carine Varène, "Die Eisnerin: Entretien avec Lotte H. Eisner," *Cinématographe* 73 (December 1981): 25–38.

30. Johannes von Moltke's sympathetic *The Curious Humanist: Siegfried Kracauer in America* (Berkeley: University of California Press, 2012) offers a detailed, highly engaging assessment of Kracauer's life and work in the United States.

31. Even Theodor Adorno's infamous, ambivalent tribute to his onetime mentor stops short of suggesting that Kracauer was unworthy of such consideration:

Theodor W. Adorno and Shierry Weber Nicholsen, "The Curious Realist: On Siegfried Kracauer," *New German Critique* 54 (Autumn 1991): 159–77.

32. Lotte Eisner, "Comment écrire l'histoire du cinéma," *Positif* 6 (April 1953): 37–40.

33. Eisner, "Comment écrire l'histoire du cinéma," 40.

34. *Monsieur Verdoux* (Charles Chaplin, 1947) and Vicki Baum serve as stable, opposing points of reference in Eisner's criticism and commentary; she consistently championed Chaplin's film (and repeatedly declared it one of the best postwar films in the critics polls in which she participated) as a pinnacle of cinematic humanism, and, as far back as her *Film-Kurier* days, she trotted out Vicki Baum's name to signify a type of popular author whose work, in Eisner's opinion, pandered to its readers.

35. This included both those within the *Cahiers* milieu and those in the (very different) Filmology group within the academy: "In contrast to the affinity of the French intelligentsia for the cinema during the period of the active avant-gardes of the 1920s, the postwar intellectual appeal of filmology was not aesthetic so much as it was sociological, arising from a humanistic concern for the power, influence and even utopian possibilities of film as a mass medium . . . couched in terms of urgency and crisis." Edward Lowry, *The Filmology Movement and Film Study in France* (Ann Arbor: UMI Research Press, 1985), 5.

36. Eisner, "Kitsch in the Cinema," in *Kitsch: The World of Bad Taste*, ed. Gillo Dorfles (New York: Bell Publishing Company, 1969): 197–217.

37. Eisner, *Ich hatte*, 291.

38. Eisner, "Kitsch in the Cinema," 215, 217.

39. Lotte H. Eisner, "Quelques aspects de l'avant-garde," *Positif* 12 (November 1954): 25–32.

40. In *Die langen Ferien der Lotte H. Eisner*, Eisner argues that turmoil in the period prior to the 1924 Dawes Plan influx of cash and resultant prevailing "materialism" among Germans allowed for the most intensely creative period in the country's history. Eisner attributes the decline in the quality of German films as the twenties drew to a close, and, similarly, with the strengthening of the West German economy postwar, to increasing stability: "Germans need metaphysical influences, they need despair and agitation to be creative. . . . Germans cannot become too content. When they do, a petit bourgeois mentality, rather than their creativity, comes to the surface." This take of Eisner's bears a fleeting resemblance to Kracauer's thesis on the post–Dawes Plan "paralysis," in *From Caligari to Hitler*.

41. Lewis Jacobs, "Avant-garde Production in America," in *Experiment in Film*, ed. Roger Manvell (London: Grey Walls, 1949).

42. Aristarco published his remarks in a review of the New American Cinema Group Exposition, May 13–23, 1967, at the Unione Culturale in Turin, a program that subsequently toured to Pesaro and other Italian cities: "Il *New American Cinema* esce dal sottosuolo," *Cinema Nuovo* (May–June 1967): 214–16. Discussing the program, curated by Jonas Mekas, Andrea Giaime Alonge summarized Aristarco's post-screening discussion contributions thusly: "According to Aristarco, the New

American Cinema Group's films were not innovative at all. They were simply remaking experiments already made by the European avant-gardes in the twenties. Moreover, they were not really revolutionary, but part of the capitalist system." Alonge's talk, titled "Underground Films in Factory Town: The New American Cinema Group Travels to Turin, Italy in 1967," was given at the Society for Cinema and Media Studies meeting March 19, 2021.

43. Irene Rozsa and Masha Salazkina, "Dissonances in 1970s European and Latin American Political Film Discourse: The Aristarco-García Espinosa Debate," *Canadian Journal of Film Studies* 24, no. 2 (Fall 2015): 72.

44. In the (English) text of the article, Eisner mixes up the French and German release titles, *Le Tigre du Bengal* and *Der Tiger von Eschnapur* (both 1959). Lotte H. Eisner, "Review: Erich von Stroheim," *Sight and Sound* 30, no. 2 (1961): 98.

45. Bezombes, et al., "Die Eisnerin," 28.

46. Luft, "Wir sind eigentlich alle vergessen worden," 94.

47. Eisner, *The Haunted Screen* (Berkeley: University of California Press, 1969), x.

48. Eisner, *The Haunted Screen*, 207.

49. Eisner, "Notes sur le style de Fritz Lang," 3.

50. Eisner, "Notes sur le style de Fritz Lang," 10.

51. Eisner, "Notes sur le style de Fritz Lang," 4.

52. McGilligan has asserted, in essence, that Eisner was browbeaten by Lang and that the process of drafting the manuscript consisted mainly in Lang micromanaging and bending Eisner's work to his own narrative, in *Fritz Lang: The Nature of the Beast* (New York: St. Martin's Press, 1997), 461–63. This highly colored biography of Lang has been faulted in some quarters for its exuberance and for the apparent relish with which its author builds a case for Lang as a murderer, liar, and bully; his descriptions of the relationship between Eisner and Lang and the book they worked on together strike me as tendentious, and his characterization of Eisner as "suffer[ing] endlessly" at Lang's hands, and her physical frailty—although almost every account of Eisner's person from the later years, most of them by then-young men, describe her as extremely thin, small, and weak—seem calculated to make such purported abuses by Lang seem all the more cruel and perverse. Nevertheless, where McGilligan makes reference to documents, such as the notes and revisions Lang made on Eisner's draft manuscripts, the infelicities of the final text of Eisner's monograph find some explanation.

53. Eisner, "Les origines du style Lubitsch," *La Revue du cinéma* 17 (September 1948): 3–15.

54. Eisner, *Ich hatte*, 39.

55. Eisner, "Les origines du style Lubitsch," 4.

56. Kalbus's original phrasing is: *wesenfremder Schnoddrigkeit*. To my eye, Joel Westerdale's translation ("impudence alien to our nature") improves upon both Kracauer's English translation ("pertness entirely alien from our true being") and Eisner's French (*effronterie*). Eisner's statement, rendered closely in English, reads as follows: "Dr. Kalbus, Nazi critic, pretends in his *Wesen* [sic] *deutscher Filmkunst*

that the effrontery of the early farces by Lubitsch were 'foreign to the German race.'" Eisner, "Les origines du style Lubitsch," 4. See Joel Westerdale, "An Accident of Resistance in Nazi Germany: Oskar Kalbus's Three-Volume History of German Film (1935–37)," *Film History* 29, no. 2 (2017): 165–91, and Siegfried Kracauer, *From Caligari to Hitler* (Princeton, NJ: Princeton University Press, 1947), 24.

57. Westerdale, "An Accident of Resistance," 175. Westerdale recuperates Kalbus on the grounds that the first two volumes of *Vom Werden deutscher Filmkunst* are ideologically inconsistent and take what Westerdale judges to be a "heterogenous" and "inclusive" approach to German film history prior to 1935, alternately invoking Nazi rhetoric and, at other moments, seeming to offer analysis or assessments uncontaminated by it. According to Westerdale, such waffling attracted negative attention to Kalbus in the party press; he compensated for this in the third, unpublished volume by rigidly toeing the party line, "seek[ing] to situate film in a Spenglerian history of decay and renewal brimming with clichés of the will and power of the racially homogeneous community." Westerdale, "An Accident of Resistance," 184. Such careful re-reading notwithstanding, it's clear that neither Eisner nor Kracauer believed that Kalbus's ambivalence in any way blunted or excused his anti-Semitic commentary and analysis.

58. Eisner, *The Haunted Screen*, n.p., excerpted from Leopold Ziegler, *Das Heilige Reich der Deutschen* (Darmstadt: O. Reichl, 1925).

59. James F. Ward, *Heidegger's Political Thinking* (Amherst: University of Massachusetts Press, 1995), 54.

60. Victor Farías, *Heidegger and Nazism* (Philadelphia: Temple University Press, 1989), 71.

61. Eisner, *The Haunted Screen*, 55–56. See Lotte H. Eisner, "Aperçus sur le costume dans les films allemands." *La Revue du cinéma* 19/20 (Autumn 1949): 68–86, and L. H. E., "Encore l'opéra de quat'sous." *Cahiers du cinéma* 37 (July 1954): 32–33 for reference to the "upside-down world of the brown shirts" and the "brown invasion."

62. Kracauer's reproach echoes in this passage if we listen carefully. He sent the apologetic admonishment I reproduced in translation above in March 1947; this article was published in September of the same year. Eisner, "Les origines du style Lubitsch," 8.

63. Eisner, "Les origines du style Lubitsch," 8.

64. Vicki Baum served as a consistent point of reference for Eisner, standing in for commercialized art that presumes a low standard of attention and discernment on the part of audiences; see earlier discussion of her 1953 piece in *Positif*. Eisner, "Comment écrire l'histoire du cinéma," 15.

65. Eisner, "Aperçus sur le costume dans les films allemands," 75.

66. Mannoni mentions in passing that Eisner said it took her five years to write and edit the volume before its initial publication in 1952, although this edition was drastically cut by request of the publisher André Bonne, and Eisner often remarked that she was dissatisfied with the 1952 edition. Mannoni, "Kurtz et Eisner," 47. Prior to the mid-sixties, a handful of French- and English-language single-subject articles

on German directors or films had appeared, but few summary works on interwar German cinema had been published outside of Germany. Eisner identified the following surveys as the peers of *L'écran démoniaque*: Alfred Bauer, *Deutscher Spielfilm Almanach, 1929–1950: Das Standardwerk des deutschen Films* (Berlin: Filmblätter Verlag, 1950), Oskar Kalbus, *Vom Werden deutscher Filmkunst* (Altona-Bahrenfeld: Cigaretten-Bilderdienst, 1935), Kracauer, *From Caligari to Hitler*, and Rudolf Kurtz, *Film und Expressionismus* (Berlin: Verlag der Lichtbildbühne, 1926).

67. Kracauer, *From Caligari to Hitler*, 96–97.

68. Eisner, "Comment écrire l'histoire du cinéma," (1953) and Luft, "Wir sind eigentlich alle vergessen worden," (1974).

69. Eisner would cite in all editions of the Murnau book her brief, but intriguing, "L'énigme des deux Nosferatu," *Cahiers du cinéma* 79 (January 1958): 22–24. For each new edition, Eisner expanded the chapter based on this article, finally declaring the case closed with the US edition in 1973.

70. Eisner did not include a foreword in the original French edition of 1964, but she comments on that edition in the 1967 foreword.

71. Eisner, *F. W. Murnau: Der Klassiker des deutschen Films* (Hannover: Friedrich Verlag, 1967), 7.

72. Eisner, *F. W. Murnau* (1967), 7. *Die Gartenlaube* was a popular weekly illustrated family magazine published from 1853 to 1944, associated with increasingly nationalist conservative bourgeois social and cultural values over time. During Eisner's lifetime, the magazine was published first by August Scherl, later Alfred Hugenberg, and in 1938 it was brought directly under the Nazi Party's control and relaunched as *Die neue Gartenlaube*. For an interesting history of the magazine's address of its female readership, see Kirsten Belgum, "Domesticating the Reader: Women and *Die Gartenlaube*," *Women in German Yearbook: Feminist Studies in German Literature & Culture* 9 (1994): 91–111.

73. Eisner, *Murnau* (Berkeley: University of California Press, 1973), 6–7.

74. Bergstrom, "In defence of F. W. Murnau," *Screen* 62, no. 3 (Autumn 2021): 400–407.

75. Eisner, *Murnau* (1973), 80. The conceit of chance-as-cinematographer harks back to the early sketch about the balloon-seller on the Kurfürstendamm, L. H. E., "Begebenheit," *Film-Kurier*, January 16, 1928 (see discussion in "Out and About," in chapter 2).

76. Eisner, *Murnau* (1973), 82.

77. Eisner, "Quelques aspects de l'avant-garde," 31, and Eisner, *Murnau* (1973), 152.

78. Many others have mobilized Murnau's optics and his sexuality in related arguments; most persuasively, Janet Bergstrom extended this basic premise to call for an expansion of Laura Mulvey's theory of the gendered and sexualized gaze. Bergstrom, "Sexuality at a Loss: The Films of F. W. Murnau," *Poetics Today* 6, no. 1–2 (1985): 185–203.

79. Eisner, *Murnau*, 222.

80. Eisner, *Murnau*, 222.

81. Baer makes this point in his note on Eisner's "A New India Film: *A Throw of the Dice*," in *The Promise of Cinema*, ed. Anton Kaes, Nicholas Baer, and Michael Cowan (Berkeley: University of California Press, 2016), 63. I would add that in several film reviews from the *Film-Kurier* days, in her chapter on *Tabu* in *Murnau*, and in at least one review from the mid-fifties, Eisner leans on dehumanizing language to describe non-European people, invoking tropes devised by and implicated in brutal colonial regimes of power and trade, while at the same time offering unreservedly critical remarks on the depredations and atrocities perpetrated by those same colonial enterprises.

82. Eisner, *The Haunted Screen*, 98.

83. Recall her formulation of kitsch as the result "when a director does not have the power of persuasion and the genius to impose the absurdity of another world on us as if it were real." Eisner, "Kitsch in the Cinema," 213.

84. Lotte Eisner, *Fritz Lang* (Berkeley: University of California Press, 1976), 7–8.

85. Charles Jameux, *F. W. Murnau* (Paris: Éditions Universitaires, 1965).

86. Eisner, *Fritz Lang*, 8.

87. In the Shahid Saless documentary, Eisner mistakenly attributes this metaphor to her earliest piece published in the *Film-Kurier*, saying, "I don't remember which film I actually saw being produced, but I published my article, which got a two-page spread—this was 1927—even though I knew very little about filmmaking; all I remember is that all the cables reminded me of lianas in the jungle. Nevertheless, they asked me if I wanted to write for them, and I said yes, as long as I can also review theater." Eisner had used the simile between cables and lianas in an earlier article about a set visit to the Ufa Kulturfilm division, but its December 1928 publication came over a year into her tenure at the *Film-Kurier*: Lotte H. Eisner, "Kulturfilm im Werden: Bei der Ufa in Neubabelsberg," *Film-Kurier*, December 8, 1928. See my translation, "Kulturfilm in Development: At Ufa in Neubabelsberg," published in DeCelles, "A Critic at Large: Lotte Eisner at the *Film-Kurier* (1927–1933)."

88. L. H. E., "Ein Wald wird ummontiert—Fritz Lang beginnt zu drehen," *Film-Kurier*, October 3, 1932.

89. Lotte Eisner, "Quand Fritz Lang réalisait *Le Testament du Docteur Mabuse*," *L'Intransigeant* (May 1933): 10.

90. L. H. E. "Chauffeurs de Taxi," *Cahiers du cinéma* 74 (August–September 1957): 38.

91. One additional example: in a 1937 article celebrating Peter Lorre's career to date, Eisner makes a point of remarking that she's been talking with him about Verlaine's poem about Gaspard Hauser and that she suggested to him that he attempt an adaptation in Hollywood, a role she says he would be uniquely adept in portraying: "Peter Lorre le Meurtier," *Cinématographe* 2 (May 1937): 13. Of course, Eisner famously inspired Herzog with her recitations of the poem, and she was invited as a special guest and sort of totemic figure to the shooting of his own *The Enigma of Kaspar Hauser* (*Jeder für sich und Gott gegen alle*, 1974), which she described,

glowingly, in Lotte H. Eisner, "In the Picture: Herzog in Dinkelsbühl," *Sight and Sound* 43, no. 4 (Fall 1974): 212–13.

CONCLUSION

1. Hamid Naficy, *An Accented Cinema* (Princeton, NJ: Princeton University Press, 2001), 204. At the time, this sum would have been equivalent to roughly $287,850 per US Department of the Treasury, *Treasury Reporting Rates of Exchange as of June 30, 1979* (1979), 2.
2. S. Mark Horowitz interview by author, February 27, 2018.
3. Michelle Langford, "Sohrab Shahid Saless: An Iranian Filmmaker in Berlin," *Screening the Past* (December 2016): www.screeningthepast.com/2016/12/sohrab-shahid-saless-an-iranian-filmmaker-in-berlin/.
4. Mamad Haghighat, "Lotte H. Eisner über Saless: Ein Interview von Mamad Haghighat," in *Sohrab Shahid Saless: Bericht über ein abgekürztes Leben* (Oldenberg: Werkstattfilm, 1999), 58–61.
5. Werner Herzog and Paul Cronin, *Herzog on Herzog* (New York: Farrar, Straus and Giroux 2002), 152–53.
6. In 1980, Herzog appealed directly to Bundespräsident Carl Carstens for funds to pay off hospital bills and contribute to the costs of physical therapy and in-home health care for Eisner in a series of letters copied to Shahid Saless, held in the Shahid Saless papers at Oldenberg. In a May 5, 1980, letter Herzog claims that Eisner's family had neglected her after she broke her hip earlier that spring and that he, Sohrab Shahid Saless, Volker Schlöndorff, and Alexander Kluge believed the West German state should step in, using money held in an arts fund to support her care.
7. The bulk of these samples are drawn from Horowitz's and Shahid Saless's films, a smaller portion from *La mort n'a pas voulu de moi* (Célémenski, Roussopoulos, and Varène, 1984).
8. David Marchese, "Werner Herzog Has Never Thought a Dog Was Cute," *New York Times Magazine*, March 23, 2020: www.nytimes.com/interactive/2020/03/23/magazine/werner-herzog-interview.html.
9. Lotte H. Eisner, *The Haunted Screen: Expressionism in the German Cinema and the Influence of Max Reinhardt*. Berkeley: University of California Press, 1969, 341.
10. The first histories of German cinema written in the postwar period, according to Sabine Hake, tended to focus on West German cinema from 1945 to 1962, construing its "seemingly harmless, trivial subject matter" as "little more than the displaced fears, desires, and resentments that gave rise to the culture of amnesia after the Second World War." This school of thought held that the Oberhausen Manifesto of 1962 marked the beginning of a German cinema worthy of serious critical attention and analysis. "Since unification," however, "comparative studies have opened up new perspectives on the intensively reciprocal relationship between East and West German cinema," and "brought into sharper relief the many connections between

West and East postwar cinema and other European cinemas." Sabine Hake, *German National Cinema* (New York: Routledge, 2002), 92–93.

11. For discussion of the MoMA Film Library's imbrication with "wartime knowledge production," see Nathaniel Brennan, "The Cinema Intelligence Apparatus," in *Cinema's Military Industrial Complex*, ed. Haidee Wasson and Lee Grieveson (Oakland: University of California Press, 2018), 137–56, and Peter Decherney, *Hollywood and the Culture Elite: How the Movies Became American* (New York: Columbia University Press, 2005).

12. Those interested in seeing the film will be gratified to learn that Horowitz recently deposited a print at the UCLA Film and Television Archive and posted a good-quality copy online; there has also been at least one 16 mm print in US public library circulation.

13. They are: "Paris, 1979," "1926: The beginning," "Film," "Emigration and exile," "The long vacation," "Escoffier," "The first years in France," "Meeting Henri Langlois," "Sunday, June 24, 1979," "May '68," "Henri Langlois is dead," "Expressionist cinema and *The Haunted Screen*," "The birth of the young German cinema," "... and the future," "The critics," "It is better to write positively," and "Yearning for the past, yearning for the lost home."

14. This may be a reference to the dancer Vaslav Nijinsky, but I am not aware of an acquaintance between Eisner and Nijinsky, either in their youth or at any later point, which his retirement ca. 1919 would seem to have prohibited.

15. Naficy, *An Accented Cinema*, 160.

16. Naficy, *An Accented Cinema*, 27.

17. Naficy, *An Accented Cinema*, 11.

18. Joan W. Scott, "Fantasy Echo: History and the Construction of Identity," *Critical Inquiry* 27, no. 2 (2001): 284–304.

19. Naficy, *An Accented Cinema*, 152.

20. Lotte Eisner, *Ich hatte einst ein schönes Vaterland: Memoiren* (Heidelberg: Wunderhorn, 1984), 346.

21. Bishnupriya Ghosh, "The Hole That Wasn't There," *GLQ* 17, no. 4 (2011): 683–85.

22. Shelley Stamp, "Feminist Media Historiography and the Work Ahead," *Screening the Past* 40 (2015): www.screeningthepast.com/2015/08/feminist-media-historiography-and-the-work-ahead/.

23. Wedel advanced these arguments in his talk, "*Faust* in America: *Sunrise* through the Looking-Glass of Lotte Eisner and Eric Rohmer," at the Lotte Eisner Symposium at King's College, London, October 26–27, 2018, and in Michael Wedel, "Through the Looking-Glass: Lotte H. Eisner and Éric Rohmer on Murnau," *Screen* 62, no. 3 (Autumn 2021): 390–99.

24. Wedel offered this assessment in the context of his talk at the Lotte Eisner Symposium, and he rephrased it slightly in "Through the Looking-Glass," 399: "Eisner was many things, but she never would have considered herself a film theorist in the full sense of the word."

25. Raymond Williams, *The Long Revolution* (London: Chatto & Windus, 1961) 47.

26. Stegner, *Angle of Repose* (New York: Penguin, 1971), 379.

27. The gleaner might also be considered a relative of Carlo Ginzburg's "low" register of the conjectural paradigm, articulated in "Clues: Roots of an Evidential Paradigm," in *Clues, Myths, and the Historical Method* (Baltimore: Johns Hopkins University Press, 1989), 125.

28. Yvonne Hartman and Sandy Darab, "A Call for Slow Scholarship: A Case Study on the Intensification of Academic Life and Its Implications for Pedagogy," *Review of Education, Pedagogy, and Cultural Studies* 34, nos. 1–2 (2012): 49–60.

29. Saidiya Hartman, "Venus in Two Acts," *Small Axe* 12, no. 2 (2008): 1–14.

30. Thomas Elsaesser critiques the historiography of German film exiles in Hollywood on somewhat similar grounds, although he posits a "Paris stopover," which elides important alternate trajectories in "Ethnicity, Authenticity, and Exile: A Counterfeit Trade?" in *Home, Exile, Homeland: Film, Media, and the Politics of Place*, ed. Hamid Naficy (New York: Routledge, 1999). Patrice Petro called for a study of the greater network of exiled filmmakers, given the fact that "Berlin during the Weimar years was a node within a network of global cities that included London and Paris, Moscow, Mexico City, Los Angeles, and New York," in "Legacies of Weimar Cinema," in *Cinema and Modernity*, ed. Murray Pomerance (New Brunswick, NJ: Rutgers University Press, 2006), 240. Masha Salazkina took up just such an inquiry with fascinating results in "Moscow-Rome-Havana: A Film-Theory Road Map," *October* 139 (2012): 97–116.

31. Hortense Powdermaker, *Hollywood, The Dream Factory: An Anthropologist Studies the Movie Makers* (London: Secker & Warburg, 1951), 327.

REFERENCES

SECONDARY SOURCES

Adler, Daniel. "Painterly Politics: Wölfflin, Formalism, and German Academic Culture, 1885–1915." *Art History* 27, no. 3 (June 2004): 431–56.
Adorno, Theodor W. *The Stars Down to Earth and Other Essays on the Irrational in Culture*. London: Routledge, 1994.
Adorno, Theodor W., and Shierry Weber Nicholsen. "The Curious Realist: On Siegfried Kracauer." *New German Critique* 54 (Autumn 1991): 159–77.
Ahmed, Sara. *The Cultural Politics of Emotion*. Edinburgh: Edinburgh University Press, 2004.
Aitken, Ian. *European Film Theory and Cinema: A Critical Introduction*. Bloomington: Indiana University Press, 2001.
Altenloh, Emilie. *Zur Soziologie des Kino*. Jena: Eugen Diederichs, 1914.
Amad, Paula. "'These Spectacles Are Never Forgotten': Memory and Reception in Colette's Film Criticism." *Camera Obscura* 20, no. 2 (2005): 118–63.
Anderson, Mark M. "Siegfried Kracauer and Meyer Schapiro: A Friendship." *New German Critique* 54 (Autumn 1991): 18–29.
Arnheim, Rudolf. *Film as Art*. Berkeley: University of California Press, 2006.
———. *Film Essays and Criticism*. Madison: University of Wisconsin Press, 1997.
Arondekar, Anjali. *For the Record*. Durham, NC: Duke University Press, 2009.
Arondekar, Anjali, Ann Cvetkovich, Christina B. Hanhardt, Regina Kunzel, Tavia Nyong'o, Juana María Rodríguez, and Susan Stryker. "Queering Archives: A Roundtable Discussion." *Radical History Review* 122 (May 2015): 211–31.
Aurich, Rolf. "Zwei Pressemenschen: Ewald André Dupont und Ernst Jäger." *Filmexil* 17 (2003): 33–38.
Aurich, Rolf, and Wolfgang Jacobsen. "Leidenschaftliche Vernunft: Der Journalist Hans Feld im Exil." *Filmexil* 22 (2005): 5–21.
———. eds. *Werkstatt Film. Selbstverständnis und Visionen von Filmleuten der zwanziger Jahre*. Munich: edition text + kritik, 1998.
Barry, Iris. *Let's Go to the Movies*. New York: Arno Press, 1972 [1926].

Behrens, Roy R. "Rudolf Arnheim: The Little Owl on the Shoulder of Athene." *Leonardo* 31, no. 3 (1998): 231–33.

Belgum, Kirsten. "Domesticating the Reader: Women and *Die Gartenlaube*." *Women in German Yearbook: Feminist Studies in German Literature & Culture* 9 (1994): 91–111.

Bergfelder, Tim, Erica Carter, Deniz Göktürk, and Claudia Sandberg, eds. *The German Cinema Book*. London: BFI, 2020.

Berg-Ganschow, Uta, and Wolfgang Jacobsen, eds. *Film . . . Stadt . . . Kino . . . Berlin*. Berlin: Argon, 1987.

Bergstrom, Janet. "In defence of F. W. Murnau." *Screen* 62, no. 3 (Autumn 2021): 400–407.

———. "Out from the Shadows: Lotte Eisner's Significance as a Collector." In *Cinema in the Eye of the Collector*, edited by André Habib, Louis Pelletier, and Jean-Pierre Sirois-Trahan. Amsterdam: Amsterdam University Press, 2022.

———. "Sexuality at a Loss: The Films of F. W. Murnau." *Poetics Today* 6, no. 1–2 (1985): 185–203.

Bezombes, Renaud, Michel Celemenski, and Carine Varène. "Die Eisnerin: Entretien avec Lotte H. Eisner." *Cinématographe* 73 (December 1981): 25–38.

Bieber, Margarete. "Necrology." *American Journal of Archaeology* 62, no. 4 (October 1958): 429–30.

Bock, Hans-Michael, and Wolfgang Jacobsen. *Recherche: Film. Quellen und Methoden der Filmforschung*. Munich: edition text + kritik, 1997.

Breger, Claudia. "Feminine Masculinities: Scientific and Literary Representation of 'Female Inversion' at the Turn of the Twentieth Century." *Journal of the History of Sexuality* 14, nos. 1–2 (January–April 2005): 76–106.

Brennan, Nathaniel. "The Cinema Intelligence Apparatus." In *Cinema's Military Industrial Complex*, edited by Haidee Wasson and Lee Grieveson, 137–56. Oakland: University of California Press, 2018.

Brockmann, Stephen. *A Critical History of German Film*. Rochester, NY: Camden House, 2010.

Celemenski, Michel, and Serge Eymann. "Lotte H. Eisner." *Cinématographe* 95 (December 1983): 80–81.

Cifor, Marika. "Affecting Relations: Introducing Affect Theory to Archival Discourse." *Archival Science* 16 (2016): 7–31.

Cvetkovich, Ann. *An Archive of Feeling: Trauma, Sexuality, and Lesbian Public Cultures*. Durham, NC: Duke University Press, 2003.

DeCelles, Naomi. "The Case for (Re)collecting Lotte Eisner's work." In *Uncanny Histories in Film and Media Studies*, edited by Patrice Petro. New Brunswick, NJ: Rutgers University Press, 2022.

———. "A Critic at Large: Lotte Eisner at the *Film-Kurier* (1927–1933)." *Journal of Cinema and Media Studies* 61, no. 3 (Spring 2022): 129–52.

———. "Mediating Displacement: Lotte Eisner's Exile on Film." *Quarterly Review of Film and Video* 37, no. 4 (2019): 384–97.

———. "Out and About: Lotte Eisner at the *Film-Kurier*, 1927–1933." *Screen* 62, no. 3 (Autumn 2021): 408–17.

Decherney, Peter. *Hollywood and the Culture Elite: How the Movies Became American*. New York: Columbia, 2005.

Dilly, Heinrich. *Kunstgeschichte als Institution. Studien zur Geschichte einer Disziplin*. Frankfurt: Suhrkamp, 1979.

Ehmann, Antje. "Rede, Gerede und Gegenrede: Film und Kultur im Diskurs der Weimarer Jahre." In *Geschichte des dokumentarischen Films in Deutschland, Band 2*, edited by Klaus Kreimeier, Antje Ehmann, Jeanpaul Goergen, 249–74. Stuttgart: Philipp Reclam jun. GmBH & Co., 2005.

Eisner, Julia. "Lotte Eisner in Exile: Reinvention and Relocation." In *Ach, sie haben ihre Sprache verloren*, edited by Erika Wottrich and Swenja Schiemann, 169–90. Munich: edition text + kritik, 2017.

———. "Lotte Eisner: Pioneer of the Art and Craft of Collecting." *Screen* 62, no. 3 (Autumn 2021): 418–23.

Eisner, Lotte. "Die Entwicklung der Komposition auf griechischen Vasenbildern." PhD diss. Rostock: University of Rostock, 1924.

Eisner, Lotte H., and David Williams. "Films in Paris." *Cinema Journal* 14, no. 3 (Spring 1975): 68–74.

Elsaesser, Thomas. "Ethnicity, Authenticity, and Exile: A Counterfeit Trade?" In *Home, Exile, Homeland: Film, Media, and the Politics of Place*, edited by Hamid Naficy, 99–123. New York: Routledge, 1999.

———. "Too Big and Too Close: Alfred Hitchcock and Fritz Lang." *Hitchcock Annual* 12 (2003–2004): 1–41.

———. *Weimar Cinema and After: Germany's Historical Imaginary*. London: Routledge, 2000.

———. "Weimar Cinema, Mobile Selves, and Anxious Males: Kracauer and Eisner Revisited." In *Expressionist Film: New Perspectives*, edited by Dietrich Scheunemann, 33–71. Rochester: Camden House, 2003.

Elsner, Jas'. "From Empirical Evidence to the Big Picture: Some Reflections on Riegl's Concept of *Kunstwollen*." *Critical Inquiry* 32 (Summer 2006): 741–66.

Fairfax, Daniel. *The Red Years of Cahiers du Cinéma (1968–1973)*. Amsterdam: Amsterdam University Press, 2021.

Farías, Victor. *Heidegger and Nazism*. Philadelphia: Temple University Press, 1989.

Feld, Hans. "Die dokumentarischen Aufgaben des Kulturfilms." *Film-Kurier*, April 7, 1928.

———. "Jews in the Development of the German Film Industry: Notes from the Recollections of a Berlin Film Critic." *Leo Baeck Institute Year Book* 27 (1982): 337–64.

———. "Lotte Eisner: Beginn einer Karriere. Eine Federzeichnung mit dem Hintergrund von Weimar." *Filmexil* 22 (2005): 37–38.

Frame, Lynne. "Gretchen, Girl, Garçonne? Weimar Science and Popular Culture in Search of the Ideal New Woman." In *Women in the Metropolis: Gender and*

Modernity in Weimar Culture, edited by Katharina von Ankum, 12–34. Berkeley: University of California Press, 1997.

Freidenreich, Harriet Pass. *Female, Jewish, and Educated: The Lives of Central European University Women*. Bloomington: Indiana University Press, 2002.

Garberson, Eric. "Art History in the University: Toelken, Hotho, Kugler." *Journal of Art Historiography* 5 (December 2011): 1–89.

Ghosh, Bishnupriya. "The Hole That Wasn't There." *GLQ* 17, no. 4 (2011): 683–85.

Ginzburg, Carlo. "Clues: Roots of an Evidential Paradigm." In *Clues, Myths, and the Historical Method*, translated by John Tedeschi and Anne C. Tedeschi, 96–125. Baltimore: Johns Hopkins University Press, 1989.

Gossman, Lionel. "Imperial Icon: The Pergamon Altar in Wilhelmine Germany." *Journal of Modern History* 78 (September 2006): 551–87.

Graham, Cooper C. "'Olympia' in America, 1938: Leni Riefenstahl, Hollywood, and the Kristallnacht." *Historical Journal of Film, Radio and Television* 13, no. 4 (September 2006): 433–50.

Greenbaum, Connie. "Entretien avec Lotte Eisner." *La Revue du cinéma: Image et son* 283 (April 1974): 67–69.

Grierson, John. *Grierson on Documentary*. Edited by Forsyth Hardy. Berkeley: University of California Press, 1966.

Gubser, Michael. "Time and History in Alois Riegl's Theory of Perception." *Journal of the History of Ideas* 66, no. 3 (July 2005): 451–74.

Hagener, Malte, ed. *The Emergence of Film Culture: Knowledge Production, Institution Building and the Fate of the Avant-Garde in Europe, 1919–1945*. New York: Berghahn, 2014.

Haghighat, Mamad. "Lotte H. Eisner über Saless: Ein Interview von Mamad Haghighat." In *Sohrab Shahid Saless: Bericht über ein abgekürztes Leben*, edited by Farschid Ali Zahedi, 58–61. Oldenberg: Werkstattfilm, 1999.

Hake, Sabine. *German National Cinema*. New York: Routledge, 2002.

Hansen, Miriam. *Cinema and Experience*. Berkeley: University of California Press, 2012.

———. "'With Skin and Hair': Kracauer's Theory of Film, Marseille 1940." *Critical Inquiry* 19, no. 3 (1993): 437–69.

Hartman, Saidiya. "Venus in Two Acts." *Small Axe* 12, no. 2 (2008): 1–14.

Hartman, Yvonne, and Sandy Darab. "A Call for Slow Scholarship: A Case Study on the Intensification of Academic Life and Its Implications for Pedagogy." *Review of Education, Pedagogy, and Cultural Studies* 34, nos. 1–2 (2012): 49–60.

Harvey, Sylvia. *May '68 and Film Culture*. London: BFI Publishing, 1978.

Hemmings, Clare. "Invoking Affect," *Cultural Studies* 19, no. 5 (2005): 548–67.

Herf, Jeffrey. *Reactionary Modernism: Technology, Culture, and Politics in Weimar and the Third Reich*. Cambridge: Cambridge University Press, 1984.

Hervo, Brigitte. "Geist und Tat." *filmfaust* 9/10 (October/November 1978): 7–12.

Herzog, Werner, and Paul Cronin. *Herzog on Herzog*. New York: Farrar, Straus and Giroux, 2002.

Higgins, Scott, ed. *Arnheim for Film and Media Studies*. New York: Routledge, 2011.

Hillier, James. *Cahiers du Cinema, the 1950s: Neo-Realism, Hollywood, New Wave*. Cambridge, MA: Harvard University Press, 1985.

Huff, Theodore. "An Index to the Films of F. W. Murnau." *Sight and Sound* (August 1948): 1–14.

Hurst, Heike, Dorothea Muenk, and Uscica Perabo. "Film . . . das ist so populo! Gespräch mit Lotte Eisner von Heike Hurst, Dorothea Muenk, and Uscica Perabo." *Frauen und Film* 11 (March 1977): 29–37.

Isenberg, Noah, ed. *Weimar Cinema: An Essential Guide to the Classic Films of the Era*. New York: Columbia University Press, 2009.

———. "Review. *Expressionist Film: New Perspectives* by Dietrich Scheunemann." *Monatshefte* 98, no. 1 (2006): 152–54.

Jacobs, Lewis. *The Compound Cinema: The Film Writings of Harry Alan Potamkin*. New York: Teachers College Press, 1977.

Jurczyk, Günter. "Voll Mut—wenn's auch nicht stimmt: Gespräch mit der Filmhistorikerin Lotte Eisner." *Süddeutsche Zeitung* 204 (September 6, 1982): 15.

Kaes, Anton. "Siegfried Kracauer: Film Historian in Exile." In *"Escape to Life": German Intellectuals in New York: A Compendium on Exile after 1933*, edited by Eckart Goebel and Sigrid Weigel, 236–69. Berlin: de Gruyter, 2013.

Kaes, Anton, Nicholas Baer, and Michael Cowan, eds. *The Promise of Cinema*. Berkeley: University of California Press, 2016.

Kracauer, Siegfried. *From Caligari to Hitler*. Princeton, NJ: Princeton University Press, 2004.

———. *The Mass Ornament*. Cambridge, MA: Harvard University Press, 1995.

Krenn, Günter, and Karin Moser. *Louise Brooks: Rebellin, Ikone, Legende*. Wien: Verlag Filmarchiv Austria, 2006.

Langford, Michelle. "Sohrab Shahid Saless: An Iranian Filmmaker in Berlin." *Screening the Past* (December 2016): www.screeningthepast.com/2016/12/sohrab-shahid-saless-an-iranian-filmmaker-in-berlin/.

Langlois, Georges. "Oeuvre et biographie d'Henri Langlois." *Films & documents* 332 (Autumn 1980): 4–19.

Layton, Roland V., Jr. "The 'Völkischer Beobachter,' 1920–1933: The Nazi Party Newspaper in the Weimar Era." *Central European History* 3, no. 4 (December 1970): 353–82.

Lenk, Sabine, and André Stufkens. "'Then Began the Battle Royal': Marion Michelle and the FIAF Crisis." *The Moving Image* 13, no. 1 (Spring 2013): 199–217.

Lenssen, Claudia. "'Die Klassiker': Die Rezeption von Lotte H. Eisner und Siegfried Kracauer." In *Recherche: Film. Quellen und Methoden der Filmforschung*, edited by Hans-Michael Bock and Wolfgang Jacobsen, 67–82. Munich: edition text + kritik, 1997.

Lowry, Edward. *The Filmology Movement and Film Study in France*. Ann Arbor: UMI Research Press, 1985.

Luce, Stephen Bleecker. "A Brief History of the Study of Greek Vase-Painting." *Proceedings of the American Philosophical Society* 57, no. 7 (1918): 649–68.

Lücken, Gottfried von. "Archaische griechische Vasenmalerei und Plastik." *Mitteilungen des deutschen archäologischen Instituts* 44 (1919): 47–174.

———. *Die Entwicklung der Parthenonskulpturen*. Augsburg: Dr. Benno Filser Verlag, 1930.

———. "Zur Entstehung des Bildes." *Zeitschrift für bildende Kunst* 57 (N.F. 33, 1922): 1–6.

Luft, Edmund. "Wir sind eigentlich alle vergessen worden; Lotte H. Eisner im Gespräch mit Edmund Luft." *Filmgeschichte* 16/17 (1974): 87–94.

MacDonald, Richard Lowell. "Film Appreciation and Cultural Leadership: Rudolf Arnheim, Roger Manvell, and Two Books Called '*Film*.'" *Canadian Journal of Film Studies* 23, no. 1 (Spring 2014): 109–27.

Mannoni, Laurent. *Histoire de la Cinémathèque française*. Paris: Gallimard, 2006.

———. "Kurtz et Eisner: Deux regards sur l'expressionnisme." In *Le cinéma expressionniste: de Caligari à Tim Burton*, edited by Jacques Aumont and Bernard Benoliel, 32–58. Rennes, France: Presses Universitaires de Rennes, 2008.

———. "Lotte Eisner, historienne des démons allemands." In *Le cinéma expressionniste allemand: Splendeurs d'une collection*. Paris: Éditions de La Martinière / La Cinémathèque Française, 2006.

Mannoni, Laurent, and Richard Crangle. "Henri Langlois and the Musée du Cinéma." *Film History* 18, no. 3 (2006): 274–87.

Marchese, David. "Werner Herzog Has Never Thought a Dog Was Cute." *New York Times Magazine*, March 23, 2020, www.nytimes.com/interactive/2020/03/23/magazine/werner-herzog-interview.html.

Martin, Marcel. "De l'archéologie à l'histoire." *La Revue du cinéma: Image et son* 377 (November 1982): 127–30.

Mazón, Patricia M. *Gender and the Modern Research University: The Admission of Women to German Higher Education, 1865–1914*. Stanford, CA: Stanford University Press, 2003.

———. "'*Fräulein Doktor*': Literary Images of the First Female University Students in Fin-de-Siècle Germany." *Women in German Yearbook* 16 (2000): 129–50.

McGilligan, Patrick. *Fritz Lang: The Nature of the Beast*. New York: St. Martin's Press, 1997.

Mendes-Flohr, Paul. "The Berlin Jew as Cosmopolitan." In *Berlin Metropolis: Jews and the New Culture, 1890–1918*, edited by Emily D. Bilski, 15–31. Berkeley: University of California Press, 2000.

Moltke, Johannes von. *The Curious Humanist: Siegfried Kracauer in America*. Berkeley: University of California Press, 2012.

Moltke, Johannes von, and Kristy Rawson. *Siegfried Kracauer's American Writings*. Berkeley: University of California Press, 2012.

Muthesius, Stefan. "Towards an 'exakte Kunstwissenschaft'? A Report on Some Recent German Books on the Progress of Mid-19th-Century Art History." *Journal of Art Historiography* 9 (December 2013): 1–37.

Myrent, Glenn, and Georges P. Langlois. *Henri Langlois: First Citizen of Cinema.* New York: Twayne Publishers, 1995.
Naficy, Hamid. *An Accented Cinema.* Princeton, NJ: Princeton University Press, 2001.
Neupert, Richard. *A History of the French New Wave Cinema.* Madison: University of Wisconsin Press, 2007.
Olin, Margaret. "Riegl, Alois." In *Encyclopedia of Aesthetics, Second Edition*, edited by Michael Kelly. Oxford: Oxford University Press, 2014.
Orbanz, Eva. *Hans Feld: Redakteur und Kulturjournalist. Bibliografie Film-Kurier 1926–1932.* Munich: edition text + kritik, 2019.
Patalas, Enno. "On the Way to '*Nosferatu.*'" *Film History* 14, no. 1 (2002): 25–31.
Patry, Lucien. "Entretien avec Lotte Eisner, le 2 février 1980." *Films & documents* 332 (Autumn 1980): 24–31.
Petro, Patrice. "Legacies of Weimar Cinema." In *Cinema and Modernity,* edited by Murray Pomerance, 235–52. New Brunswick, NJ: Rutgers University Press, 2006.
———. "Perceptions of Difference: Woman as Spectator and Spectacle." In *Women in the Metropolis*, edited by Katharina von Ankum, 41–62. Berkeley: University of California Press, 1997.
Powdermaker, Hortense. *Hollywood, The Dream Factory: An Anthropologist Studies the Movie Makers.* London: Secker & Warburg, 1951.
Quaresima, Leonardo. "De faux amis: Kracauer et la filmologie." *Cinémas* 19, nos. 2–3 (2009): 333–58.
———. "Introduction to the 2004 Edition: Rereading Kracauer." In *From Caligari to Hitler*, xv–xlix. Princeton, NJ: Princeton University Press, 2004.
Riegl, Alois. "Die Stimmung als Inhalt der modernen Kunst" [1899]. In *Gesammelte Aufsätze*, edited by K. M. Swoboda, 28–39. Augsburg, Germany: Filser, 1929.
Ringer, Fritz K. *The Decline of the German Mandarins.* Cambridge, MA: Harvard University Press, 1969.
Robinson, J. Bradford. "The Jazz Essays of Theodor Adorno: Some Thoughts on Jazz Reception in Weimar Germany." *Popular Music* 13, no. 1 (January 1994): 1–25.
Roud, Richard. "The Moral Taste of Lotte H. Eisner." *Sight & Sound* 53, no. 2 (Spring 1984): 139–40.
———. *A Passion for Films.* New York: Viking, 1983.
Rozsa, Irene, and Masha Salazkina. "Dissonances in 1970s European and Latin American Political Film Discourse: The Aristarco-García Espinosa Debate." *Revue Canadienne d'Études cinématographiques/Canadian Journal of Film Studies* 24, no. 2 (Fall 2015): 66–81.
Salazkina, Masha. "Moscow-Rome-Havana: A Film-Theory Road Map." *October* 139 (2012): 97–116.
Salis, Arnold von. *Die Kunst der Griechen.* Leipzig: S. Hirzel, 1919.
Salt, Barry. "From Caligari to Who?" *Sight and Sound* 48, no. 2 (1979): 119–23.
Saunders, Thomas J. *Hollywood in Berlin.* Berkeley: University of California Press, 1994.
Scheunemann, Dietrich, ed. *Expressionist Film: New Perspectives.* Rochester, NY: Camden House, 2003.
Schlüpmann, Heide. "Kinosucht." *Frauen und Film* 33 (October 1982): 45–52

Schollmeyer, Patrick. "Lotte Eisner: Eine Archäologin als Filmkritikerin." *Thersites* 11 (2020): 324–42.
Scott, Joan. "Fantasy Echo: History and the Construction of Identity." *Critical Inquiry* 27, no. 2 (2001): 284–304.
Sedgwick, Eve Kosofsky. *Epistemology of the Closet*. Berkeley: University of California Press, 1990.
Sitton, Robert. *Lady in the Dark: Iris Barry and the Art of Film*. New York: Columbia University Press, 2014.
Stamp, Shelley. "Feminist Media Historiography and the Work Ahead." *Screening the Past* 40 (2015): www.screeningthepast.com/2015/08/feminist-media-historiography-and-the-work-ahead/.
Stegner, Wallace. *Angle of Repose*. New York: Penguin Books, 1971.
Sudendorf, Werner. "Hans Feld. 15. Juli 1902–15. Juli 1992: Ein Gedenkblatt." *Filmexil* 1 (1992): 53–54.
———. "'Nicht zur Öffentlichung': Zur Biographie des Filmjournalisten Ernst (Ejott) Jäger." *Filmexil* 5 (1994): 61–66.
———. "Täglich: Der *Film-Kurier*," in *Film . . . Stadt . . . Kino . . . Berlin . . .* , ed. Uta Berg-Ganschow and Wolfgang Jacobsen (Berlin: Argon Verlag, 1987),
Thurman, Kira. "Singing the Civilizing Mission in the Land of Bach, Beethoven, and Brahms: The Fisk Jubilee Singers in Nineteenth-Century Germany." *Journal of World History* 27, no. 3 (September 2016): 443–71.
VanHaitsma, Pamela. "Gossip as Rhetorical Methodology for Queer and Feminist Historiography." *Rhetoric Review* 35, no. 2 (2016): 135–47.
Ward, James F. *Heidegger's Political Thinking*. Amherst: University of Massachusetts Press, 1995
Warnke, Martin. "On Heinrich Wölfflin." *Representations* 27 (Summer 1989): 172–87.
Wasson, Haidee. *Museum Movies*. Berkeley: University of California Press, 2005.
Wedel, Michael. "Through the Looking-Glass: Lotte H. Eisner and Éric Rohmer on Murnau." *Screen* 62, no. 3 (Autumn 2021): 390–99.
Weinberg, Herman G. "Review: *The Haunted Screen: Expressionism in the German Cinema and the Influence of Max Reinhardt*." *Film Comment* 6, no. 2 (1970): 60–62.
Wellbery, David, and Rebecca Pohl. "Stimmung." *new formations: a journal of culture/theory/politics* 93 (February 2017): 6–45.
Werner, Gösta. "Fritz Lang and Goebbels: Myth and Facts" *Film Quarterly* 43, no. 3 (Spring 1990): 24–27.
Westerdale, Joel. "An Accident of Resistance in Nazi Germany: Oskar Kalbus's Three-Volume History of German Film (1935–37)." *Film History* 29, no. 2 (2017): 165–91.
Williams, Linda. *Playing the Race Card*. Princeton, NJ: Princeton University Press, 2001.
Williams, Raymond. *The Long Revolution*. London: Chatto & Windus, 1961.
Wipplinger, Jonathan O. *The Jazz Republic: Music, Race, and American Culture in Weimar Germany*. Ann Arbor: University of Michigan Press, 2017.
Witte, Karsten. "Ein oft gemischtes Glück." *Der Zeit*, October 31, 1986.

Zimmermann, Konrad. "Gottfried von Lücken." *Gnomon* 50, no. 2 (April 1978): 221–24.

SELECTED *FILM-KURIER* BIBLIOGRAPHY ARRANGED CHRONOLOGICALLY

Eisner, Lotte H. "Bürger, schützt Eure Anlagen!" *Film-Kurier*, August 9, 1927.
———. "The Utica Jubilee Singers." *Film-Kurier*, August 16, 1927.
———. "Zu einem Spießerfilm." *Film-Kurier*, September 14, 1927.
———. "Kunst in Metern." *Film-Kurier*, November 10, 1927.
———. "'Große Szene' in Staaken." *Film-Kurier*, November 24, 1927.
———. "'Großkampftag' in Johannistal." *Film-Kurier*, December 7, 1927.
L. H. E. "Berufe." *Film-Kurier*, December 10, 1927.
Eisner, Lotte H. "Theater im Film." *Film-Kurier*, December 15, 1927.
———. "Die neue Jugend und der Film." *Film-Kurier*, January 1, 1928.
L. H. E. "Begebenheit." *Film-Kurier*, January 16, 1928.
———. "Mitmenschen." *Film-Kurier*, February 1, 1928.
Lo-Ha. "Glashaus. 'Haus Nr. 17' und ein Schornstein, der rauchen soll." *Film-Kurier*, February 15, 1928.
L. H. E. "Der Maler der Objekte: Ausstellung Fernand Léger bei Flechtheim." *Film-Kurier*, February 17, 1928.
———. "Schauspielerinnen." *Film-Kurier*, February 18, 1928.
———. "Vom Tage: Aktualität oder Sensation." *Film-Kurier*, February 18, 1928.
Lo–Ha. "Glashaus: Mord in der Großstadt." *Film-Kurier*, February 22, 1928.
Flapper. "Wir haben Frühlingssorgen." *Film-Kurier*, March 10, 1928.
Anon. "Margot Walter-Landa: Meine großen weichen Hüte," *Film-Kurier*, March 10, 1928.
L. H. E. "Vom Tage: Die Probe aufs Exempel." *Film-Kurier*, March 13, 1928.
Eisner, Lotte H. "Kultur-Film-Sondervorführung für die Berliner Presse (Universum Film A-G.)." *Film-Kurier*, March 17, 1928.
Eisner, Dr. L. H. "Beiblatt zum Film-Kurier: Der Kulturfilm." *Film-Kurier*, March 21, 1928.
L. H. E. "Alfred Kerr über den Kritiker." *Film-Kurier*, March 23, 1928.
Flapper. "Kurze Naturgeschichte der 'Dame von Welt.'" *Film-Kurier*, March 24, 1928.
Lolott. "Das Mädel von heute." *Film-Kurier*, March 24, 1928.
Eisner, Lotte H. "*Aloma, die Blume der Südsee*." *Film-Kurier*, March 29, 1928.
———. "Die schöne deutsche Heimat." *Film-Kurier*, April 7, 1928.
L. H. E. "Der Film in der Schule." *Film-Kurier*, April 12, 1928.
Eisner, Dr. L. H. "Der deutsche Kulturfilm in Gefahr? Der italienische Krieg. Geheimpolitik im Bund." *Film-Kurier*, April 13, 1928.
Lolott. "Sieben im Autobus." *Film-Kurier*, April 14, 1928.
L. H. E. "Vor der Haager Konferenz." *Film-Kurier*, April 21, 1928.

Eisner, L. H. "Film-Kritik: Pressevorführung des Lehrfilmbundes." *Film-Kurier*, April 27, 1928.
Eisner, Lotte H. "Weitere Zuspitzung im Haag: Vierter Tag der Haager Lehrfilm-Konferenz." *Film-Kurier*, May 5, 1928.
———. "Otto Rombach: Der heilige Krieg." *Film-Kurier*, May 24, 1928.
L. H. E. "Wie gefällt dir Dein Nachbar?" and "Zeitschriften." *Film-Kurier*, May 26, 1928.
Eisner, Lotte H. "'Avantgarde—Achtung!'" *Film-Kurier*, May 26, 1928.
Eisner, Dr. Lotte H. "Von einem, der auszog das 'Filmwesen' zu lernen. Was die Preussische Staatsbibliothek vom Film weiß." *Film-Kurier*, May 26, 1928.
Lo-Ha. "Neue Gesichter für den Film Barbara Dju." *Film-Kurier*, July 14, 1928.
Flapper. "Tausend Beinchen suchen." *Film-Kurier*, August 28, 1928.
———. "Die Baker in Berlin: Josephine wird photovraphiert [*sic*]." *Film-Kurier*, September 10, 1928.
L. H. E. "Für den Lehrer!" *Film-Kurier*, September 15, 1928.
-ner. "Der Kulturfilm: Der Lehrfilm braucht die Schere." *Film-Kurier*, September 15, 1928.
Eisner, Lotte H. "Der Kulturfilm: Tabak-Kulturfilm der Ufa." *Film-Kurier*, September 22, 1928.
-ner. "Neuer Weg für den Landschaftsfilm." *Film-Kurier*, September 22, 1928.
Eisner, Lotte H. "Kino-Sonntag in Amsterdam." *Film-Kurier*, October 20, 1928.
———. "Kulturfilm im Werden: Bei der Ufa in Neubabelsberg." *Film-Kurier*, December 8, 1928.
Eisner, Dr. L. H. "Der Kulturfilm: Forderungen für 1929." *Film-Kurier*, January 12, 1929.
L. H. E. "Der Kulturfilm: Wo bleibt das gute Beiprogramm?" *Film-Kurier*, February 9, 1929.
-ner. "Der Wissenschaftsfilm fordert: Mehr Einsicht bei Wissenschaftlern—Unterstützung beim Reich!" *Film-Kurier*, March 15, 1929.
Eisner, L. H. "Der Kulturfilm: Gläserne Wundertiere." *Film-Kurier*, August 5, 1929.
L. H. E. "'Weltkongreß sabotiert den Film!'" *Film-Kurier*, August 14, 1929.
Eisner, Lotte H. "R.C. Sheriff: Die andere Seite." *Film-Kurier*, August 30, 1929.
Eisner, L. H. "Avantgarde der Massen." *Film-Kurier*, August 31, 1929.
———. "Sommertheater . . . René Schickele: Hans im Schnakenloch." *Film-Kurier*, September 5, 1929.
———. "Film-Kritik. *§173 Blutschande*." *Film-Kurier*, October 18, 1929.
L. H. E. "Staatliche Kulturfilmaufgaben." *Film-Kurier*, November 2, 1929.
Eisner, L. H. "Film-Kritik. *The Jazz Singer*." *Film-Kurier*, November 27, 1929.
Eisner, Lotte H. "Berliner Bühnen: Karl Kraus, Die letzte Nacht." *Film-Kurier*, January 16, 1930.
L. H. E. "Das Kino braucht den Kulturfilm." *Film-Kurier*, September 27, 1930.
-ner. "Der Lehrer sieht es anders" and "Ufa-Filmschau vor Lehrern" *Film-Kurier*, October 13, 1930.
———. "Mehr Montage für den Kulturfilm." *Film-Kurier*, December 13, 1930.

———. "Der Kulturfilm. Dilemma des Kulturfilmproduzenten." *Film-Kurier*, December 20, 1930.
Eisner, Lotte H. "Spanischer Frühling. Jacobinermützen in Barcelona." *Film-Kurier*, May 2, 1931.
Eisner, L. H. "Zum Internationalen Lehrfilmkongreß: Was geschieht in Wien?" *Film-Kurier*, May 23, 1931.
—lo—. "Kleines Rivierakino." *Film-Kurier*, June 20, 1931.
Lo-Ha., "Carmen hat unrecht! Ich lad Euch allen ein, dort in Sevillas Mauern . . ." *Film-Kurier*, July 4, 1931.
-ner. "Hans Fischingers erster abstrakter Film." *Film-Kurier*, October 23, 1931.
L. H. E. "Ein Komödiant könnt einen Autor lehren . . . Der produktive Schauspieler." *Film-Kurier*, November 12, 1931.
———. "Der produktive Kameramann wird zum Mitschöpfer. Wege zur Manuskript-Verwirklichung." *Film-Kurier*, November 26, 1931.
Eisner, Lotte H. "Film-Kritik: Mädchen in Uniform." *Film-Kurier*, November 28, 1931.
—lo—. "Formkünstler werden Autoren: Ein interessantes Film-Triumvirat." *Film-Kurier*, May 19, 1932.
Eisner, Lotte H. "Arnolt Bronnen sagt: "Funk und Film haben nichts Gemeinsames." *Film-Kurier*, June 9, 1932.
L. H. E. "Ein Wald wird ummontiert—Fritz Lang beginnt zu drehen," *Film-Kurier*, October 3, 1932.

SELECTED POST-*FILM-KURIER* BIBLIOGRAPHY ARRANGED CHRONOLOGICALLY

Eisner, Lotte. "Quand Fritz Lang réalisait Le Testament du Docteur Mabuse," *L'Intransigeant* (May 1933): 10.
Eisner, Lotte H. "Le sujet que voudrait tourner G.-W. Pabst." *Cinématographe* 1 (March 1937): 7.
———. "Notes sur le style du Fritz Lang." *La Revue du cinéma* 5 (February 1947): 3–26.
———. "Peter Lorre le Meutrier." *Cinématographe* 2 (May 1937): 13.
———. "The German Films of Fritz Lang." *The Penguin Film Review* 6 (April 1948): 53–61.
———. "Les origines de style Lubitsch." *La Revue du cinéma* 17 (September 1948): 3–16.
———. "Aperçus sur le costume dans les films allemands." *La Revue du cinéma* 19/20 (Autumn 1949): 68–86.
———. *L'écran démoniaque: Influence de Max Reinhardt et de l'expressionnisme*. Paris: André Bonne, 1952.
———. "Décor Démoniaque." *L'Âge du cinéma* 6 (1952): 29–31.
———. "Aperçus sur le Kammerspielfilm." *Cahiers du cinéma* 10 (March 1952): 4–10.

———. "A la seconde vision." *Cahiers du cinéma* 20 (February 1953): 57–60.
———. "Comment écrire l'histoire du cinéma." *Positif* 6 (April 1953): 37–40.
L. H. E. "Une 'Cinema-Dramaturgie' Suisse-Allemande." *Cahiers du cinéma* 24 (June 1953): 63.
Eisner, Lotte H. "Impressions de deux festivals." *Cahiers du cinéma* 26 (August–September 1953): 36–40.
———. "En marge du festival de Venise." *Cahiers du cinéma* 28 (November 1953): 36–37.
———. "Les affamés du film de qualité." *Cahiers du cinéma* 29 (December 1953): 36–37.
———. "Asta Nielsen." *Cahiers du cinéma* 30 (Winter 1953): 36–38.
L. H. E. "Le peintre Reveron." *Cahiers du cinéma* 32 (February 1954): 52.
Eisner, Lotte H. "De la pièce et du film au … ballet d'opéra (à propos de l'opéra de Quat'Sous." *Cahiers du cinéma* 36 (June 1954): 33–37.
L. H. E. "Encore l'opéra de quat'sous." *Cahiers du cinéma* 37 (July 1954): 32–33.
Eisner, Lotte H. "La semaine du film à Vienne." *Cahiers du cinéma* 37 (July 1954): 30–31.
———. "Au Lido: Deux festivals avant courreurs [sic]." *Cahiers du cinéma* 38 (August–September 1954): 23–26.
———. "La rétrospective du film allemand au Festival de Venise." *Cahiers du cinéma* 40 (November 1954): 24–25.
———. "Mise en garde et mise au point: l'école expressionniste." *Cinéma* 1 (November 1954): 14–23.
———. "Quelques aspects de l'avant-garde." *Positif* 12 (November 1954): 25–32.
———. "Lettre de Bad Ems." *Cahiers du cinéma* 41 (December 1954): 21–23.
———. "Un livre à traduire et des autres livres allemands." *Cahiers du cinéma* 45 (March 1955): 58–60.
———. "French Cinema." *Film Culture* 1, no. 2 (March–April 1955): 33–34.
———. "Petit voyage cinématographique." *Cinéma* 5 (April 1955): 60–63, 95.
———. "Post-war Realism in France." *Film Culture* 1, no. 3 (May–June 1955): 21–22.
———. "Rencontre avec Carl Dreyer." *Cahiers du cinéma* 48 (June 1955): 1–5.
———. "Reflections on the Cannes Festival." *Film Culture* 1, no. 4 (Summer 1955): 13–15.
———. "The Painter Reveron" *Sight and Sound* 25, no. 2 (Fall 1955): 105–6.
———. "60 Years of Cinema in France." *Film Culture* 1, no. 5/6 (Winter 1955): 25–26.
———. "Trois livres sur trois acteurs allemands." *Cahiers du cinéma* 55 (January 1956): 51–54.
———. "Dans les studios des deux Berlin." *Cinéma* 9 (February 1956): 69–71.
———. "Venice Film Festival (Part II)." *Film Culture* 2, no. 7 (1956): 24, 31.
———. "Les Grands Manoeuvres." *Film Culture* 2, no. 7 (1956): 27, 29.
———. "Les films japonais hors festival." *Cahiers du cinéma* 51 (June 1956): 17–18.
———. "Cannes Festival—Day by Day." *Film Culture* 2, no. 8 (1956): 11–15.
———. "Cayatte: A New Style and A New Film." *Film Culture* 2, no. 10 (1956): 26–27.

———. "Children's Films at Lido." *Film Culture* 2, no. 10 (1956): 31–32.
———. "Documentaries at Lido." *Film Culture* 2, no. 10 (1956): 32–33.
———. "Réalisme et irréel chez Dreyer." *Cahiers du cinéma* 65 (December 1956): 17–18.
———. "*Tarde de toros.*" *Cinéma* 13 (December 1956): 74.
———. "Notes sur le style de Stroheim." *Cahiers du cinéma* 67 (January 1957): 8–18.
———. "Cinema." In *Enciclopedia dello spettacolo* Volume 4, edited by Silvio d'Amico, 1644–48. Rome: Casa Editrice Le Maschere, 1957.
Eisner, Lotte. "Sur le procès de l'Opéra de quat'sous." *Europe* 35 (January–February 1957): 133–34.
Eisner, Lotte H. "The Style of René Clément. Part I." *Film Culture* 3, no. 12 (1957): 21.
———. "Quelques souvenirs sur Erich von Stroheim." *Cahiers du cinéma* 72 (June 1957): 3–6.
———. "Le fantastique dans le film allemand." *Cinéma* 20 (July 1957): 106–10.
L. H. E. "Berlin Est." *Cahiers du cinéma* 74 (August–September 1957): 38.
———. "Chauffeurs de Taxi." *Cahiers du cinéma* 74 (August–September 1957): 38.
———. "Retrospective Mizoguchi." *Cahiers du cinéma* 75 (October 1957): 46.
Eisner, Lotte H. "The Style of René Clément. Part II." *Film Culture* 3, no. 13 (October 1957): 11.
———. "L'énigme des deux Nosferatu." *Cahiers du cinéma* 79 (January 1958): 22–24.
L. H. E. "Musidora." *Cahiers du cinéma* 79 (January 1958): 39.
Eisner, Lotte H. "Homage to an Artist." *Film Culture* 4, no. 18 (April 1958): 7–8.
———. "Notes on the Style of Stroheim." *Film Culture* 4, no. 18 (April 1958): 13–19.
L. H. E. "Carl Boese et le tournage du Golem." *Cahiers du cinéma* 88 (October 1958): 45–46.
———. "Mort de F.-A. Wagner." *Cahiers du cinéma* 88 (October 1958): 46.
Eisner, Lotte H. "Note sur quelques films allemands." *Cahiers du cinéma* 90 (December 1958): 18–19.
———. "Filmdialog und Zwischentitel," "Filmkamera," "Filmmontage," "Filmschauspieler," "Musik im Film," "Stile und Gattungen des Films." In *Film Rundfunk Fernsehen*, edited by Dr. Lotte H. Eisner and Heinz Friedrich. Frankfurt am Main: Fischer Bücherei KG, 1958.
———. "The Seine Meets Paris." *Film Quarterly* 13, no. 2 (Winter 1959): 60–61.
L. H. E. "Hertha Thiele à Paris." *Cahiers du cinéma* 93 (March 1959): 41.
Eisner, Lotte H. "Note sur le baroque dans le cinéma allemand." *Etudes cinématographiques* 1 (Spring 1960): 86–89.
———. "Zu Ehren von Asta Nielsen." *Kosmorama* 50 (October 1960): 6–7.
———. "Review: *Eric Von Stroheim* by Bob Bergut" *Sight and Sound* 30, no. 2 (Spring 1961): 98–99.
Eisner, Lotte. "Murnau et L'Aurore." *Cinéma* 84 (March 1964): 42–72.
Eisner, Lotte H. "Les Secrets de Murnau," *Cinéma* 86 (May 1964): 105–6.
———. "Le style de 'M' le Maudit." *L'avant-scène cinéma* 39 (July 1964): 5–6.
———. "Hommage à Peter Lorre." *L'avant-scène cinéma* 39 (July 1964): 45.
———. *F. W. Murnau*. Paris: Le Terrain Vague, 1964.

———. *L'écran démoniaque: Édition définitive*. Paris: Le Terrain Vague, 1965.
———. *Murnau: der Klassiker des deutschen Films*. Hannover: Friedrich, 1967.
Eisner, Lotte. "Meetings with Pabst." *Sight and Sound* 36, no. 4 (Fall 1967): 209–10.
Eisner, Lotte H. "Louvre der Filmkunst: Henri Langlois und seine Cinémathèque." *Die Welt* 115 (May 17, 1968): 13.
———. "Kitsch in the Cinema." In *Kitsch: An Anthology of Bad Taste*, edited by Gillo Dorfles, 197–217. London: Studio Vista, 1969.
———. *The Haunted Screen: Expressionism in the German Cinema and the Influence of Max Reinhardt*. Berkeley: University of California Press, 1969.
———. "A Contribution to the Definition of Expressionist Film." In *Expressionism as an International Literary Phenomenon*, edited by Ulrich Weisstein, 161–66. Paris: Librairie Marcel Didier, 1973.
———. *Murnau*. Berkeley: University of California Press, 1973.
———. "In the Picture: Herzog in Dinkelsbühl." *Sight and Sound* 43, no. 4 (Fall 1974): 212–13.
Eisner, Lotte. "Einige Erinnerungen an Erich von Stroheim." *Filmkritik* 20, no. 2 (February 1976): 64–67.
———. "Ambivalences du film Expressioniste." *Obliques* 6/7 (1976): 173–74.
Eisner, Lotte H. *Fritz Lang*. London: Secker & Warburg, 1976.
———. "Rede an die jungen deutschen Filmemacher." *Filmfaust* 9/10 (October 1978): 4–5.
———. *Vingt ans de cinéma allemand, 1913–1933*. Paris: Centre Georges Pompidou, 1978.
———. *Murnau: mit dem Faksimile des von Murnau beim Drehen verwendeten Orignalskripts von Nosferatu*. Frankfurt: Kommunales Kino, 1979.
———. "Introduction." *Great Film Stills of the German Silent Era: 125 Stills from the Stiftung Deutsche Kinemathek*. New York: Dover Publications, 1981.
Eisner, Lotte. "Naissance de Fury." *Cinématographe* 65 (February 1981): 25–26.
———. "A Witness Speaks." In *Lulu in Hollywood*, by Louise Brooks, 107–10. New York: Knopf, 1982.
Eisner, Lotte H. "Retour à Berlin" *Cinématographe* 89 (May 1983): 3–4.
———. "Grandeur et décadence du décor" *Cahiers du cinéma* 355 (January) 1984: 42–44.
Eisner, Lotte. *Fritz Lang*. Translated by Bernard Eisenschitz. Paris: Cahiers du cinéma, Éditions de l'Étoile, Cinémathèque Française, 1984.
———. *Ich hatte einst ein schönes Vaterland: Memoiren*. Heidelberg: Wunderhorn, 1984.

INDEX

§173 St.G.B. Blutschande (Bauer), 60, 181n60

Abitur, 27, 172n26
accented cinema, 148–53
actuality, 61. *See also* documentary
Adorno, Theodor, 159, 179nn39,43, 180n45, 197n31
affect, 85, 94–98, 100–104, 149, 152, 162
affect theory, 94, 104, 190n56, 191nn61, 194n86
Âge du cinéma, L', 109, 217
Aloma of the South Seas (Tourneur), 70, 71
Amsterdam, Eisner's travel writing on, 56
Andokides, 34, 173n34
Andrejew, André, 90, 93
Anger, Kenneth, 121, 135, 136
animation, 65
anti-racism, 70–73, 154, 161, 185n94
anti-Semitism, 27, 70, 73, 84, 96, 102, 161
archaeology, 18, 29, 30, 39, 91, 108, 117, 123, 133
Arendt, Hannah, 159
Ärgernis, Das (Wilhelm Hegeler, 1908), 73
Aristarco, Guido, 122–23, 190n42
Arnheim, Rudolf, 2, 65, 67–69, 77, 95, 159, 161, 184n86
Artaud, Antonin, 129
art history, 2, 14, 31–39, 108, 118, 123, 124, 130, 155
assimilation, 27, 72, 144, 152, 161
Astruc, Alexandre, 111
Attic black-figure painting, 31, 34

Attic red-figure painting, 31–35
Auch Einer (Vischer), and the "perfidy of objects," 58, 180n55
audiences, 55, 59–60, 64, 65, 67–69, 119, 121, 159, 181n59
Auriol, Jean George, 85, 113, 196n16
auteur theory, 9, 91, 107, 109–11, 123, 124
avant-garde, 43, 46, 69–70, 119, 121–22
Avant-scène cinéma, L', 109, 219

Baal (Brecht), 150
Baker, Josephine, 178n36
Balázs, Béla, 2, 43, 65, 161
baroque, 32, 34–35, 37, 174n42
Barry, Iris, 65, 67, 69, 95, 129, 161, 188n32
Bauer, Alfred, 201n66
Baum, Vicki, 119, 130, 198n34, 200n64
Bazin, André, 2, 20, 99, 109–13, 122
Beazley, John, 32–33, 36
Beiprogramm, 56, 61, 65
Benjamin, Walter, 101, 158, 186n8
Bergen-Belsen, 85, 188n27
Bergut, Bob, 123
Berlin, 28–30, 39, 40, 46, 56–57, 58, 74, 102–4, 126–27, 130, 148, 150
Berlinale, 143, 145
Berliner Tageblatt, 40, 45, 73
Bildeinheit, 31–33, 35, 38
biography, 4, 155–56
blackface, 71–73, 185n94
Brecht, Bertolt, 2, 3, 29, 90, 149–50
British Film Institute, 83, 192n66
Brooks, Louise, 2, 90, 97, 150, 193nn76,77

221

Bryher, Winifred, 161
Büchse der Pandora, Die (Pabst), 10–11, 169n27
Bund der Lehr- und Kulturfilmhersteller, 63
Buñuel, Luis, 3, 122
Busch, Ernst, 96

Cabinet of Dr. Caligari, The (Wiene), 121, 125, 131
Cahiers du cinéma, 9, 91–92, 106, 109–13, 123, 139, 140, 190n53, 196nn7,9
Caligarism, 131. See also *Cabinet of Dr. Caligari, The*
Canudo, Riciotto, 129, 130
Carstens, Carl, 203n6
cercle du cinéma, Le, 82, 99
chant d'amour, Un (Jean Genet, 1950), 121, 135
Chaparral, Ernst, 43, 176n5, 177n10
Chaplin, Charles, 45, 129, 198n34
Chevalier de l'ordre national de la Légion d'honneur, 96
chosen family, 103, 152
chronotope, 151–52
cinécriture, 158
cinemagoing. See audiences
cinema of exile, 149, 151
cinematographers, 9, 36, 58, 70, 117, 130–31, 134–35, 139, 168n10
Cinématographie française, La, 78, 79, 83
cinephilia, 99, 109, 154
classical style, 32, 34, 37, 91, 168n10, 190n50
Cocteau, Jean, 82
Colette, 161, 196n7
colonialism, 55, 63, 70–71, 136, 162, 182n70, 202n81
Conservative Revolution, 6, 127–28
Constructivism, 126, 168n12
Corinth, Lovis, 63
Cürlis, Hans, 63–64, 67, 90, 182n69
Curtius, Ludwig von, 30

Dadaism, 121
Dawes Plan (1924), 121, 198n40
Deren, Maya, 121–22, 159
Deutsche Kinemathek, 91
diaspora, 70, 72, 152

Dietrich, Marlene, 103
Dinesen, Robert, 13
Dju, Barbara, 55, 180n48
documentary: film criticism by Eisner, 48, 61–67, 121, 183n74; films about Eisner, 142–54
Douy, Max, 93–94
Dreyer, Carl Theodor, 129
Dulac, Germaine, 122

Educational and Documentary Filmmakers Union. See Bund der Lehr- und Kulturfilmhersteller
Ehrenbaum-Degele, Hans, 93
Eisenschitz, Bernard, 21, 137, 145
Elsaesser, Thomas, 8, 9, 14–15, 110–11, 168n12, 169nn27,28
Epstein, Jean, 83
Epstein, Marie, 83, 89, 189n44
Escoffier, Louise Hélène, 84, 115, 186n10
eugenics, 70, 161
Euthymides, 34
Expeditionsfilm, 61, 62, 65

fantasy echo, 151
Faust (Murnau), 93, 133, 136. See also Murnau, F. W.
Feld, Hans, 40–41, 44–45, 66–67, 69, 73–74, 76, 161, 175n2, 176n3, 177nn16,17, 185n99
feminism, Eisner's comments on, 51–53, 102, 104, 108, 144, 154. See also misogyny, Eisner's
feminist media historiography, 4–5, 20, 155–59, 160–62
FIAF (International Federation of Film Archives), 83, 89, 189n46
Figeac, 84–85, 188n27
Film as Art (Arnheim), 68–69, 184n86. See also Arnheim, Rudolf
Film Culture, 109
Film-Kurier: changes in Eisner's writing published in, 56–61, 70–74, 119, 121, 178n31, 184n89; contributors to, 40–42, 43, 176n5; Eisner's bylines, 48–49, 79–81; Eisner's tenure, 9–10, 43–48, 153–54, 178n33, 183n79, 186n101; Hans Feld's tenure and writing, 40–41,

44–45, 66–67, 73–74, 177nn16,17, 185n99; profile of, 42–43
Filmology, 198n35
Films Albatros, 83
film studies, disciplinary history, 2–4, 5, 17, 107–8, 109, 154, 155–56, 159, 162
Finanzen des Großherzogs, Die (Murnau), 135. *See also* Murnau, F. W.
Fireworks (Kenneth Anger, 1947), 121, 135
4 Devils (Murnau), 93. *See also* Murnau, F. W.
Franju, Georges, 78, 79, 81, 82, 83
Frankfurt School, 54, 179n43
Frauenstudium, 28–30
French naturalization, Eisner's, 151
French New Wave. *See* Nouvelle Vague
freudlose Gasse, Die (Pabst), 112, 168n14
Freund, Karl, 36, 90, 134–35
From Caligari to Hitler (Kracauer), 6–14, 106, 115–18, 129–32, 147, 160, 168nn18,19, 169n28
Fun in a Chinese Laundry (Sternberg), 88

Galeen, Henrik, 13
Garbo, Greta, 104, 168n14, 194n93
Gartenlaube, Die, 135, 201n72
Geheimagent (Piel), 73–74
gender: Eisner's writing on, 48–51 53–56, 154; identity, and dysphoria, Eisner's, 17–18, 24–25, 102–3, 104, 151, 171nn7,14; performance, Eisner's, 25–27, 44, 52–53, 102–103, 104. *See also* feminism, Eisner's comments on; misogyny, Eisner's
genre, as a topic in Eisner's writing, 9–10, 13–14, 106, 108, 113, 126–31. *See also* kitsch
Genuine (Wiene), 131, 132
German Expressionism, 12–14, 106, 113, 126, 127, 130–31
Gert, Valeska, 90, 104
Geschminkte Jugend (Boese), 60
glaneurs et la glaneuse, Les (Varda), 158
Gliese, Rochus, 88, 90, 94, 98, 135
Golem, wie er in die Welt kam, Der (Boese and Wegener), 121
Goslar, Hans, 71
gossip, 23, 50, 51, 101–3, 117, 136–37
Grierson, John, 64, 65

Grohmann, Martje, 3, 22, 145, 153–54
Grune, Karl, 11, 90
Guderian, Paul Gerd, 131
Gurs, 84, 192n68

Haas, Willy, 43, 161, 176n5
Hake, Sabine, 7, 8, 9, 203n10
Hammid, Alexander, 122
Harbou, Thea von, 90, 95
Harlé, Paul-Auguste, 79, 82, 83
Harrington, Curtis, 190n53
Hasler, Emil, 90, 94, 139
Haunted Screen, The, 5–13, 38, 85, 106, 113–14, 124–30; Eisner's remarks on, 117–18, 123, 138, 140
Haus Nummer 17 (Bolváry), 58
heilige Reich der Deutschen, Das (Ziegler), 128
Hensel, Frank, 83, 84, 187n25
Herkt, Günther, 46
Herlth, Robert, 36, 90, 91, 92, 94, 135, 190n51
Herzberg, Georg, 43, 176n5
Herzog, Werner, 1, 16, 19, 98, 139, 142–43; Eisner's relationship with, 144–47, 151, 151–54, 203n6
Hirschfeld, Magnus, 50
Hitchcock, Alfred, 111, 123
Hoesch, Eduard, 158
Hoffmann, Carl, 43, 131, 135
Holl, Gussy, 95–96, 192n69
Hollywood Babylon (Anger), 136
Hoppin, J. M., 32, 33
Horowitz, S. M., 142, 147. *See also Lotte Eisner in Germany*
Huff, Theodore, 114
Hunte, Otto, 87, 88, 90, 91, 131

Ihering, Herbert, 120, 161
Industriefilm, 61, 65
Institut für Kulturforschung (Institute for Cultural Research), 63, 67, 182n69, 183n76
intellectual history: Eisner's place in, 1, 3–5, 12, 20, 35, 86, 100, 104–8; of film studies, 155–58, 160–61
Internationale Filmschau, 77, 78
Intransigeant, L', 77, 139

Jäger, Ernst, 41–42, 43, 46, 52, 73–74
Jannings, Emil, 10–11, 57, 96, 192n69
Jazz Singer, The (Crosland), 71–72
Jeder für sich und Gott gegen Alle (Herzog), 202n91
Jerven, Walter, 46, 176n5
Jewish identity, Eisner's, 27, 70, 72–78, 96, 102, 126, 152, 161–62
Jolson, Al, 71–72, 185n94
Junge, Alfred, 88, 90
Junge, Ewald, 88–89, 90

Kalbus, Oskar, 125–28, 130, 147, 199nn56,57
Kamenka, Alexandre, 83
Kammerspielfilme, 124, 113, 132, 134–35
Karlsruhe, 27
Kerr, Alfred, 59, 161
Kettelhut, Erich, 90, 131
kitsch, 119–121
Klein, César, 114, 131, 132
Kortner, Fritz, 10–11
Kracauer, Siegfried, 2, 53–55, 65, 69, 77, 159; correspondence with Eisner, 114–16, 179n44, 197nn24,27; exile, 69, 77, 116, 129, 184n86, 186n8, 200n62; *The Mass Ornament*, 53–55, 179n43, 180nn45,46. See also *From Caligari to Hitler*
Krauss, Werner, 95–96
Kritik, Die, 76
Kulturfilm, 43, 44, 49, 61–67, 119, 183n79, 202n87
Kunst der Griechen, Die (Salis), 34, 174n42
Kunstwollen, 37, 168n12, 175n51
Kurtz, Rudolf, 113
Kurzfilm, 61, 62–65

Lampe, Felix, 62, 67, 184n83
Lamprecht, Gerhardt, 90, 91, 95
Landschaftsfilm, 61, 66
Lang, Fritz, 57, 91, 93, 97, 109–11, 123, 193n78, 194n87, 199n52; Eisner's publications about the work of, 5, 8, 12, 21, 125–26, 137–40
Langbehn, Julius, 128
langen Ferien der Lotte H. Eisner, Die (Shahid Saless), 19, 95, 142–45, 148–54
Langlois, Henri, 3, 80, 116, 153, 187n25, 190n48, 194n83, 196n18; and the Cinémathèque française, 83–84, 86–88, 91, 98–100, 189nn45,46; friendship with Eisner, 78–79, 80, 84–85, 193n77; the Langlois Affair, 188n32, 189n37; working relationship with Eisner, 15, 78, 80, 85–90, 97–100, 113, 169n28, 193n75
Lehrfilme, 61, 62, 63–65, 69
Lejeune, C. A., 161
Lenssen, Claudia, 7
letzte Mann, Der (Murnau), 57, 93, 121, 124, 133. See also Murnau, F. W.
Lindgren, Ernest, 82, 95, 192n66
Literarische Welt, 40
Lorre, Peter, 3, 139, 202n91
Lotte Eisner in Germany (Horowitz), 7*fig.*, 19, 23*fig.*, 95, 100*fig.*, 108*fig.*, 142, 149–54, 204n12
Lubitsch, Ernst, 110, 126–30, 137, 161, 199n56
Lücken, Gottfried von, 30–31, 35–37, 39, 76, 85, 188n29

M (Lang), 123, 125. See also Lang, Fritz
Mädchen, hütet Euch! (Arnheim), 57
Mädchen in Uniform (Sagan), 178n35
Mahler, Margaret Schoenberger, 25
Mann, Heinrich, 48
Mann, Klaus, 104, 194n93
Mann, Thomas, 128, 159
Mannoni, Laurent, 16, 83, 91, 94, 104, 145, 193n75
Mayer, Carl, 14, 131–32, 134–35
Medina, Paul, 43, 176n5
Meerson, Mary, 83, 87, 97, 193nn76,77, 194n87, 196n18
Mekas, Jonas, 109, 198n42
Méliès, Georges, 121, 122
Meshes of the Afternoon (Deren), 121
Metropolis (Lang), 14, 58, 125. See also Lang, Fritz
Metzner, Ernő, and Grace Metzner, 97–98, 193n79
Michelle, Marion, 90, 189n46
misogyny, Eisner's, 49, 50, 52, 55, 104, 154, 171n7, 177n6, 192n68
Mitry, Jean, 83, 85
MoMA Film Library, 83, 115, 169n28, 188n32, 192n66, 204n11

Monsieur Verdoux (Chaplin), 119, 198n34
müde Tod, Der (Lang), 125, 189n45. *See also* Lang, Fritz
Murnau, F. W., 57, 90–96, 145, 151, 195n94, 201n78; Eisner's publications about the work of, 5, 8, 9, 13–15, 114, 132–38, 140, 197n21. *See also Faust; Finanzen des Großherzogs, Die; 4 Devils; letzte Mann, Der; Nosferatu; Sehnsucht; Sunrise: A Song of Two Humans; Tabu: A Story of the South Seas; Tartuffe*

Nazi party, Nazism, 2, 6, 41, 63, 77, 85, 133, 144, 176n7; cultural policies and historiography of, 92, 95–96, 125, 127–29, 146–47, 159. *See also* Kalbus, Oskar
New American Cinema, 122, 198n42
New German Cinema, 98, 143–47, 153, 154, 203n10
Nibelungen, Die (Lang), 57, 126, 131. *See also* Lang, Fritz
Nielsen, Asta, 13, 112, 178n14, 196n15
Nosferatu (Murnau), 121, 134, 147, 189n45. *See also* Murnau, F. W.
Nosferatu the Vampyre (Herzog), 147. *See also* Herzog, Werner; Horowitz, S. M.
nostalgia, 148–49, 150
Nouvelle Vague, 15, 19, 144
Nussbaum, Anna, 71, 185n93

Of Walking in Ice (Herzog), 145. *See also* Herzog, Werner

Pabst, G. W., 9, 10–11, 195, 133, 139, 168n14, 192n72
Pierre, Sylvie, 111, 196n9
Pinschewer, Julius, 90, 91
Plumpe-Murnau, Robert, 90, 92–93; other Plumpe family members, 90, 134
Pommer, Erich, 43, 140
Positif, 109, 111, 117, 123
Potamkin, Harry Alan, 11, 65, 67
Powdermaker, Hortense, 159, 160
Preussische Staatsbibliothek, 79, 80

queer historiography, 5, 94–95, 101–5, 157, 160, 190n56, 191n61

reception. *See* audiences
Regiensitzungen, 8, 168n10
Reichsfilmarchiv, 83, 84
Reimann, Walter, 131
Reinhardt, Max, 9, 13–14, 113–14, 128–30
Reiniger, Lotte, 65
Revue du cinéma, La, 13, 14, 109, 110, 113–14, 130, 196n16
Richter, Hans, 121, 122
Richter, Heinrich, 58
Riefenstahl, Leni, 2, 95, 150, 176n7
Riegl, Alois, 31, 37–38, 118, 168n12 174n48, 175n50
Rivette, Jacques, 111, 112, 148
Roditi, Edouard, 4, 75, 97, 193n78
Rohmer, Éric, 17, 111
Röhrig, Peter, 88, 90, 91
Röhrig, Walter, 36, 88, 90, 125, 131, 135
Rohrscheidt, Anneliese von, 27, 102
Romanticism, 6, 131, 173n33
Rosher, Charles, 135
Rotha, Paul, 65
Rotmil, Jacek, 58
Roud, Richard, 16, 19, 99, 154
Roussell, Henry, 129, 130
Rundt, Arthur, 71, 185n93
Rye, Stellan, 13

Sadoul, Georges, 130
Salis, Arnold von, 32, 34–35, 37, 174n42
Salt, Barry, 12–14
salvage, 92–94, 146, 154, 157, 160, 162, 190n56
Schaffende Hände, 63, 67
Schapiro, Meyer, 186n8
Schinderhannes (Bernhardt), 58
Schlöndorff, Volker, 145, 203n6
Schramm, Wolfgang, 134
Schüfftan, Eugen, 36, 58, 90
Seeber, Guido, 43
Sehnsucht (Murnau), 95–96, 192n69. *See also* Murnau, F. W.
Seldes, Gilbert, 126
Shahid Saless, Sohrab, 143–45, 148, 153, 203n6. *See also langen Ferien der Lotte H. Eisner, Die*
Sight and Sound, 109
Simple Event, A (Shahid Saless), 143

Singing Fool, The (Bacon), 72; Hans Feld's review of, 177n16
Soviet Cinema, 56, 65, 161, 183n74
Spätrömische Kunstindustrie (Riegl), 37. See also Riegl, Alois
Spengler, Oswald, 128, 200n57
Städtefilme, 61
Steglitzer Tragedy, 60
Sternberg, Josef von, 88, 90
Stilfragen: Grundlegungen zu einer Geschichte der Ornamentik (Riegl), 38. See also Riegl, Alois
Still Life (Shahid Saless), 143
Stimmung, 17, 32, 38, 156, 120, 124, 170n32, 175n53
Stindt, Georg Otto, 46, 176n5
Straus-Ernst, Louise, 161
Stroheim, Erich von, 110, 120–21, 123, 139
stylistic analysis, 8, 11, 18, 107–9, 124–25, 129–32, 159; in Eisner's dissertation, 31, 36
Sunrise: A Song of Two Humans (Murnau), 93, 134. See also Murnau, F. W.
surrealism, 78, 121

Tabu: A Story of the South Seas (Murnau), 122, 135, 136, 202n81. See also Murnau, F. W.
Tartuffe (Murnau), 133, 134. See also Murnau, F. W.
Testament des Dr. Mabuse, Das (Lang), 77, 139. See also Lang, Fritz
Tigre du Bengal, Le (*Der Tiger von Eschnapur,* Lang), 123, 199n44. See also Lang, Fritz
Theory of Film (Kracauer), 116. See also Kracauer, Siegfried
Thérèse Raquin (Feyder), 57
Theresienstadt (Terezín), 85, 188n29
Tiller Girls, 53–54, 55
To Be or Not to Be (Lubitsch), 130. See also Lubitsch, Ernst
translation, 20–21, 71, 87, 89, 168n19, 193n78, 199n56

trauma, 85, 92–96, 98–105, 114, 137, 148, 154, 160
Trotta, Margarethe von, 179n37. See also New German Cinema
Truffaut, François, 99, 111, 112, 196n17. See also Nouvelle Vague

Umwelt, 17, 124, 156, 170n32
Universität Rostock, 30, 31, 39, 172n26
Utica Jubilee Singers, 70–72

Vargas, Alberto, 53
Variété (Dupont), 10, 121
Veidt, Conrad, 192n69
Vélodrome d'Hiver, 83, 192n68
Vergangenheitsbewältigung, 144
Verlaine, Paul, 150, 202n91
Viertel, Salka, 133
Völkischer Beobachter, 74, 186n101
Vollbrecht, Karl, 87, 90, 139
Vom Täter fehlt jede Spur (David), 58

Wagner, Fritz Arno, 90, 134, 135, 137, 139
Warburg, Aby, 31
Warm, Hermann, 88, 90, 125, 131
Weg ins Leben, Der (Ekk), 73
Weinberg, Herman, 116, 126, 193n78
Weiß, Leo, 43, 176n5
Weltgeschichte als Kolonialgeschichte, Die (Hans Cürlis, 1926), 63, 182n70
Weltreklamekongress, 62
Wenders, Wim, 143, 145
Werbefilm, 61–65, 181n66
Wiene, Robert, 125, 131, 132
Wiener Tag, Der, 71
Wölfflin, Heinrich, 30–31, 38, 39, 173n37
Woman in the Window, The (Lang), 125. See also Lang, Fritz
World Advertising Congress. See Weltreklamekongress
Worringer, Wilhelm, 127

Zadek, Walter, 40
Ziegfeld Follies, 53–54
Ziegler, Leopold, 6, 127–28

Founded in 1893,
UNIVERSITY OF CALIFORNIA PRESS
publishes bold, progressive books and journals
on topics in the arts, humanities, social sciences,
and natural sciences—with a focus on social
justice issues—that inspire thought and action
among readers worldwide.

The UC PRESS FOUNDATION
raises funds to uphold the press's vital role
as an independent, nonprofit publisher, and
receives philanthropic support from a wide
range of individuals and institutions—and from
committed readers like you. To learn more, visit
ucpress.edu/supportus.

www.ingramcontent.com/pod-product-compliance
Lightning Source LLC
Chambersburg PA
CBHW020811230426
43666CB00007B/968